WORLD BANK INDEPENDENT EVALUATION GROUP

IEG

Engaging with Fragile States

An IEG Review of World Bank Support
to Low-Income Countries Under Stress

http://www.worldbank.org/ieg

2006
The World Bank
Washington, D.C.

Photo credit: "The Horror, the Hope." Child in refugee camp for people fleeing war in Rwanda; Democratic Republic of Congo. ©Mikkel Ostergaard.

ISBN-10: 0-8213-6847-8
ISBN-13: 978-0-8213-6847-3
eISBN: 0-8213-6848-6
DOI: 10.1596/978-0-8213-6847-3

Library of Congress Cataloging-in-Publication Data
Carvalho, Soniya.
    Engaging with fragile states : an IEG review of World Bank support to low-income countries under stress / author, Soniya Carvalho.
        p. cm. — (Independent Evaluation Group study series)
    Includes bibliographical references.
    ISBN-13: 978-0-8213-6847-3
    ISBN-10: 0-8213-6847-8
    ISBN-10: 0-8213-6848-6 (electronic)
    1. World Bank—Evaluation. 2. Economic development projects—Evaluation. 3. Economic assistance—Developing countries—Evaluation. I. World Bank. Independent Evaluation Group. II. Title. III. Title: IEG review of World Bank support to low-income countries under stress.
    HG3881.5.W57C37 2006
    332.1'532—dc22
                                                                                                2006034735

World Bank InfoShop
E-mail: pic@worldbank.org
Telephone: 202-458-5454
Facsimile: 202-522-1500

Printed on Recycled Paper

Independent Evaluation Group
Knowledge Programs and Evaluation Capacity
Development (IEGKE)
E-mail: eline@worldbank.org
Telephone: 202-458-4497
Facsimile: 202-522-3125

Contents

Boxes

Figures

Tables

Acknowledgments

This review was prepared by a team led by Soniya Carvalho. Manuel Penalver provided advice, and Marcello Basani, Alexandru Cojocaru, Tara Lonnberg, and Anju Vajja contributed to all aspects of the review. Howard White provided guidance to the work on aid effectiveness and aid allocation.

Fieldwork and thematic background analysis were undertaken by Nils Boesen, Alison Evans, Stephen Jones, Kavita Mathur, Desmond McCarthy, Marina Ottaway, Manuel Penalver, Hans Rothenbuhler, Roger Slade, Inder Sud, and Peter Whitford.

Reviewers included Jens Andvig, Stein Eriksen, Alan Gelb, Paul Isenman, Hasan Tuluy, and Indra Øverland. Alberto Agbonyitor, Ivar Andersen, Sarah Cliffe, Meron Desta, Alison Vale Gillies, Blair Stephen Glencorse, Barbry Keller, Xavier Legrain, Christian Lotz, Trayambkeshwar Sinha, Frederik van Bolhuis, Melvin Vaz, and Per Egil Wam shared knowledge and insights. Deepa Chakrapani, Catherine Gwin, Fareed Hassan, Nalini Kumar, Shonar Lala, and S. Ramachandran commented on sections of the review.

William Kraus, Mary McIntosh, and Matthew Petri helped design and administer the Stakeholder Survey. William Hurlbut edited the original manuscript and provided document production support. Heather Dittbrenner and Caroline McEuen edited and produced the report for publication. The team was assisted by Romayne Pereira.

The External Advisory Panel comprised Olayinka Creighton-Randall, John Githongo, Pieter Stek, and Gunnar Sørbø.

The review was conducted in partnership with the Evaluation Department of the Norwegian Agency for International Development (Norad), which provided both substantive and financial support.

The review was prepared under the direction of Alain Barbu, Manager of the Independent Evaluation Group, Sector, Thematic, and Global Evaluation Division.

Director-General, Evaluation: *Vinod Thomas*
Director, Independent Evaluation Group–World Bank: *Ajay Chhibber*
Manager, Sector, Thematic, and Global Evaluation Division: *Alain Barbu*
Task Manager: *Soniya Carvalho*

Note: The World Bank used the term "Low-Income Countries Under Stress (LICUS)" until January 2006, when the Bank adopted the term "fragile states." Given that this report evaluates the Bank's fragile state experience—most of which occurred before the change in terminology—it uses the term "LICUS." The term "fragile states" is used when it appears in titles and when discussing these countries in a broader international context.

Foreword

Home to almost 500 million people, roughly half of whom earn less than a dollar a day, fragile states, until recently known in the World Bank as Low-Income Countries Under Stress (LICUS), have attracted increasing attention. Concern is growing about the ability of these countries to reach development goals as well as about the adverse economic effects they have on neighboring countries and the global spillovers that may follow.

With their multiplicity of chronic problems, LICUS pose some of the toughest development challenges. Most have poor governance. Many, like Sudan, are embroiled in extended internal conflicts. Some, like Timor-Leste, are struggling through tenuous post-conflict transitions. All face similar hurdles: weak security, fractured societal relations, corruption, breakdown in the rule of law, and lack of mechanisms for generating legitimate power and authority. As low-income countries, these countries also have a huge backlog of investment needs and limited government resources to meet them.

Past international engagement with these countries has failed to yield significant improvements, and donors and others continue to struggle with how best to assist fragile states. LICUS, as the Bank has called fragile states since 2002, are characterized by weak policies, institutions, and governance. The Bank identified 25 such countries in fiscal 2005 based on their income and Country Policy and Institutional Assessment (CPIA) rating.

These 25 countries have a number of similarities: their infant mortality rate is a third higher than that of other low-income countries, life expectancy is 12 years lower, and their maternal mortality rate is about 20 percent higher. There are also important differences among LICUS. Some, Angola and Cambodia among them, grew at around 4 percent per annum during 1995–2003; others, such as the Solomon Islands, the Democratic Republic of Congo, and Guinea-Bissau, had negative growth rates of similar magnitude. Some, such as Angola, the Democratic Republic of Congo, Nigeria, and Papua New Guinea, have abundant natural resources, but others, such as Burundi and Haiti, are resource-poor. These differences are recognized in specific business models the Bank has developed to work with countries in crisis: deterioration, prolonged crisis or impasse, post-conflict or political transition, and gradual improvement.

During fiscal 2003–05, lending and administrative budgets to LICUS stood at $4.1 billion and

$161 million—increases of 67 percent and 55 percent compared with fiscal 2000–02. The LICUS approach has evolved from general aid effectiveness concerns in 2002 to state-building and peace-building objectives in 2005. IEG's assessment of experience with the Bank's LICUS approach found some early successes, but significant remaining challenges.

Early Successes

The Bank has improved its operational readiness to engage with LICUS. It has increased its analytical work and introduced the use of Interim Strategy Notes to design strategies covering a shorter period to accommodate volatile LICUS conditions. LICUS managers have also gained greater access to senior Bank management and increased guidance on a number of important issues. The Bank has also initiated the LICUS Trust Fund to finance countries in non-accrual; these countries previously had little access to finance.

These moves have helped the Bank contribute to improved macroeconomic stability and deliver significant amounts of physical infrastructure, especially in post-conflict LICUS. Substantial progress has also been made on donor coordination at the international policy level.

Challenges

Significant challenges remain, however. The reforms in some LICUS have lacked selectivity and prioritization. The Bank's effectiveness needs to be improved after the immediate post-conflict phase when structural change is needed. The Bank has not yet sufficiently internalized political understanding in its country strategies. The strong donor coordination at the international policy level has not carried over to the country level. Most important, the Bank has made state building a central focus without adequately demonstrating how past weaknesses will be avoided and better capacity development and governance outcomes ensured.

Internally, progress remains unsatisfactory on critical human resource reforms relating to staffing numbers, staffing quality, and incentives to undertake LICUS work. There is significant duplication and confusion about the roles and responsibilities of the LICUS Unit and the Conflict Prevention and Reconstruction Unit. Finally, the Bank has yet to address the allocation of aid for LICUS in a way that reflects its objectives for these countries and ensures that LICUS are not under- or over-aided.

With regard to effectiveness, it remains too early to judge the outcomes of the Bank's efforts. However, some indicators suggest that the overall impact may have been limited. The CPIA rating for LICUS has shown an improving trend since the launch of the LICUS Initiative, but the Kaufmann, Kraay, and Mastruzzi (KKZ) governance indicator for LICUS shows a deteriorating trend over the same period. Neither trend is necessarily attributable to the donor actions, but sustained effort seems to be warranted.

Lessons for the Bank and Other Donors

Engagement needs to be quickly followed by a clear and relevant reform agenda. In the Central African Republic, good initial results are now at risk of being diminished due to inadequate attention to the budget situation.

Donor efforts need to focus on internalizing political analysis in strategy design and implementation. While the Interim Strategy in Papua New Guinea contained a good discussion of the political system and recognized problems such as clan loyalties, political patronage, corruption, and lack of capacity, it treated these problems as technical in nature and did not adequately use them to underpin the overall approach.

The analysis does not have to be developed internally, however. In Lao People's Democratic Republic, the Bank effectively tapped existing political analysis and avoided the higher costs of preparing its own analysis, as well as potential tension with the government.

Appropriate sequencing of reforms and sufficient time to implement them are crucial for achieving results without overwhelming country capacity. In Afghanistan, donor reforms have not been selective enough and have led to 120 pieces of legislation. In São Tomé and Principe, the Bank was far too ambitious and many of the Country Assistance Strategy (CAS) objectives were not achieved or were only partially achieved.

Donor coordination cannot succeed without a shared vision and purpose. In Afghanistan and Tajikistan, donors did not subscribe to a single clear objective, which made it difficult to achieve policy coherence.

Monitoring and evaluation are at least as important in LICUS as they are in any other country. In volatile country environments, where progress is often non-linear, program adaptation is essential. Close tracking of performance can help determine when adaptation is necessary and what kind may be appropriate.

Effective country strategy implementation requires not only field presence but also adequate communication between field and headquarters staff, as well as an adequate number of field staff with the appropriate authority and skills. In Cambodia, the Bank's field presence has significantly improved understanding of the political situation, but this knowledge may still be highly concentrated in a few managers and staff, with relatively limited dissemination to the broader country team. In Angola, the initial lack of operational staff in the field office who could work with ministry staff to prepare for high-level meetings between ministers and the Bank resulted in issues moving too quickly to the top, which created unnecessary tensions.

Better operational guidance is needed for tailoring donor approaches. In addition to recently issued notes, guidance is especially needed for countries in *deterioration* and *prolonged crisis or impasse,* and for the transition and development phases that follow the immediate reconstruction phase in *post-conflict or political transition* countries.

Recommendations

- Clarify the scope and content of the Bank's state-building agenda and strengthen the design and delivery of capacity development and governance support in LICUS to ensure better outcomes.
- Develop aid-allocation criteria to ensure that LICUS are not under- or over-aided.
- Strengthen internal support for LICUS work over the next three years. It is particularly important to ensure adequate incentives to attract qualified staff—both at headquarters and in field offices—to work in LICUS and to ensure an efficient organizational arrangement that removes duplication and fragmentation between LICUS and the Conflict Prevention and Reconstruction Units.
- Reassess the value added by the LICUS approach after three years, when sufficient experience on the outcomes of the approach will be available, and base continued Bank support for the LICUS category and approach on the findings of that reassessment.

Vinod Thomas
Director-General
Evaluation

Avant-propos

Avec près de 500 millions d'habitants dont la moitié gagnent moins de 1 dollar par jour, les États fragiles (jusqu' à récemment dénommés « pays à faible revenu en difficulté » par la Banque mondiale) attirent une attention grandissante. Il y a tout lieu de douter de l'aptitude de ces pays à atteindre leurs objectifs de développement et de craindre des effets économiques défavorables sur les pays voisins ainsi que les retombées qui pourraient s'ensuivre au niveau mondial.

Accablés de problèmes chroniques, ces pays ont des impératifs de développement qui présentent d'énormes défis. La plupart de ces pays souffrent d'une mauvaise gouvernance. Beaucoup, comme le Soudan, sont en proie à des conflits internes de longue date. Certains, comme le Timor-Leste, connaissent des difficultés de transition post-conflictuelle. Tous sont confrontés aux mêmes problèmes : manque de sécurité, relations sociales fragmentées, corruption, détérioration de l'ordre public et absence de mécanismes de mise en place de pouvoirs légitimes. En tant que pays à faible revenu, ils ont également d'énormes besoins d'investissement en souffrance et des ressources publiques limitées pour faire face à ces besoins.

L'action internationale menée jusqu'à présent dans ces pays n'a pas produit d'améliorations notables et les bailleurs de fonds et tous ceux concernés continuent de s'interroger sur les meilleurs moyens d'aider les États fragiles. Les LICUS, terme adopté par la Banque en 2002 pour désigner les États fragiles, se caractérisent par des politiques, des institutions et une governance faibles. La Banque a recensé 25 LICUS durant l'exercice 2005, sur la base de leur revenu et de leur performance dans le cadre des évaluations de la politique et des institutions nationales (CPIA).

Ces 25 pays présentent plusieurs similarités : taux de mortalité infantile supérieur de 33 % à celui des autres pays à faible revenu, espérance de vie inférieure de 12 ans, et taux de mortalité maternelle supérieur de quelque 20 %. Il existe également des différences importantes entre les LICUS. Certains, parmi lesquels l'Angola et le Cambodge, ont enregistré une croissance annuelle de quelque 4 % durant la période 1995-2003 ; d'autres, tels que les Iles Salomon, la République démocratique du Congo et la Guinée-Bissau, ont vu leur croissance ralentir d'autant. Certains, comme l'Angola, la République démocratique du Congo, le Nigeria et la Papouasie-Nouvelle-Guinée, possèdent d'abondantes ressources naturelles, tandis que d'autres, comme le Burundi et Haïti, sont dotés de ressources limitées. Les modèles d'intervention spécifiques établis par la Banque pour travailler avec ces pays en crise tiennent compte de ces divergences : détérioration, crise prolongée ou impasse, situation post-conflictuelle ou transition politique, et amélioration graduelle.

Durant l'exercice 03-05, les prêts et les budgets administratifs en faveur des LICUS se sont établis à 4,1 milliards de dollars et 161 millions de dollars – soit une hausse de 67 % et 55 %, respectivement, par rapport à l'exercice 00-02. La démarche suivie pour les LICUS a évolué entre 2002 et 2005, le centre des préoccupations étant passé de l'efficacité globale de l'aide à l'édification de l'État et à la consolidation de la paix. D'après l'évaluation de l'IEG, la démarche suivie par la Banque pour les LICUS a été initialement couronnée de succès mais il reste d'importants obstacles à surmonter.

Succès initiaux

La Banque a amélioré ses capacités opérationnelles d'intervention dans les LICUS. Elle a accru ses travaux d'analyse et utilise à présent des Notes de stratégie intérimaire pour élaborer des stratégies portant sur une plus courte période afin de tenir compte de l'instabilité de la situation dans les LICUS. Les responsables des LICUS ont aussi plus facilement accès à l'équipe de direction de la Banque et reçoivent davantage d'orientations sur les questions importantes. La Banque a d'autre part créé le Fonds fiduciaire LICUS pour fournir une aide financière aux pays dont la dette est improductive ; dans le passé, ces pays avaient difficilement accès à des moyens de financement.

Ces initiatives ont permis à la Banque d'aider à améliorer la stabilité macroéconomique et à mettre en place une importante infrastructure matérielle, notamment dans les LICUS sortant d'un conflit. D'importants progrès ont également été réalisés dans le domaine de la coordination des bailleurs de fonds sur le plan de la politique internationale.

Défis à relever

Il reste cependant des défis de taille à relever. Par exemple, les réformes mises en place dans certains LICUS n'ont pas été assez sélectives quant à la définition des priorités. Il importe d'accroître l'efficacité de la Banque dans la phase post-conflictuelle, lorsque des changements structurels s'imposent. La Banque ne tient pas ensore suffisamment compte des réalités politiques dans ses stratégies-pays. L'étroite coordination des bailleurs de fonds sur le plan international ne s'est pas répercutée au niveau national. Aussi et surtout, la Banque a mis l'accent sur l'édification de l'État sans démontrer de manière adéquate de quelle façon les faiblesses passées seront évitées ni comment les résultats seront améliorés sur le plan du développement des capacités et de la gouvernance.

Sur le plan interne, les progrès accomplis restent insuffisants en ce qui concerne les importantes réformes à effectuer dans le domaine des ressources humaines (effectifs, qualité du personnel et mesures d'encouragement en faveur des travaux effectués au titre des LICUS). Les doubles emplois sont fréquents et il règne une grande confusion quant au rôle et aux responsabilités de l'équipe chargée des LICUS d'une part, et celle chargée de la prévention des conflits et de la reconstruction d'autre part. Enfin, la Banque doit encore déterminer comment allouer l'aide aux LICUS en tenant compte de ses objectifs pour ces pays et en évitant que cette aide soit insuffisante ou excessive.

S'agissant de l'efficacité, il est encore trop tôt pour évaluer l'impact des mesures prises par la Banque. Certains indicateurs donnent cependant à penser que l'impact global risque d'être limité. Bien que la performance des LICUS se soit améliorée sur le plan de la politique et des institutions nationales depuis le lancement de l'initiative en faveur de ces pays, l'indicateur de gouvernance KKZ pour les LICUS reflète une détérioration sur la même période. Ni l'une ni l'autre tendance n'est nécessairement attribuable à l'action des bailleurs de fonds, mais il y a lieu de poursuivre les efforts.

Enseignements à tirer par la Banque et les autres bailleurs de fonds

Les engagements pris doivent être rapidement suivis d'un programme de réforme clair et pertinent. En République centrafricaine, les résultats initialement favorables risquent aujourd'hui d'être compromis par le manque d'attention à la situation budgétaire.

Les bailleurs de fonds doivent s'attacher à tenir compte des réalités politiques dans la conception et la mise en œuvre des stratégies. Alors que la stratégie intérimaire en Papouasie-Nouvelle-Guinée contenait une bonne analyse du système politique et reconnaissait les problèmes en présence, tels que les allégeances de clan, le clientélisme politique, la corruption et le manque de capacité, elle les a traités comme des problèmes techniques et n'en a pas convenablement tenu compte pour étayer la démarche globale.

Cela ne signifie cependant pas que l'analyse doit être effectuée de manière interne. En République démocratique populaire lao, la Banque a mis à profit les analyses politiques existantes et évité ainsi d'effectuer ell-même une analyse plus coûteuse, tout en écartant les risques de friction avec les autorités locales.

Il est impératif de bien échelonner les réformes et de prévoir suffisamment de temps pour les mettre en oeuvre si l'on entend produire les résultats escomptés sans trop lourdement grever les capacités nationales. En Afghanistan, les réformes introduites par les bailleurs de fonds n'ont pas été assez sélectives et ont abouti à la publication de 120 textes de loi. À São Tomé-et-Principe, la Banque s'est montrée beaucoup trop ambitieuse et bon nombre des objectifs de la stratégie d'aide-pays n'ont pas été atteints ou ne l'ont été que partiellement.

La coordination des bailleurs de fonds ne peut être efficace sans une vision et un objectif communs. En Afghanistan et au Tadjikistan, les bailleurs de fonds n'avaient pas clairement défini un objectif commun et il a donc été difficile d'assurer la cohérence des politiques.

Le suivi et l'évaluation sont au moins aussi importants dans les LICUS que dans tout autre pays. Dans les pays où la situation est instable et où les progrès sont souvent en dents de scie, il est essentiel d'adapter les programmes. Le suivi rigoureux des résultats peut aider à déterminer si une adaptation est nécessaire et quelle forme elle doit revêtir.

La bonne exécution d'une stratégie-pays exige à la fois une présence sur le terrain et une communication adéquate entre les services extérieurs et le siège, ainsi qu'un personnel de terrain suffisamment nombreux et doté des pouvoirs et des compétences voulus. Au Cambodge, la présence de représentants de la Banque a sensiblement amélioré la compréhension de la situation politique, mais ce savoir reste probablement l'apanage de quelques dirigeants et leurs collaborateurs, avec une diffusion relativement limitée dans l'ensemble de l'équipe-pays. En Angola, en raison du manque initial de personnel opérationnel au bureau extérieur pouvant travailler avec les services ministériels pour préparer les réunions de haut niveau entre les ministres et la Banque, les questions ont été adressées trop rapidement aux instances supérieures, ce qui a créé des tensions inutiles.

Il faut de meilleures directives opérationnelles pour adapter les démarches des bailleurs de fonds. En plus des notes récemment publiées, des directives sont tout particulièrement nécessaires pour les pays en situation de *détérioration, de crise prolongée ou d'impasse,* et pour les phases de transition et de développement qui suivent la phase de reconstruction immédiate dans les pays *sortant d'un conflit ou en transition politique.*

Recommandations

- Préciser la teneur et la portée du programme d'édification de l'État de la Banque et renforcer la conception et la mise en place des mesures d'aide au développement des capacités et à la gouvernance dans les LICUS pour améliorer les résultats.
- Formuler des critères d'affectation de l'aide pour faire en sorte que les LICUS reçoivent une aide qui n'est ni insuffisante ni excessive.
- Renforcer l'appui interne aux travaux sur les LICUS au cours des trois prochaines années. Il est particulièrement important d'offrir des incitations de nature à attirer un personnel qualifié – tant au siège que dans les bureaux extérieurs – pour travailler sur les LICUS, et de mettre en place une organisation efficace qui élimine les doubles emplois et la fragmentation

entre l'équipe chargée des LICUS et celle chargée de la prévention des conflits et de la reconstruction.

- Réexaminer la valeur ajoutée de la démarche suivie pour les LICUS au bout de trois ans, lorsqu'on possédera suffisamment de données d'expérience sur les résultats de cette approche, et baser la poursuite de l'aide de la Banque aux LICUS ainsi que l'approche à adopter sur les résultats de ce réexamen.

Vinod Thomas
Directeur général de l'évaluation

Prefacio

En los Estados frágiles, hasta recientemente conocidos en el Banco Mundial como países de ingreso bajo en dificultades, viven casi 500 millones de personas, aproximadamente la mitad de las cuales ganan menos de un dólar por día; por ese motivo, la situación de esos países despierta cada vez más atención. Es causa de creciente preocupación la posibilidad de que esos países no logren alcanzar sus objetivos de desarrollo, así como los efectos económicos desfavorables que provoca su situación en países vecinos y la consiguiente posibilidad de que sus problemas se propaguen al resto del mundo.

Dada la multiplicidad de problemas crónicos que padecen, esos países plantean algunos de los desafíos más arduos en materia de desarrollo. En la mayoría de ellos la gestión de los asuntos públicos es insatisfactoria. Muchos de esos países —por ejemplo, Sudán— están sumidos en vastos y complicados conflictos internos. Algunos, como Timor-Leste, se debaten en medio de delicados procesos de transición posteriores a conflictos. Todos tienen ante sí obstáculos similares: inadecuada seguridad, fractura de las relaciones sociales, corrupción, desintegración del Estado de derecho y falta de mecanismos de generación de poder y autoridad legítimos. Además, por tratarse de países de ingreso bajo, han acumulado enormes necesidades de inversión y no disponen de suficientes recursos públicos para atenderlas.

La labor internacional llevada a cabo con esos países no ha generado mejoras significativas, por lo cual los donantes y otras instituciones siguen batallando por hallar la manera más eficaz de ayudarlos. Los PIBD, como el Banco denomina desde 2002 a los Estados frágiles, se caracterizan por lo insatisfactorio de sus políticas, instituciones y gestión pública. En el ejercicio de 2005, el Banco identificó a 25 de esos países, basándose en sus ingresos y en el puntaje que les corresponde en la evaluación de las políticas e instituciones nacionales (CPIA).

Esos 25 países presentan ciertas semejanzas: en comparación con otros países de ingreso bajo, su tasa de mortalidad infantil es un tercio más alta; la esperanza de vida es 12 años menor, y la tasa de mortalidad materna es alrededor de un 20% más alta. A esto se agregan importantes diferencias entre distintos PIBD. Algunos, como Angola y Camboya, registraron un crecimiento económico de alrededor del 4% por año en el período 1995–2003; en otros, como Islas Salomón, República Democrática del Congo y Guinea-Bissau, las tasas de crecimiento económico fueron de magnitud similar, pero negativas. Algunos, como Angola, Nigeria, Papua Nueva Guinea y República Democrática del Congo, poseen abundantes recursos naturales; otros, como Burundi y Haití, son pobres en recursos. Esas diferencias se reconocen en modelos económicos específicos —de deterioro, crisis o estancamiento prolongados, situaciones posteriores a conflictos o de transición política, y mejora gradual— que el Banco ha elaborado para trabajar con países en crisis.

En los ejercicios de 2003–05, el monto del presupuesto para otorgamiento de préstamos y del presupuesto administrativo destinados a los PIBD fue de US$4.100 millones y US$161 millones, respectivamente; esas sumas superan en 67% y 55% las de los ejercicios de 2000–02. El enfoque de la Iniciativa para los PIBD ha evolucionado: las preocupaciones generales sobre la eficacia de la ayuda en 2002 dejaron paso, en 2005, a objetivos de fortalecimiento del Estado y de consecución de la paz. La evaluación de la experiencia en la aplicación del enfoque sobre los PIBD del Banco realizada por el Grupo de Evaluación Independiente (IEG) revela algunos éxitos iniciales, pero subsisten considerables dificultades.

Éxitos iniciales

El Banco se ha puesto en mejores condiciones operativas para ocuparse de los PIBD. Ha intensificado su labor de análisis y ha comenzado a usar las Notas de la Estrategia Provisional para diseñar estrategias para un período más breve, a fin de dar cabida a las condiciones inestables de los PIBD. Además los gerentes que se ocupan de esos países han obtenido un acceso más amplio a la administración superior del Banco, y reciben mayor orientación en relación con varios temas importantes. Por otra parte, el Banco ha comenzado a utilizar el Fondo Fiduciario PIBD para financiar a países excluidos del régimen de contabilidad en valores devengados, que tenían limitado acceso al financiamiento.

Esas medidas han ayudado al Banco a lograr mejoras en cuanto a estabilidad macroeconómica y a proporcionar un volumen significativo de infraestructura física, en especial a PIBD en

situaciones posteriores a conflictos. También se han logrado avances sustanciales en materia de coordinación de los donantes a nivel de la política internacional.

Dificultades

No obstante, subsisten considerables dificultades. Por ejemplo, las reformas introducidas en algunos PIBD no han sido selectivas ni se han priorizado. El Banco debe actuar más eficazmente al concluir la fase que sigue inmediatamente a un conflicto, en que se requieren reformas estructurales. Las estrategias para los países que elabora el Banco no permiten afirmar que se hayan captado, en suficiente medida, las realidades políticas de los países. No se ha llevado al nivel de países la firme coordinación de los donantes lograda en el nivel de las políticas internacionales. Lo más importante es que el Banco ha centrado la atención en la construcción del Estado, sin poner adecuadamente de manifiesto la manera de evitar las fallas del pasado y garantizar mejores resultados en cuanto a creación de capacidad y gestión de los asuntos públicos.

En la esfera interna, el avance sigue siendo insatisfactorio en relación con las reformas esenciales en materia de recursos humanos referentes a número de funcionarios, calidad de sus aptitudes e incentivos para la realización de la labor de la Iniciativa para los PIBD. Existe considerable duplicación de esfuerzos y confusión con respecto a las funciones y responsabilidades de la Unidad de PIBD y la Unidad de prevención de conflictos y de reconstrucción. Finalmente, el Banco aún no ha abordado el tema de una asignación de ayuda para los PIBD que refleje los objetivos de la institución en esos países y confiera certeza de que los PIBD no reciben menos ni más asistencia de la que necesitan.

Con respecto a la eficacia, aún sería prematuro abrir juicio sobre los resultados de la labor del Banco, pero algunos indicadores llevan a pensar que el impacto puede haber sido limitado. El puntaje de la CPIA referente a los PIBD pone de manifiesto un mejoramiento de la tendencia desde la puesta en marcha de la Iniciativa para los PIBD, pero el indicador de gobernabilidad de Kaufmann, Kraay, Mastruzzi (KKZ) muestra, en el mismo período, una tendencia al deterioro de la situación. Ninguna de las dos tendencias es necesariamente atribuible a las actividades de los donantes, pero parece justificarse la realización de un esfuerzo sostenido.

Enseñanzas para el Banco y para otros donantes

Iniciada la participación, es preciso establecer, sin dilación, objetivos de reforma claros y pertinentes. En la República Centroafricana existe el peligro de que una inadecuada atención de la situación presupuestaria comprometa ahora los satisfactorios resultados iniciales.

Es preciso que la labor de los donantes se centre en la inserción del análisis político en el diseño y la ejecución de la estrategia. Aunque en Papua Nueva Guinea la estrategia provisional daba cabida a un adecuado debate del sistema político y en ella se reconocían problemas tales como lealtades de clanes, clientelismo político, corrupción y falta de capacidad, esos problemas se trataban como dificultades técnicas; y no se los utilizó del modo adecuado para basar en ellos el enfoque general.

No obstante, puede prescindirse de un análisis interno. En la República Democrática Popular Lao, el Banco aprovechó eficazmente los análisis políticos existentes y evitó los mayores costos que implicaba la preparación de sus propios análisis, así como las posibles tensiones con el gobierno.

Establecer una adecuada secuencia de reformas y disponer de tiempo suficiente para ejecutarlas son factores esenciales para lograr resultados sin hacer recaer una carga abrumadora sobre la capacidad del país. En Afganistán las reformas de los donantes no han sido suficientemente selectivas y han dado lugar a 120 leyes. En Santo Tomé y Príncipe, el Banco adoptó objetivos excesivamente ambiciosos, lo que impidió alcanzar —por lo menos totalmente— muchos de los objetivos de la Estrategia de asistencia al país.

No puede lograrse la coordinación de los donantes sin una visión y una finalidad compartidas. En Afganistán los donantes no coincidieron en un único objetivo claro, lo que impidió la consecución de coherencia en las políticas.

El seguimiento y la evaluación no revisten menos importancia en los PIBD que en los restantes países. En entornos nacionales inestables, en que el progreso suele no ser lineal, es esencial adaptar los programas a esa realidad. Un estrecho seguimiento del desempeño puede contribuir a establecer el momento en que deben realizarse adaptaciones, y de qué tipo.

Una eficaz ejecución de la estrategia para el país requiere no sólo una presencia in situ, sino también adecuada comunicación entre el personal que opera sobre el terreno y el de la sede, así como un adecuado número de funcionarios sobre el terreno, dotados de facultades y aptitudes apropiadas. En Camboya, la presencia in situ del Banco ha permitido conocer bastante mejor la situación política del país, pero ese saber tal vez esté muy concentrado en unos pocos gerentes y funcionarios; poco se ha difundido al resto del grupo a cargo del país. En la oficina de Angola, la falta inicial de personal operativo en condiciones de colaborar con el personal de los ministerios en los preparativos para reuniones de alto nivel entre ministros y representantes del Banco, aceleró excesivamente el avance del trámite hacia la cúspide administrativa, lo que creó tensiones innecesarias.

Se requiere una mejor orientación operativa para adaptar a las necesidades locales los enfoques de los donantes. Además de los estudios recientemente publicados, existe una especial necesidad de orientación para países en *proceso de deterioro* y *sujetos a crisis o estancamiento prolongados*, y para las fases de transición y desarrollo que siguen a la fase de reconstrucción inmediata en los países en *situaciones posteriores a conflictos o en transición política*.

Recomendaciones

• Establecer claramente el alcance y contenido de los objetivos de fortalecimiento del Estado que persigue el Banco y reforzar el diseño y el suministro de respaldo en materia de desarrollo de capacidad y gestión de los asuntos públicos en los PIBD, para lograr mejores resultados.

- Elaborar criterios de asignación de la ayuda, para que los PIBD no reciban menos ni más ayuda de la necesaria.
- Reforzar el apoyo interno para la labor referente a los PIBD en los próximos tres años. Reviste especial importancia contar con adecuados incentivos que atraigan personal calificado — en la sede y en las oficinas en los países— que se ocupe de los PIBD, y establecer una estructura institucional eficiente que elimine la duplicación y fragmentación de esfuerzos entre la Unidad de PIBD y la Unidad de prevención de conflictos y de reconstrucción.
- Al cabo de tres años, volver a evaluar el valor agregado del enfoque de la Iniciativa para los PIBD, cuando se disponga de experiencia suficiente sobre los resultados de ese enfoque, y basar en las conclusiones de esa nueva evaluación el continuo apoyo del Banco para la categoría de los PIBD y para el enfoque que a ellos se refiere.

Vinod Thomas
Director General, Evaluación

Main Evaluation Messages

- Low-Income Countries Under Stress (LICUS) present some of the toughest development challenges, and the donor community continues to grapple with the question of how best to assist them. The World Bank has been an active participant in international policy discussions on LICUS and has improved its operational readiness to support them since introducing the LICUS Initiative in 2002.
- Before the LICUS Initiative, outcomes of the Bank's assistance programs in LICUS were mostly in the unsatisfactory range. The initiative has increased Bank attention to LICUS, but it is too early to assess outcomes. Implementation experience has been mixed, and outcomes of the few country strategies that have been assessed by the Independent Evaluation Group (IEG) mostly indicate underachievement of objectives.
- By adopting state building as a central objective, the Bank has made an area of traditional weakness (capacity development and governance) a part of its main focus in LICUS. Focusing the LICUS Initiative on the complex state-building agenda requires that the Bank clarify its areas of comparative advantage and the scope and content of the agenda. The Bank also needs to identify innovative approaches to improve the weak capacity development and governance record, and performance indicators to measure state-building outcomes.
- Little progress has been made on critical human resource reforms relating to staffing numbers, staffing quality, and incentives to undertake LICUS work in the three years since the LICUS approach was implemented.
- Although the Bank has recently emphasized the need to increase its field presence in LICUS, that emphasis alone will be insufficient for the effective implementation of country strategies. Increased field presence needs to be complemented by stronger communication between the Bank's field and headquarters staff. An adequate number of field staff with the appropriate authority and skills is also required.
- Donor reform agendas in LICUS could be more selective. In complex LICUS environments, where virtually every sector requires reform, appropriate sequencing of reforms and sufficient time to implement them are crucial for achieving results without overwhelming limited LICUS capacity.

Executive Summary

Home to almost 500 million people, roughly half of whom earn less than a dollar a day, fragile states, until recently known in the World Bank as Low-Income Countries Under Stress (LICUS), have attracted increasing attention. Concern is growing about the ability of these countries to reach the Millennium Development Goals (MDGs) as well as about the adverse economic effects they have on neighboring countries and the global spillovers that may follow.

With their multiplicity of chronic problems, LICUS pose some of the toughest development challenges. Most have poor governance and are embroiled in extended internal conflicts or are struggling through tenuous post-conflict transitions. They face similar hurdles of widespread lack of security, fractured relations among societal groups, significant corruption, breakdown in the rule of law, absence of mechanisms for generating legitimate power and authority, a huge backlog of investment needs, and limited government resources for development. Past international engagement with these countries has generally failed to yield significant improvements.

The donor community is grappling with the question of how best to assist countries faced with such challenging problems. With their differing motivations and objectives, donors and researchers have chosen to address different aspects of these problems, which has led them to focus on slightly varying groups of countries. For instance, recent research by the Center for Global

Development focuses on stagnant low-income countries (defined by gross national product per capita and growth rates), and the Failed States Index of *Foreign Policy* focuses on state failure, identifying countries based on such factors as the level of economic decline, security, factionalized elites, displaced persons, human rights breaches, and external intervention. The U.S. Agency for International Development aims to address issues surrounding vulnerability and crisis, many pertaining to the political environment. The U.K. Department for International Development (DFID) and the Organisation for Economic Co-operation and Development–Development Assistance Committee's (OECD-DAC's) definitions of fragile states are similar to those used by the World Bank.

As defined by the World Bank, all LICUS are characterized by weak policies, institutions, and governance. The Bank has used two criteria to define *core* and *severe* LICUS (henceforth LICUS refers to core and severe LICUS, not *marginal* LICUS, which are identified by the Bank only for monitoring purposes): per capita income within the threshold of International Development Association (IDA) eligibility and performance of 3.0 or less (2.5 or less for severe and 2.6–3.0 for core) on both the overall Country Policy and Institutional Assessment (CPIA) rating and the CPIA rating for Public Sector Management and Institutions.

Some low-income countries without CPIA data are also included. In fiscal 2005, the Bank identified 25 countries as LICUS. Six fiscal 2005 LICUS did not have a CPIA rating: Afghanistan, Liberia, Myanmar, Somalia, Timor-Leste, and the territory of Kosovo. This review bases its evaluation on the Bank's assistance to the 25 countries classified as LICUS in fiscal 2005.

Lending and administrative budgets to LICUS have increased since the LICUS Initiative began. Lending to LICUS increased from about $2.5 billion during fiscal 2000–02 (before the LICUS Initiative) to about $4.1 billion during fiscal 2003–05 (since the launch of the LICUS Initiative). On a per capita basis, lending to LICUS ranged from $0 to $25.4 during fiscal 2003–05. Administrative budgets for LICUS increased from about $104 million during fiscal 2000–02 to about $161 million during fiscal 2003–05. On a per capita basis, administrative budgets for LICUS ranged from $0.002 to $4.5 during fiscal 2003–05.

A large share of lending to LICUS during fiscal 2003–05 went to post-conflict LICUS (post-conflict countries are identified based on Post-Conflict Progress Indicators, for purposes of determining exceptional IDA grants), while administrative budgets have been more evenly distributed across the LICUS group (7 post-conflict LICUS out of the 25 received 64 percent of total LICUS lending, and 34 percent of the total LICUS administrative budget).

While the large proportion of lending to post-conflict LICUS might have occurred even without the LICUS Initiative (given that IDA's exceptional post-conflict allocations predate the initiative), the initiative likely contributed to the more even distribution of administrative budgets across the group (given an increase of 400 percent or more in administrative budgets between fiscal 2000–02 and 2003–05 for three LICUS—Liberia, Somalia, and Sudan—that

would have received minuscule amounts of administrative budgets prior to the initiative because of their non-accrual status).

The Bank's LICUS approach has evolved since its initial articulation in 2002, which was grounded in country-level core principles (see table ES.1). The original rationale for the initiative was that of improving aid effectiveness by using other instruments, such as analytical work and knowledge transfers where necessary, supplemented by financial transfers to promote change.

In 2005, the objectives and scope of the LICUS Initiative shifted from general aid effectiveness to state-building and peace-building objectives. The LICUS Initiative also introduced four business models (deterioration, prolonged political crisis or impasse, post-conflict or political transition, and gradual improvement) that provided for varying treatment of different types of LICUS. Learning by doing and the focus on organizational issues in the 2002 approach were retained and further reinforced in the 2005 approach.

This review set out to answer three questions:

- How effective has the Bank's LICUS approach been?
- How operationally useful are the Bank's criteria for identifying and classifying LICUS, and how useful is the aid-allocation system for them?
- How appropriate and adequate has the Bank's internal support for LICUS work been?

Main Findings and Conclusions

Effectiveness of the Bank's LICUS approach

Implementation experience across the core country-level LICUS principles has been mixed (see table ES.1). Problems encountered in implementation sometimes arose from overambitious Bank objectives (thus requiring the scaling down of objectives) and sometimes from inadequate Bank effort or inappropriate input, as suggested by IEG's fieldwork and its CAS Completion Report Reviews (thus requiring scaling up of effort).

The majority of stakeholders interviewed in IEG's Stakeholder Survey said that the Bank's

Table ES.1: Implementation Experience on the Core Country-Level LICUS Principles

LICUS principle	Implementation experience rating
Stay engaged	Substantial
Anchor strategies in stronger sociopolitical analysis	Medium
• Political understanding	• Medium-substantial
• Internalizing political understanding in strategy design and implementation	• Medium-low
Promote domestic demand and capacity for positive change	Low
Support simple and feasible entry-level reforms	Medium-low
• Macroeconomic reforms	• Substantial
• Delivery of physical infrastructure	• Substantial
• Transition from the immediate post-conflict reconstruction phase to the development phase	• Low
• Selectivity and prioritization	• Low
Explore innovative mechanisms for social service delivery	Medium
Donor collaboration	Medium
• At international policy level	• Substantial
• At country level	• Medium-low
Measure and monitor results[a]	Low

Sources: Fieldwork and thematic background analysis done for this review by IEG, 2005.

a. Not specifically mentioned as a separate core principle by the Bank, but included by IEG because it is pivotal to the Bank's learning-by-doing LICUS agenda.

overall program in LICUS has made a small positive contribution to development—a view that refers to Bank support generally, and not to the LICUS approach per se.

There have been some notable early successes with regard to the LICUS principles. The Bank's LICUS Initiative has allowed for increased Bank engagement in countries where such engagement would likely have been lower. The Bank has recently engaged with a number of LICUS from the early days of peace or political transition. The Bank has also contributed to macroeconomic stability and to the delivery of significant amounts of physical infrastructure, especially in post-conflict LICUS. Substantial progress has been made in donor coordination at the international policy level, as exemplified by the recent agreement of a wide spectrum of donors, including the Bank, to the 12 OECD-DAC principles of international engagement.

The Bank has often played a leading role as co-chair of international donor events and co-author of joint policy papers. The Bank's recently introduced business models, which differentiate among different types of LICUS,

are likely to permit a more tailored response to LICUS. The percentage of closed LICUS projects rated satisfactory on outcome by IEG increased from 50 percent in fiscal 2002, before the LICUS Initiative, to 58 percent in 2003, 65 percent in 2004, and 82 percent in 2005. The corresponding numbers for projects in non-LICUS low-income countries ranged from 70 to 79 percent.

But several significant challenges remain. The Bank's initial engagement with a number of LICUS has not been adequately followed up by a focused and well-sequenced reform agenda. Furthermore, the Bank has yet to internalize sufficient political understanding in country strategy design and implementation. The Bank also needs to strengthen the quality of its country-level coordination with other donors, especially in implementation follow-through that goes beyond policy agreements.

In addition, the Bank has made one of its areas of traditional weaknesses (capacity development and governance) a central part of its focus by adopting the more complex state-building objective. This new emphasis requires the Bank to identify its comparative advantage more effectively; improve performance, including through the development of innovative approaches; and identify partners who can complement its work to ensure achievement of the intended outcomes. Finally, the choice of the term *state building* may itself be inappropriate, given its political and ideological connotations.

The Bank needs to develop its operational approaches in LICUS, especially for the *deterioration* and *prolonged crisis or impasse* business models. Further refinement of the business models by more explicitly factoring in differences in capacity to perform core state functions (for example, resource generation, resource allocation, basic social service and infrastructure provision, and political accommodation of dissent and security) is also needed to enable the Bank to achieve a better fit between its operational approaches and the varying institutional environments of LICUS.

The Bank's work on post-conflict countries predates the LICUS approach, and the corresponding business model for post-conflict LICUS is articulated more clearly than the other business models. However, it has shortcomings and needs to be further developed to guide the transition and development phases that follow the immediate post-conflict reconstruction phase. Furthermore, while the Bank has given increasing attention to conflict prevention, there is limited knowledge about the effectiveness of its efforts in this area.

The Bank's role and comparative advantage in conflict prevention have yet to be clearly established, especially because conflict prevention requires the Bank to give greater attention to the *root causes* of conflict and address ethnic, sociological, and political factors. The Bank needs to define better what its peace-building objective does and does not include and how it will be achieved.

Operational utility of the Bank's LICUS identification, classification, and aid-allocation mechanisms

Despite the move to state- and peace-building objectives, the Bank continues to rely almost exclusively on the CPIA to identify LICUS. The CPIA, however, fails to capture some key aspects of state fragility (such as accommodation of political dissent) and conflict (such as political instability and security or susceptibility to conflict), and may need to be supplemented. A stronger approach to the identification of LICUS would require an analytical framework that more explicitly focuses on the objectives of the LICUS Initiative.

The policy selectivity of the system the Bank uses to allocate IDA resources (called performance-based allocation, or PBA) has increased over the years, and less IDA funding has been available for countries with weaker policies, institutions, and governance. This has raised the question of whether LICUS are receiving appropriate amounts of IDA resources. Adjustments to the PBA have resulted in increased IDA financing, including to some post-conflict LICUS and LICUS undergoing political transitions. Yet it remains far from clear whether the current levels of IDA funding ensure that LICUS are not under- or over-aided.

The aid-allocation issue has once again come to the fore with some research questioning the empirical evidence for the positive link between policies and aid effectiveness (which underlies the PBA). Other research argues that aid can be effective in promoting sustainable policy turnarounds in failing states by building and strengthening the preconditions for reform or by enhancing the chances that the reform will be sustained once it is set in place. The latter research finds that potential returns from aid to LICUS can be extraordinarily high, even though the risks of failure are substantial.

For its part, the Bank has yet to address the aid-allocation issue for LICUS in a way that reflects its objectives for these countries and ensures that LICUS are not under- or over-aided.

Appropriateness and adequacy of internal Bank support for LICUS work

The Bank's internal support for LICUS work has progressed in several areas:

- Expanding analytical work by de-linking administrative budgets for economic and sector

work and technical assistance from lending volumes
- Using Interim Strategy Notes that allow for the design of strategies that cover a shorter period to accommodate the volatile LICUS conditions
- Providing LICUS managers access to the Bank's senior management
- Introducing the LICUS Trust Fund to finance countries in non-accrual (for which the Bank previously lacked an instrument).

Based on country experience, the LICUS Unit has distilled guidance on a number of important issues and has fed this guidance into both operational advice to country teams and broader external policy debates.

However, three years after the Bank recognized the need for an internal culture shift to implement the LICUS approach effectively, the Bank's internal support for LICUS work has progressed little. It remains unsatisfactory on critical human resource reforms relating to staffing numbers, staffing quality, and incentives to undertake LICUS work. Bank staff comments about the importance of working on both a non-

LICUS and a LICUS country demonstrate inadequate recognition of LICUS work within the Bank and point to an incentive system in need of reform.

The uneven attention of individual country directors, especially if they are also covering a larger, more "successful," or higher-profile country, was mentioned by staff as an issue, indicating the need to ensure consistent attention to LICUS work throughout the management hierarchy. In IEG's Stakeholder Survey, the majority of Bank respondents said that there has been no change when working on LICUS with respect to several human resource matters (see figure ES.1).

There is significant duplication and confusion surrounding the roles and responsibilities of the LICUS and the Conflict Prevention and Reconstruction (CPR) Units. Staff is concerned with the practical questions of which unit to turn to for specific types of advice and what kinds of support to expect from each unit. In IEG's Stakeholder Survey, about two-thirds of Bank respondents saw some problem with the current organizational arrangement: 37 percent

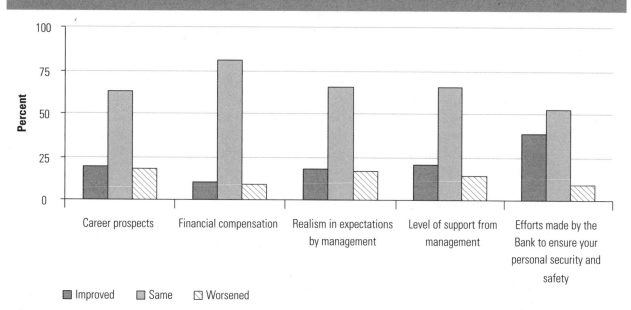

Figure ES.1: The Majority of Bank Respondents Said There Has Been No Change When Working on LICUS in Several Areas (listed below)

Legend: ■ Improved ■ Same ◩ Worsened

Source: Appendix Z (Stakeholder Survey results).

Note: Number of valid responses ranges from 213 to 238. The question in the survey did not differentiate between staff who had worked in a LICUS and those who had worked in a non-LICUS in their previous assignment.

said that there is some duplication between the support of the Bank's LICUS Unit and that of the CPR Unit, 15 percent that there is a lot of duplication, and 12 percent that there is a conflict or contradiction.

Lessons of Experience for the Bank and Other Donors

Several lessons emerge from this review's assessment of the Bank's experience in implementing the core principles of the LICUS approach. Many of the issues covered under these lessons were noted as areas in need of improvement in the 2002 LICUS Task Force report (World Bank 2002)—such as the need to anchor strategies in stronger sociopolitical analysis or to support highly focused reform agendas—and have also been emphasized in the Bank's 2005 LICUS reports. The lessons derive from the Bank's own implementation experience, but may also be useful in guiding other donor assistance in LICUS.

LICUS engagement

Staying engaged is only a means to an end and needs to be quickly followed by a clear and relevant reform agenda in LICUS. In the absence of a clear and relevant reform agenda, early successes of engagement may be short lived and contribute little to the achievement of country strategy objectives. The examples of the Central African Republic and Haiti show that various obstacles may make the follow-up to a successful initial LICUS engagement difficult. Because political successes were insufficiently backed up on the economic side, the government of the Central African Republic is now faced with a potentially disastrous budget crisis. In Haiti, the donor community seems to have given inadequate attention to ensuring a minimum level of security. In both cases, good initial results of the LICUS Initiative are now at risk of being diminished.

In certain instances, strategic disengagement—with the exception of in-house analytical work—may be needed, at least for periods of time. This is a particularly appropriate strategy when involvement with the Bank is seen as inappropriately giving legitimacy to the LICUS government or

when it dampens internal pressure for reform, thus potentially hindering the emergence of conditions needed to bring about serious and sustainable political reform.

In the deterioration and prolonged crisis or impasse business models, where there is often little consensus between donors and government on development strategy, engagement needs to include policy dialogue aimed at creating an opening for reform, while simultaneously working on a reform agenda should a window of opportunity appear. In the post-conflict or political transition and gradual improvement business models, engagement will need to have more of a technical content and a stronger focus on implementing the reform agenda, given the greater reform consensus between donors and government.

The Bank's guidance for prolonged conflict or political impasse countries states that "relatively non-controversial development issues may provide an entry point for constructive dialogue between the parties to a conflict." For deteriorating governance countries, the Bank's guidance states that the Bank should provide "input on specific economic issues which are important for mediation efforts and may serve as a way to restart dialogue" (World Bank 2005e).

Country ownership and absorptive capacity constraints apply as much to knowledge products as to financial products. The involvement of country counterparts in the Bank's analytical work remains limited to administrative aspects, with much less country-client participation in selecting topics and undertaking analysis, thereby reducing national buy-in. Yet the involvement of country counterparts is essential to ensuring client ownership and improving the impact of analytical work.

In Tajikistan, the lack of government involvement in the selection and preparation of the Bank's analytical work limited the government's interest in the results, which hindered effective implementation. In Angola, some Bank-led analytical work (for instance, the recent Country Economic Memorandum) was perceived by senior government officials as an imposition of Bank views on their internal affairs, which led to limited ownership and capacity development. Without country ownership, the chance of analytical work influencing government policy is small.

LICUS governments' absorptive capacity constraints in using analytical work may also limit possible knowledge transfer. The Angolan government, for instance, endorsed the Bank Interim Strategy Note but expressed concern about the amount of analytical and advisory activities foreseen. This has raised doubt about whether the analytical products would be fully utilized by the government. The absorptive capacity of the government is severely limited, and analytical and advisory activities undertaken mostly by the Bank risk straining relations with the government, regardless of their technical quality. In Cambodia, plans for analytical and advisory services in the 2005 Country Assistance Strategy (CAS)—totaling 30 tasks to be completed over fiscal 2005–07—appear overly ambitious considering the country's limited institutional capacity.

Political understanding and its use in country strategy

Commissioning and consuming—not necessarily producing—good political analysis is critical for donors in LICUS. The objective of a country team should be to commission or consume (not necessarily produce) analysis that is directly relevant to, and usable in, the development of a strategy. In LICUS, especially in environments where speed is critical, donors need to ensure that existing political analysis is mined before commissioning new analysis.

In Lao People's Democratic Republic, the Bank effectively tapped existing political analysis and invited a political scientist who had published extensively about the country to make a presentation to the country team on politics and reform in the country. This allowed for the preparation of an independent summary of relevant political analysis (tailored to the needs of the donor community in general and the Bank in particular) and its dissemination to a relevant group of Bank staff and other donors. It avoided the higher costs of preparing a "Bank" analysis, as well as potential

tension with the government, by allowing the Bank to avoid getting bogged down in some of the sensitivities surrounding the analysis. For the Bank, the acquisition of existing knowledge, as well as its dissemination, proved more important and effective in this case than knowledge creation.

The main focus of donor efforts needs to be on helping staff internalize political analysis in strategy design and implementation. Although the Bank has conducted or had access to good political analysis in some LICUS, such analysis has not been adequately reflected in its strategy. For example, the Interim Strategy in Papua New Guinea contains a good discussion of the political system and recognizes problems such as clan loyalties, political patronage, corruption, and lack of capacity. Yet the strategy treats these problems as technical matters and does not adequately use them to underpin the overall approach.

Focused reform agenda

In complex LICUS environments, where virtually every sector requires reform, appropriate sequencing of reforms and sufficient time to implement them are crucial for achieving results without overwhelming limited LICUS capacity. While donors must strive for collective donor selectivity, this is far from being achieved, as the examples of Afghanistan's donor-endorsed reform agenda and Haiti's Interim Cooperation Framework (ICF), presented below, indicate. However, even if collective donor selectivity is not immediately achieved, the Bank needs to ensure focus and selectivity in its own assistance program, based on its core competences. Such Bank selectivity has been increasing in recent years but remains a challenge.

In Afghanistan, the reforms covered by donors are wide ranging, show lack of sufficient priority, and have led to 120 pieces of pending legislation. These reforms, dealing with virtually every economic and social aspect of the country, need to be carefully prioritized and sequenced, but donors have yet to do so. In Haiti, the ICF is meant to guide international assistance and cooperation with Haiti through September 2006, and covers practically all basic state functions, ranging from security, to national dialogue, to economic governance, to economic recovery, to basic services. Individually, each of these areas seems important, but together they add up to a formidable agenda.

With respect to the Bank's own assistance program, São Tomé and Principe is an example where the Bank was far too ambitious in relation to the resources allocated to the country, with the result that many of the CAS objectives were not achieved or were only partially achieved.

Beyond selectivity in CASs, it is critical to ensure that actual reform agendas on the ground are focused and well prioritized. The lack of selectivity and prioritization in the reform agendas raises questions of effectiveness, especially given the limited capacity in LICUS. While it is difficult to be selective in a country where there is an urgent need to fix many things, the appropriate sequencing of reforms is crucial to ensuring that limited LICUS capacity is not overtaxed, while also avoiding partial solutions. Well-sequenced reforms spanning a sufficient number of years, along with donor commitment to see them through, will be essential.

In Timor-Leste, donors may have pulled out too quickly, without sufficiently dealing with the country's pressing capacity needs. In Haiti, development assistance has greatly fluctuated over the years. The country has gone through several "feast or famine" cycles in its relations with the donor community. This might have been avoided had various donors better timed and sequenced their aid.

Capacity development in post-conflict LICUS

Capacity development and governance programs need to start early, even in post-conflict LICUS. Immediately following the cessation of conflict, the international donor community tends to focus its assistance on physical reconstruction. Because capacity to use aid effectively in post-conflict LICUS is low and governance is often poor, the focus from the beginning also needs to be on the development of capacity and improvement of governance, not merely the reconstruction of physical infrastructure. This may require the creation or strengthening of public institutions, civil service reform, and use of local

expertise. If foreign experts are brought in to provide technical assistance, it must be ensured that this will not compromise the long-term development of *local* capacity.

Donor coordination

Donor coordination cannot succeed without a common vision and purpose among donors—when donor objectives cannot be fully harmonized, it is important that they at least be complementary. The Bank's approach has not fully recognized the differing motivations of donors for engaging with LICUS. Although the broad concept of fragility is widely understood and accepted, the countries identified by donors as fragile vary. The motivations for supporting fragile states range from security, to aid effectiveness, to equitable development, to poverty reduction, to state building, to peace building and conflict prevention.

In both Afghanistan and Tajikistan, IEG's fieldwork found that major donors did not subscribe to a single clear objective. Without a common overall objective, policy coherence is unlikely. The Bank's donor coordination efforts and modalities are insufficiently informed by the objectives of the different players in a country. That said, donor coordination is a form of collective action, requiring that other donors similarly improve their outreach to the Bank and subordinate bilateral agendas to agreed multilateral objectives.

Coordination needs to begin within each donor agency. Coordination is not only important among multilateral and bilateral donor agencies. It is also a vital issue *within* each donor agency. Projects in different sectors of the same country often work in parallel and fail to tap synergies. This was the case in the Bank's Community Empowerment and Agricultural Projects in Timor-Leste.

A side-effect of the Bank's decentralization to country offices has been the concentration of country knowledge among local staff and inadequate dissemination of this knowledge to the country team, especially to those based in Washington. Addressing the problems of coordination across the various departments of donor agencies (such as among Bank departments dealing with public sector management, conflict prevention and reconstruction, LICUS, capacity development, and research) is particularly important in LICUS, where problems are complex and widespread and often require multisectoral solutions.

Results measurement and monitoring

Monitoring and evaluation are at least as important in LICUS as they are in any other country. Monitoring and evaluation are crucial in LICUS for a number of reasons:

- First, the Bank, like other donors, is still learning what approaches work in LICUS contexts. Closely monitoring experiences in order to draw lessons is critical, and learning and sharing needs to become a more prominent feature of LICUS work.
- Second, given that progress is often slow in these countries, it is important to reassess continually whether the program is on course to achieve the desired outcomes.
- Third, a constantly changing and volatile LICUS environment where progress is often nonlinear means that program adaptation is essential—closely tracking performance will help determine when and what kind of adaptation is necessary.

Effective learning by doing to improve the Bank's future effectiveness in LICUS can only happen with strong monitoring and evaluation.

The Bank has stated that state and peace building should be the goals used to measure the LICUS Initiative's success. But the Bank has yet to identify performance indicators for this purpose or yardsticks against which performance may be measured. Change is often more process oriented, especially in the deterioration and prolonged crisis or impasse business models, and outputs and outcomes that may be expected in the other business models may not be appropriate yardsticks of success. Objectives should be appropriate to particular LICUS contexts, which would, in turn, determine

yardsticks and ensure that the bar of success is set at an appropriate height.

Improving internal organizational support for LICUS work

Field presence alone is insufficient for effective country strategy implementation—it needs to be complemented by adequate communication between field and headquarters donor agency staff, as well as by an adequate number of field staff with the appropriate authority and skills. Understanding of country circumstances is often best achieved through substantial field presence, although that alone is not enough. Internalizing analysis of the country conditions throughout all donor agency departments involved and applying its lessons to all interventions is equally important. In Cambodia, for example, the Bank's field presence has significantly improved understanding of the political situation, but discussions with country team members and other stakeholders suggest that this knowledge may still be highly concentrated among a few managers and staff (mostly in the country office and Bangkok hub), with relatively limited dissemination to the broader country team.

The issue appears to have shifted from a partial understanding of the political realities of Cambodia to a question of where within the Bank's country team this knowledge is located and how it is used to guide decision making in strategy and program implementation. The concentration of in-depth country knowledge among just a few staff members implies that only some Bank activities and interventions benefit. In general, greater knowledge transfer is needed between donor country offices and their headquarters-based country and sector staff.

Despite the cost, field offices need to be adequately staffed if they are to engage effectively with clients. In Angola, the initially small group of field staff faced a multiplicity of tasks, from strategic dialogue with government and donors to logistics such as moving the office to new premises. The situation was made more difficult by the lack of operational-level staff in the field office who could, in consultation with Ministry staff, prepare the ground before high-level meetings between the ministers and the Bank. Moving issues to the top too quickly—because the lower levels were not staffed—led to unnecessary tensions. Donor decisions regarding the number of staff in each LICUS should reflect the extent and nature of intended engagement, considering respective donors' objectives in those countries.

Apart from the absolute numbers, field office staff also need sufficient authority in relation to headquarters to ensure that not every decision has to be approved by headquarters. An effective field presence requires that the right kind of staff be involved in the country. In semistructured interviews done for this review, several donors emphasized that coordination is unusually susceptible to the strengths and the foibles of the individuals involved. More appropriate training for staff being posted to difficult field assignments and improved incentives within the Bank that encourage staff to collaborate with other donors might ameliorate these idiosyncratic risks.

In the deterioration business model, where there might be a breakdown of dialogue with the government, donor agency staff will need strong diplomatic and persuasive skills to ensure that the door remains open for a dialogue with the government, while simultaneously mobilizing nongovernmental groups, including civil society.

In the prolonged crisis or impasse business model, where problems are chronic or there is political stalemate, the necessary staff skills will include immense patience as well as creativity, with constant innovation to break persistent logjams.

In the post-conflict or political transition business model, the necessary staff skills will include specific technical knowledge of how to develop sound economic systems, institutions, and key infrastructure. Staff should also possess the ability to act quickly and decisively in these environments, before the optimism following peace dissipates, and to help guard against the countries falling back into conflict. Since these situations often attract massive international aid, donor staff need strong coordination and sequencing skills to organize both development partners and their activities.

In the gradual improvement business model, the primary staff skill needed is the ability to provide customized technical assistance and work hand-in-hand with a client that is already reforming.

Sharing experiences —both positive and negative— is essential for learning, but doing so effectively requires a receptive institutional environment and management support. Sharing experiences of what is working in different LICUS situations, and what is not, can foster learning. Learning is especially important in LICUS work because the donor community is continuing to grapple with the question of how best to assist these challenging countries. Although the Bank has shared some lessons through its LICUS Learning Group Seminar Series, much more attention is needed to intensify the systematic stock-taking and dissemination of emerging LICUS experiences—both those of the Bank and of other donors, and both positive and negative.

Creating a more receptive institutional environment and ensuring management support for the sharing of negative experiences will be critical. So far, the Bank seems mainly willing to share positive examples, as in its recent LICUS reports.

Effective communication is essential both for ensuring country acceptance of donor approaches for LICUS and for tempering unrealistic country expectations about what can be achieved, especially immediately following the cessation of conflict. Better communication of donor objectives and approaches in LICUS will be needed to ensure country buy-in. It can also prevent disillusionment by tempering unrealistic expectations among stakeholders about what can be achieved in a specific period of time.

In the Bank's deterioration and prolonged crisis or impasse business models, where the economic and social situation is for the most part worsening or stagnant, the communication strategy would need to disseminate actively the benefits of reform to both the government and civil society. In the Bank's post-conflict or political transition business model, in order to prevent the disillusionment that follows unrealistic expectations, the communication strategy should target the entire population and be explicit about what donors will do, when, how, and what results should be expected. The communication strategy in the gradual improvement business model will need to be more informational, presenting relevant cross-country and cross-sectoral experiences.

Immediately following the cessation of conflict, international donors, including the Bank, have often committed large amounts of aid coupled with overly ambitious agendas. This has frequently created high expectations among the population and led to disillusionment when expectations have remained unfulfilled and there are few tangible improvements day to day. Avoiding overambitious agendas and utilizing better communication are critical, and the Bank needs to invest in such strategies.

Better operational guidance is needed for tailoring donor approaches to the special conditions of LICUS. The LICUS Initiative has raised awareness of the need to act differently in LICUS, but the Bank and other donors have yet to identify precisely *how* to do so. The extent to which donor approaches to LICUS need to, and can, efficiently address the causes—not just symptoms—of countries becoming or remaining LICUS also needs greater attention. Solutions that view causes as givens may miss all-important contextual factors. Donor operational guidance must ensure that areas outside the comparative advantage of particular donors be left to others, while their own work both adequately factors in and complements the work done by others.

The Bank's deterioration and prolonged crisis or impasse business models, and the transition and development phases that follow the immediate reconstruction phase in the post-conflict or political transition business model, pose some of the biggest challenges faced by the donor community. These are also areas where there has been relatively little innovative thinking. There is a pressing need for operational guidance in several areas, including ways to prioritize and sequence reforms while avoiding partial solutions; ways to deliver services quickly

without harming long-term government capacity development; ways to foster political reconciliation while also contributing to effective and legitimate governance; ways to internalize political understanding in country strategy design and implementation; and ways to address linkages among politics, security, and development effectively.

The balance of the Bank's recent guidance on LICUS is tilted more toward what instruments should be used rather than outlining actual operational approaches for what needs to be done differently—and how—in varying groups of LICUS. LICUS country teams would also benefit from more narrative-based guidance, of the kind presented in chapter 2 of this review, and from short, problem-oriented notes, rather than the more formal guidance notes that are often too condensed and devoid of sufficient country context.

Recommendations

- ***Clarify the scope and content of the Bank's state-building agenda and strengthen the design and delivery of capacity development and governance support in LICUS.***

Given its weak record on capacity development and governance, as well as its current focus on the more ambitious and complex state-building objective in LICUS, the Bank needs to clarify its areas of comparative advantage in relation to other donors and adopt innovative approaches that ensure better capacity and governance outcomes. Innovative approaches need to be developed for achieving a better fit between the Bank's interventions and the capacity of a LICUS to perform core state functions; ensuring implementation of focused and well-sequenced interventions in LICUS environments, where virtually every aspect of capacity and governance may need significant improvement; and effectively monitoring capacity and governance outcomes.

- ***Develop aid-allocation criteria for LICUS*** *that en-sure they are not under- or over-aided.*

The Bank needs to conduct a technical review of the cumulative effect of the various adjustments to the performance-based allocation system on aid volumes to LICUS. Aid-allocation criteria that reflect the Bank's objectives in LICUS and ensure that these countries are not under- or over-aided need to be developed. Whether and to what extent the criteria should be based on factors other than policy performance (such as levels of other donor assistance, assessment of potential risks and rewards, and regional and global spillovers) needs to be examined, keeping in mind that aid is limited and trade-offs will have to be made.

- **Strengthen internal Bank support for LICUS work over the next three years.**

Two aspects of internal Bank support need attention. **First,** staffing numbers, skills, and incentives for working on LICUS need to be prioritized. Ensuring adequate incentives to attract qualified staff—both at headquarters and in field offices—to work on LICUS will require giving clear signals of what is deemed to be success in LICUS, what outcomes staff will be held accountable for, how much risk it is reasonable to take, how failure will be judged, and how overall performance evaluation ratings and staff career development will take these into account.

As in Olympic diving, where the scoring system factors in both the technical perfection and the difficulty of the dive, staff performance in LICUS should be judged by assigning appropriate weight to the extent of challenges presented by varying LICUS environments. Signaling the importance of LICUS work throughout the management hierarchy will also be required.

Apart from incentives, the Bank needs to ensure that staff working on LICUS has relevant skills, such as in public sector management; are capable of seeking and using political knowledge; and are willing and able to work in interdisciplinary teams. Current plans to address these issues in the forthcoming *Strengthening the Organizational Response to Fragile States* paper are welcome, even if late.

More systematic thinking is needed about staffing decisions for LICUS within the context of the Bank's overall staffing, recognizing that assigning more and better-qualified staff to work on LICUS would likely mean trade-offs for other Bank country teams. Trade-offs to benefit LICUS may or may not be justified, depending on the Bank's objectives for LICUS as well as other Bank clients' needs for assistance.

Second, the organizational structure for LICUS and conflict work needs to be streamlined. The Bank needs to ensure an efficient organizational arrangement that removes duplication and fragmentation of support between the LICUS and the CPR Units.

- **Reassess the value added of the LICUS approach after three years.**

The value of the LICUS category and approach, including the operational usefulness of the business models, needs to be independently evaluated after three years, when sufficient experience with the outcomes of the approach will be available. At that time it should be possible to address the more fundamental question of whether and to what extent Bank assistance can effectively support sustainable state building. Continued Bank support for the LICUS category and approach should be based on the findings of that reassessment.

Principaux messages de l'évaluation

- Le développement est un défi extrêmement difficile à relever dans les États fragiles et la communauté des bailleurs de fonds continue de s'interroger sur la meilleure façon de leur venir en aide. La Banque mondiale participe activement aux débats internationaux sur les LICUS et a amélioré ses capacités opérationnelles d'assistance depuis le lancement de l'initiative en faveur des LICUS en 2002.

- Avant la mise en place de cette initiative, les programmes d'aide de la Banque aux LICUS avaient donné des résultats généralement peu satisfaisants. L'initiative a attiré l'attention de la Banque sur les LICUS mais il est encore trop tôt pour évaluer les résultats. L'expérience sur le terrain est mitigée et les conclusions de l'évaluation effectuée par le Groupe indépendant d'évaluation (IEG) indiquent pour la plupart que les objectifs n'ont pas été entièrement atteints.

- En adoptant l'édification de l'État comme objectif central, la Banque a placé le renforcement des capacités et la gouvernance, deux domaines historiquement faibles, au cœur de son action dans les LICUS. Pour centrer l'initiative en faveur des LICUS sur le programme complexe d'édification de l'État, la Banque doit préciser les domaines dans lesquels elle a un avantage relatif, ainsi que la portée et la teneur de ce programme. Elle doit également trouver de nouveaux moyens d'améliorer les résultats en matière de renforcement des capacités et de gouvernance et définir des indicateurs de performance pour mesurer les résultats obtenus sur le plan de l'édification de l'État.

- Trois ans après le lancement de l'initiative en faveur des LICUS, des progrès limités ont été accomplis sur le front des importantes réformes à effectuer dans le domaine des ressources humaines, qu'il s'agisse des effectifs, de la qualité du personnel ou des mesures d'encouragement offerts au personnel qui mène des travaux au titre des LICUS.

- Bien que la Banque ait récemment souligné la nécessité d'accroître sa présence dans les LICUS, cela ne suffira pas à garantir la bonne mise en œuvre des stratégies-pays. L'accroissement de sa présence sur le terrain doit être allié à une meilleure communication entre les bureaux extérieurs de la Banque et le siège. Il importe également de déployer un personnel de terrain suffisamment nombreux et doté des pouvoirs et des compétences voulus.

- Les programmes de réformes des bailleurs de fonds dans les LICUS pourraient être plus sélectifs. Dans l'environnement complexe des LICUS, où des réformes s'imposent dans pratiquement tous les secteurs, il est impératif de bien échelonner les réformes et de prévoir suffisamment de temps pour les mettre en oeuvre si l'on entend produire les résultats escomptés sans trop lourdement grever les capacités limitées des LICUS.

Résumé analytique

Avec près de 500 millions d'habitants dont la moitié gagnent moins de 1 dollar par jour, les pays à faible revenu en difficulté (jusqu' à récemment dénommés LICUS) attirent une attention grandissante. Il y a tout lieu de douter de l'aptitude de ces pays à atteindre les objectifs de développement pour le Millénaire (ODM) et de craindre des effets économiques défavorables sur les pays voisins ainsi que les retombées mondiales qui pourraient s'ensuivre.

Accablés de problèmes chroniques, les LICUS ont des impératifs de développement qui présentent d'énormes défis. La plupart de ces pays souffrent d'une mauvaise gouvernance et sont en proie à des conflits internes de longue date ou connaissent des difficultés de transition post-conflictuelle. Tous sont confrontés aux mêmes problèmes : manque de sécurité, relations sociales fragmentées, grave corruption, détérioration de l'ordre public, absence de mécanismes de mise en place de pouvoirs légitimes, énormes besoins d'investissement en souffrance et ressources publiques limitées pour le développement. Les interventions internationales dans ces pays n'ont jusqu'à présent pas produit d'améliorations notables.

Les bailleurs de fonds s'interrogent sur les meilleurs moyens d'aider les pays confrontés à des problèmes aussi épineux. Du fait qu'ils ont des motivations et des objectifs différents, les bailleurs de fonds et les chercheurs ont choisi de s'attaquer à différents aspects de ces problèmes, ce qui les a conduits à mettre l'accent sur différents groupes de pays. Par exemple, les études récemment menées par le Center for Global Development portent sur les pays à faible revenu en stagnation (sur la base du produit national brut par habitant et des taux de croissance), tandis que l'indice des pays en situation de faillite de *Foreign Policy* met l'accent sur l'échec de l'État en identifiant les pays sur la base de critères tels que le niveau de déclin économique, la sécurité, les élites divisées en factions, les personnes déplacées, les violations des droits de l'homme et les interventions extérieures. L'Agence des États-Unis pour le développement international (USAID) se concentre sur les problèmes de vulnérabilité et les situations de crise, généralement dans l'arène politique. L'Agence britannique pour le développement international (DFID) et l'Organisation de coopération et de développement économiques/Comité d'aide au développement (OCDE/CAD) utilisent la même définition que la Banque mondiale pour identifier les États fragiles.

Tels que définis par la Banque mondiale, tous les LICUS se caractérisent par des politiques, des institutions et une gouvernance faibles. La Banque a utilisé deux critères pour définir les pays à faible revenu les moins performants et les plus en difficulté (le terme LICUS ne désigne donc pas les pays à faible revenu qui éprouvent tout juste quelques difficultés, lesquels sont identifiés par la Banque uniquement aux fins de suivi) : revenu par habitant inférieur au seuil d'éligibilité défini par l'Association internationale du développement (IDA) et note égale ou inférieure à 3 (égale ou inférieure à 2,5 pour les pays à faible revenu les plus en difficulté) dans le cadre des Évaluations de la politique et des institutions nationales (CPIA) et des Évaluations CPIA de la gestion et des institutions du secteur public.

Certains pays à faible revenu pour lesquels il n'existe pas de données CPIA sont également inclus. Pour l'exercice 05, la Banque a identifié 25 pays faisant partie des LICUS. Six LICUS recensés durant l'exercice 05 n'avaient pas reçu de notation CPIA (Afghanistan, Liberia, Myanmar, Somalie, Timor-Leste et territoire du Kosovo). Ces données sont basées sur l'évaluation de l'aide fournie par la Banque aux 25 pays classés dans le groupe des LICUS durant l'exercice 05.

Les prêts et les budgets administratifs affectés aux LICUS ont augmenté depuis le lancement de l'initiative en faveur de ces pays. Les prêts aux LICUS ont augmenté de quelque 2,5 milliards de dollars durant l'exercice 00–02 (avant le lancement de l'initiative) à environ 4,1 milliards de dollars durant l'exercice 03–05 (depuis le lancement de l'initiative). En valeur par habitant, les prêts aux LICUS ont varié entre 0 et 25,4 dollars durant l'exercice 03–05. Les budgets administratifs affectés aux LICUS ont augmenté de quelque 104 millions de dollars durant l'exercice 00–02 à environ 161 millions de dollars durant l'exercice 03–05. En valeur par habitant, les budgets administratifs affectés aux LICUS se sont établis entre 0,002 et 4,5 durant l'exercice 03–05.

Une grande partie des prêts alloués aux LICUS durant l'exercice 03–05 est allée aux LICUS sortant d'un conflit (les pays sortant d'un conflit sont identifiés sur la base des indicateurs de progrès post-conflit, ou PCPI, afin de déterminer les dons accordés par l'IDA à titre

exceptionnel), tandis que les budgets administratifs ont été plus également répartis entre les LICUS (7 LICUS sortant d'un conflit sur les 25 LICUS ont reçu 64 % du montant total des prêts aux LICUS et 34 % du budget administratif total affecté à ces pays).

Même si les LICUS sortant d'un conflit auraient peut-être reçu une grande partie des prêts en l'absence de l'initiative en faveur des LICUS (étant donné que l'IDA accordait déjà des fonds à titre exceptionnel aux pays sortant d'un conflit avant le lancement de cette initiative), l'initiative a probablement contribué à une répartition plus égale des budgets administratifs entre les pays du groupe (sachant que les budgets administratifs ont augmenté de 400 % entre les exercices 00–02 et 03–05 pour trois LICUS, le Liberia, la Somalie et le Soudan, qui auraient reçu une minuscule portion des budgets administratifs avant l'initiative car les prêts accordés à ces pays sont classés improductifs).

La démarche adoptée par la Banque pour les LICUS a évolué depuis sa formulation initiale en 2002, suivant six principes fondamentaux définis pour ces pays (voir le tableau ES.1). Au départ, l'initiative visait à fournir une aide plus efficace en utilisant d'autres instruments, tels que des travaux d'analyse et des transferts de connaissances, assortis de transferts financiers pour promouvoir le changement.

En 2005, les objectifs et la portée de l'initiative en faveur des LICUS ont été modifiés en privilégiant l'efficacité générale de l'aide au détriment de l'édification de l'État. Dans le cadre de l'initiative, quatre modèles d'intervention (détérioration, crise prolongée ou impasse, situation post-conflictuelle ou transition politique, et amélioration graduelle) ont également été adoptés pour traiter séparément les différents types de LICUS. La démarche adoptée en 2005 est restée axée sur les thèmes retenus en 2002, à savoir l'apprentissage par l'action et les questions organisationnelles, tout en renforçant l'action dans ces domaines.

La présente étude a pour objet de répondre à trois questions :

• Dans quelle mesure la démarche suivie par la Banque pour les LICUS est-elle efficace ?

- Dans quelle mesure les critères retenus par la Banque pour identifier et classer les LICUS sont-ils utiles sur le plan opérationnel, et dans quelle mesure le système de répartition de l'aide est-il utile à cet égard ?
- L'appui interne fourni par la Banque aux travaux sur les LICUS est-il approprié?

Principaux résultats et conclusions

Efficacité de la démarche suivie par la Banque pour les LICUS

L'expérience montre que les principes fondamentaux définis pour les LICUS ont été plus ou moins bien appliqués (voir le tableau RA.1). Les problèmes rencontrés au niveau de l'exécution sont attribuables dans certains cas aux objectifs trop ambitieux de la Banque (qui doit donc réviser ses objectifs à la baisse), et dans d'autres cas au niveau inadéquat des efforts ou des apports de la Banque, comme l'indiquent les enquêtes réalisées par l'IEG et son évaluation des rapports d'achèvement des stratégies d'aide-pays (ce qui nécessite d'intensifier les efforts).

La majorité des parties prenantes interrogées dans le cadre de l'enquête menée par l'IEG a indiqué que le programme général de la Banque dans les LICUS avait contribué dans une faible mesure au développement—opinion qui concerne l'appui global de la Banque et non la démarche proprement dite adoptée pour les LICUS.

Les principes définis pour les LICUS ont initialement produit des résultats positifs. L'initiative de la Banque en faveur des LICUS a permis à la Banque d'accroître ses opérations dans les pays où elles auraient probablement été moins importantes. La Banque a récemment lancé des opérations dans plusieurs LICUS où la paix vient d'être rétablie ou qui amorcent une phase de transition politique. La Banque a également contribué à la stabilité macroéconomique et à la mise en place d'une importante infrastructure matérielle, notamment dans les LICUS sortant d'un conflit. D'importants progrès ont été réalisés en matière de coordination des bailleurs de fonds sur le plan de la

Tableau RA.1 : Mise en oeuvre des principes fondamentaux définis pour les LICUS

Principes définis pour les LICUS	Mise en oeuvre
Rester mobilisés	**Substantielle**
Ancrer les stratégies dans une analyse sociopolitique plus robuste	**Moyenne**
• Comprendre la situation politique	• Moyenne à substantielle
• Intégrer la compréhension politique à la conception et à la mise en œuvre des stratégies	• Moyenne à faible
Promouvoir la demande et les capacités internes de changement positif	**Faible**
Promouvoir une première série de réformes simples et réalisables	**Moyenne à faible**
• Réformes macroéconomiques	• Substantielle
• Mise en place d'une infrastructure matérielle	• Substantielle
• Transition de la phase de reconstruction post-conflit à la phase de développement	• Faible
• Sélectivité et définition des priorités	• Faible
Étudier de nouveaux mécanismes de fourniture des services sociaux	**Moyenne**
Collaboration des bailleurs de fonds	**Moyenne**
• Au niveau des politiques internationales	• Substantielle
• Au niveau national	• Moyenne à faible
Mesure et suivi des résultats[a]	**Faible**

Sources : Fnquêtes et analyses thématiques de base effectuées pour cette étude, IEG, 2005.

a. Pas considéré par la Banque comme un principe fondamental en soi, mais inclus par l'IEG car cette activité est cruciale pour le programme d'apprentissage par l'action de la Banque dans les LICUS.

politique internationale, comme en témoigne l'adhésion récente d'un large éventail de bailleurs de fonds, dont la Banque, aux douze principes d'intervention internationale définis par l'OCDE/CAD.

La Banque a souvent joué un rôle de chef de file en tant que coprésident des réunions internationales des bailleurs de fonds et co-auteur de documents d'orientation communs. Les modèles d'intervention récemment adoptés par la Banque pour tenir compte des différents types de LICUS devraient permettre de prendre des mesures mieux adaptées à la situation de chaque pays. Le pourcentage de projets achevés dans les LICUS qui ont donné des résultats jugés satisfaisants par l'IEG est passé de 50 % durant l'exercice 02, avant le lancement de l'initiative en faveur des LICUS, à 58 % en 2004 et à 82 % en 2005. Les chiffres correspondants pour les projets réalisés dans les pays à faible revenu non classés dans le groupe des LICUS varient entre 70 et 79 %.

Mais il reste de sérieux défis à relever. Les opérations initiales de la Banque dans certains LICUS n'ont pas toujours été suivies par un programme de réformes ciblées et bien échelonnées. D'autre part, il reste à mieux intégrer les réalités politiques dans la conception et la mise en œuvre des stratégies-pays de la Banque. Celle-ci doit également améliorer la qualité de la coordination de ses opérations dans les pays avec celles des autres bailleurs de fonds, notamment en assurant un suivi de l'exécution qui aille au-delà des accords de principe.

Par ailleurs, la Banque a placé le renforcement des capacités et la gouvernance, deux domaines historiquement faibles, au cœur de son action en adoptant l'objectif plus complexe d'édification de l'État. Ce recentrage signifie que la Banque doit identifier plus efficacement son avantage relatif, améliorer sa performance, notamment en définissant de nouvelles approches, et identifier des partenaires à même de compléter ses travaux pour produire les résultats visés. Enfin, le choix du terme *édification de l'État* n'est peut-être pas heureux, car il a des connotations politiques et idéologiques.

La Banque doit élaborer ses méthodes opérationnelles pour les LICUS, notamment pour les modèles d'intervention dans les pays en situation de *détérioration, de crise prolongée ou d'impasse*. Il est également nécessaire de perfectionner les modèles en tenant plus explicitement compte des écarts de capacité d'exécution des fonctions centrales de l'État (mobilisation des ressources, répartition des ressources, fourniture des services sociaux et des infrastructures de base, et dispositions politiques pour faire face à l'opposition et aux problèmes de sécurité) pour permettre à la Banque de mieux adapter ses méthodes opérationnelles à l'environnement institutionnel des LICUS.

Les travaux de la Banque sur les pays sortant d'un conflit sont plus anciens que l'initiative en faveur des LICUS et le modèle d'intervention correspondant pour les LICUS sortant d'un conflit est plus clairement défini que les autres modèles d'intervention. Il présente cependant des lacunes et doit être encore mis au point pour guider les phases de transition et de développement qui suivent la phase de reconstruction post-conflit. D'autre part, bien que la Banque accorde une attention grandissante à la prévention des conflits, on dispose de données limitées sur l'efficacité de ses efforts dans ce domaine.

Il reste à définir clairement le rôle et l'avantage relatif de la Banque en matière de prévention des conflits, d'autant plus que les mesures à prendre dans ce domaine nécessitent que la Banque accorde une plus grande attention aux *causes véritables* des conflits et examine les facteurs ethniques, sociologiques et politiques. La Banque doit mieux définir en quoi consiste son objectif de consolidation de la paix et comment atteindre cet objectif.

Utilité opérationnelle des mécanismes retenus par la Banque pour l'identification et le classement des LICUS, ainsi que pour l'affectation de l'aide à ces pays

Malgré le recentrage sur des objectifs d'édification de l'État et de consolidation de la paix, la Banque continue d'utiliser presque exclusivement les CPIA pour identifier les LICUS. Ces évaluations ne tiennent cependant pas compte de certains aspects fondamentaux de la fragilité des États (tels que les moyens de faire faire à l'opposition politique) et des conflits (tels que l'instabilité politique et la sécurité ou le risque de conflit) et il serait bon de les compléter par d'autres dispositifs. Un meilleur moyen d'identifier les LICUS serait d'utiliser un cadre analytique qui est plus explicitement axé sur les objectifs de l'initiative en faveur des LICUS.

Le système utilisé par la Banque pour allouer les ressources de l'IDA (appelé système d'affectation des fonds en fonction de la performance) est devenu plus sélectif au fil des années et les pays dont les politiques, les institutions et la gouvernance sont plus faibles reçoivent moins de ressources de l'IDA. Cela a soulevé la question de savoir si l'IDA alloue des montants appropriés aux LICUS. Les modifications apportées au système d'affectation des fonds en fonction de la performance se sont traduites par un accroissement des ressources allouées par l'IDA, notamment à certains LICUS sortant d'un conflit ou en transition politique. Mais il est difficile de dire si les niveaux actuels de financement IDA garantissent que les LICUS ne reçoivent pas une aide insuffisante ou excessive.

La question de la répartition de l'aide a ressurgi, certaines études mettant en cause les preuves empiriques de la corrélation positive entre les politiques et l'efficacité de l'aide (sur laquelle repose le système d'affectation des fonds en fonction de la performance). D'autres études montrent que l'aide peut contribuer à promouvoir des changements d'orientation durables dans les États en situation de faillite en créant et renforçant les conditions nécessaires aux réformes ou en accroissant les chances que les réformes mises en place s'inscrivent dans la durée. Ces études concluent que l'aide fournie aux LICUS peut produire des résultats exceptionnels, bien que les risques d'échec soient substantiels.

Pour sa part, la Banque doit aborder la question de l'affectation de l'aide aux LICUS d'une manière qui tienne compte de ses objectifs pour ces pays et garantisse que les LICUS ne reçoivent pas une aide insuffisante ou excessive.

Validité et efficacité de l'appui interne de la Banque aux travaux menés au titre des LICUS

L'appui interne fourni par la Banque aux travaux menés au titre des LICUS s'est amélioré sur plusieurs fronts :

- Etoffement des travaux d'analyse en dissociant les budgets administratifs affectés aux études économiques et sectorielles et à l'assistance technique d'une part, des volumes de financement d'autre part
- Utilisation de Notes de stratégie intérimaire qui permettent de concevoir des stratégies portant sur une plus courte période pour tenir compte de l'instabilité de la situation dans les LICUS
- Accès des responsables des LICUS à l'équipe de direction de la Banque
- Création du Fonds fiduciaire LICUS pour fournir des financements aux pays dont la dette est improductive (la Banque n'avait jusqu'alors pas d'instrument à cet effet).

À la lumière des données d'expérience des pays, l'équipe chargée des LICUS a établi des directives sur un certain nombre de questions importantes pour enrichir les conseils opérationnels fournis aux équipes-pays et les débats plus généraux sur la politique extérieure.

Cependant, trois ans après avoir reconnu la nécessité de modifier sa culture interne afin de bien mettre en œuvre la démarche adoptée pour les LICUS, la Banque a peu progressé sur le plan de l'appui interne fourni aux travaux sur les LICUS. Il reste beaucoup à faire en matière de réformes des ressources humaines, qu'il s'agisse des effectifs, de la qualité du personnel et des incitations offertes pour encourager à poursuivre les travaux sur les LICUS. Les commentaires du personnel de la Banque sur l'importance de travailler à la fois sur les LICUS et sur les autres pays montrent que les travaux accomplis au titre des LICUS ne sont pas suffisamment pris en compte au sein de la Banque et soulignent la nécessité de réformer le système d'incitation.

Les membres du personnel interrogés ont indiqué que les directeurs des opérations pour les pays n'accordent pas tous la même attention aux LICUS, tout particulièrement s'ils sont également chargés d'un pays plus vaste, plus « performant » ou plus médiatisé, ce qui souligne la nécessité d'accorder une attention soutenue aux travaux sur les LICUS à tous les niveaux de la direction. Dans l'enquête menée par l'IEG auprès des parties prenantes, la majorité des personnes interrogées à la Banque ont indiqué que le fait de travailler sur les LICUS n'avait rien changé dans plusieurs aspects des ressources humaines (voir la figure RA.1).

Il y a de nombreux doubles emplois et il règne une grande confusion sur le rôle et les responsabilités de l'équipe chargée des LICUS d'une part, et celle chargée de la prévention des conflits et de la reconstruction d'autre part. Les personnes interrogées ont indiqué qu'elles ne savent pas à quelle équipe s'adresser pour obtenir des conseils spécifiques ni quel type de soutien elles peuvent attendre de chaque équipe. Environ les deux tiers des membres du personnel de la Banque ayant participé à l'enquête de l'IEG auprès des parties prenantes ont indiqué que l'organisation actuelle n'était pas satisfaisante : 37 % ont dit qu'il y avait des doubles emplois entre l'appui fourni par l'équipe de la Banque chargée des LICUS et celui fourni par l'équipe chargée de la prévention des conflits et la reconstruction ; 15 % estiment qu'il y a de nombreux doubles emplois et 12 % disent qu'il y a un conflit ou une contradiction.

Leçons tirées de l'expérience de la Banque et des autres bailleurs de fonds

Il y a plusieurs enseignements à tirer de cette évaluation de l'application par la Banque des principes fondamentaux régissant la démarche suivie pour les LICUS. Le rapport 2002 du groupe de travail sur les LICUS (Banque mondiale 2002) indique qu'il y a des améliorations à apporter dans bon nombre des domaines couverts dans le cadre de ce bilan et les rapports 2005 de la Banque sur les LICUS soulignent également cette nécessité. Par exemple, il importe d'ancrer les stratégies dans une analyse sociopolitique plus rigoureuse et de promouvoir des programmes de réformes très ciblés. Les enseignements tirés reposent sur l'expérience de la Banque mais ils peuvent également fournir des orientations aux autres bailleurs de fonds sur l'aide à fournir aux LICUS.

Intervention dans les LICUS

Rester mobilisés n'est pas une fin en soi et il faut rapidement mettre en place un programme de réforme clair et approprié dans les LICUS. En

Figure RA.1 : La majorité des personnes interrogées à la Banque ont indiqué que le fait de travailler sur les LICUS n'avait rien changé dans plusieurs domaines (voir ci-dessous)

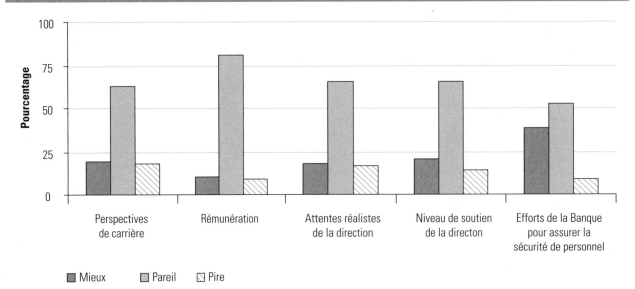

Source : Annexe Z (Résultats de l'enquête auprès des parties prenantes).

Note : Le nombre de réponses valides varie entre 213 et 238. La question a été posée sans distinction à des personnes qui avaient travaillé sur un LICUS ou sur des pays ne faisant pas partie de ce groupe.

l'absence d'un programme de réforme clair et approprié, les premiers succès remportés par les opérations dans les pays risquent d'être de courte durée et de peu contribuer à la réalisation des objetifs des stratégies-pays. Les exemples de la République centrafricaine et de Haïti montrent qu'il peut être difficile de poursuivre sur la lancée des premiers succès remportés dans les LICUS. Les progrès politiques ne s'étant pas répercutés dans l'arène économique, le gouvernement de la République centrafricaine est aujourd'hui confronté à une crise budgétaire qui pourrait être lourde de conséquences. À Haïti, il semble que les bailleurs de fonds n'aient pas accordé l'attention voulue au maintien d'un niveau minimum de sécurité. Dans les deux cas, les résultats initialement favorables de l'initiative en faveur des LICUS risquent de ne pas s'inscrire dans la durée.

Dans certains cas, le retrait stratégique – à l'exception des travaux d'analyse internes – pourrait être nécessaire, du moins temporairement. C'est une stratégie particulièrement appropriée lorsque l'intervention de la Banque donne l'impression de légitimer à tort le gouvernement d'un LICUS ou lorsque que cela atténue les pressions exercées en faveur des réformes, ce qui pourrait entraver la mise en place des conditions nécessaires à une réforme politique réelle et durable.

Dans les scénarios de détérioration ou de crise prolongée, où les bailleurs de fonds et les autorités locales ne sont souvent pas d'accord sur la stratégie de développement, l'intervention doit inclure un dialogue sur l'action à mener pour ouvrir la voie aux réformes, tout en préparant un programme de réforme au cas où les conditions deviendraient favorables. Dans les scénarios de situation post-conflictuelle ou de transition politique et d'amélioration graduelle, l'intervention devra être de nature plus technique et mettre davantage l'accent sur la mise en œuvre du programme de réforme, compte tenu du plus haut degré de consensus entre les bailleurs de fonds et le gouvernement sur les réformes à entreprendre.

Les directives de la Banque pour les pays en conflit prolongé ou dans l'impasse politique stipulent que « les questions de développement relativement peu controversées peuvent fournir le point de départ d'un dialogue constructif entre les parties en conflit ». Pour les pays où la gouvernance se dégrade, les directives indiquent que la Banque devrait « donner son avis sur les questions économiques particulièrement importantes pour les efforts de médiation et susceptibles d'aider à relancer le dialogue » (Banque mondiale 2005e).

Les obstacles à la prise en main des opérations par le pays et à l'amélioration des capacités d'absorption concernent tant les produits de diffusion du savoir que les produits financiers. La participation des homologues nationaux aux travaux d'analyse de la Banque reste limitée aux questions administratives. Les pays clients participent beaucoup moins à la sélection des sujets d'étude et à la réalisation des analyses, ce qui réduit l'adhésion nationale. La participation des homologues nationaux est cependant indispensable pour assurer la prise en charge des opérations par le pays client et accroître l'impact des travaux d'analyse.

Au Tadjikistan, la faible participation des autorités locales à la sélection et à la réalisation des travaux d'analyse de la Banque a limité leur intérêt pour les résultats, ce qui a empêché le bon déroulement des travaux. En Angola, certains travaux d'analyse menés par la Banque (tels que le récent Mémorandum économique sur le pays) ont été considérés par les hauts responsables politiques comme une ingérence de la Banque dans leurs affaires internes, ce qui a limité l'adhésion nationale et le renforcement des capacités. Sans adhésion nationale, il y a peu de chances que les travaux d'analyse influencent la politique du gouvernement.

Le manque de capacité d'absorption des autorités des LICUS pour utiliser les travaux d'analyse pourrait également limiter les possibilités de transfert de connaissances. Par exemple, le gouvernement angolais a approuvé la Note de stratégie intérimaire de la Banque mais exprimé son inquiétude face au volume des travaux d'analyse et de conseil envisagé, ce qui a soulevé la question de savoir si le gouvernement utiliserait pleinement les services d'analyse et de conseil. La capacité d'absorption du gouvernement est très faible, et les travaux d'analyse et de conseil effectués essentiellement par la Banque risquent de créer des tensions avec le gouvernement, quelle que soit leur qualité technique. Au Cambodge, les services d'analyse et de conseil prévus dans la stratégie d'aide au pays (CAS) définie en 2005, qui représentent 30 activités à mener à bien durant l'exercice 05-07, semblent trop ambitieux compte tenu des faibles capacités institutionnelles du pays.

Analyse politique et son utilisation dans la stratégie-pays

Il est essentiel que les bailleurs de fonds demandent et utilisent de bonnes analyses politiques dans les LICUS, sans nécessairement les réaliser eux-mêmes. L'objectif d'une équipe-pays devrait être de demander ou utiliser (sans forcément les réaliser) des analyses qui se rapportent ou servent directement à l'élaboration d'une stratégie. Dans les LICUS, notamment lorsqu'il est essentiel d'agir vite, les bailleurs de fonds doivent veiller à ce que les analyses politiques existantes soient exploitées avant de faire réaliser de nouvelles analyses.

En République démocratique populaire lao, la Banque a mis à profit les analyses politiques existantes et invité un politologue qui avait publié de nombreux articles sur le pays à présenter un exposé à l'équipe-pays sur la situation politique et la réforme dans le pays. Cela a permis d'établir un résumé indépendant des analyses politiques pertinentes (adapté aux besoins des bailleurs de fonds, en particulier de la Banque) qui a été distribué aux membres du personnel de la Banque concernés et à d'autres bailleurs de fonds. Cela a également évité d'effectuer une analyse « maison » plus coûteuse, ainsi que des tensions potentielles avec le gouvernement, en permettant à la Banque de ne pas se noyer dans les détails de l'analyse. Pour la Banque, l'acquisition et la diffusion des connaissances existantes se sont avérées plus importantes et efficaces que la création de savoir.

Les bailleurs de fonds doivent s'attacher à aider les services concernés à intégrer les analyses politiques à la conception et à la mise en œuvre de la stratégie. Bien que la Banque ait effectué ou ait eu accès à de bonnes analyses politiques dans certains LICUS, elle n'a pas suffisamment tenu compte de ces analyses dans sa stratégie. Par exemple, la stratégie intérimaire en Papouasie-Nouvelle-Guinée contient une bonne analyse du système politique et reconnaît les problèmes en présence, tels que les allégeances de clan, le clientélisme politique, la corruption et le manque de capacité, mais elle les traite comme des problèmes techniques et n'en tient pas convenablement compte pour étayer la démarche globale.

Un programme de réforme ciblé

Dans l'environnement complexe des LICUS, où des réformes s'imposent dans pratiquement tous les secteurs, il est impératif de bien échelonner les réformes et de prévoir suffisamment de temps pour les mettre en oeuvre si l'on entend produire les résultats escomptés sans trop lourdement grever les capacités limitées des LICUS. Alors que les bailleurs de fonds doivent collectivement faire preuve de sélectivité, c'est loin d'être le cas, comme le montrent les exemples du programme de réforme parrainé par les bailleurs de fonds en Afghanistan et aussi le cadre de coopération intérimaire à Haïti décrits ci-après. Cependant, même si tous les bailleurs de fonds ne parviennent pas immédiatement à appliquer le principe de sélectivité, la Banque doit veiller à ce que son propre programme d'aide soit ciblé et sélectif, en faisant appel à ses compétences de base. La Banque a fait preuve d'une plus grande sélectivité au cours des dernières années, mais cela reste une gageure.

En Afghanistan, les réformes parrainées par les bailleurs de fonds sont de nature très diverse, manquent de sélectivité et ont conduit à l'élaboration de 120 projets de loi. Il est impératif que les bailleurs de fonds définissent les priorités et le calendrier de ces réformes, qui portent sur pratiquement tous les secteurs économiques et sociaux du pays. À Haïti, le cadre de coopération intérimaire est censé fournir des orientations pour l'aide internationale et la coopération avec le pays jusqu'en septembre 2006. Il couvre pratiquement toutes les fonctions de base de l'État, que ce soit la sécurité, le dialogue national, la gouvernance économique, le redressement économique ou les services essentiels. Individuellement, chacun de ces domaines semble important, mais ensemble ils représentent un programme monumental.

S'agissant du propre programme d'aide de la Banque, l'évaluation par l'IEG du rapport d'achèvement de la CAS à São Tomé-et-Principe pour les exercices 01-05 montre que la Banque avait des objectifs beaucoup trop ambitieux par rapport aux ressources allouées au pays. Au total, nombre des objectifs de la CAS n'ont pas été réalisés ou ne l'ont été que partiellement.

Outre la sélectivité dans les CAS, il faut bien veiller à ce que les réformes mises en œuvre dans les pays soient ciblées et hiérarchisées. Le manque de sélectivité et l'absence d'un ordre de priorité dans les programmes de réforme soulèvent des questions d'efficacité, compte tenu des capacités limitées des LICUS. Bien qu'il soit difficile d'être sélectif dans un pays où il faut trouver une solution rapide à de nombreux problèmes, il est essentiel de bien échelonner les réformes pour éviter de trop lourdement grever les capacités limitées des LICUS, tout en évitant des solutions partielles. L'étalement des réformes sur un nombre suffisant d'années est essentiel, de même que la volonté des bailleurs de fonds de veiller à leur mise en œuvre.

Au Timor-Leste, les bailleurs de fonds se sont peut-être retirés trop tôt, sans accorder l'attention voulue aux pressants besoins de capacités du pays. À Haïti, l'aide au développement a été très variable au fil du temps. Le pays a connu des hauts et des bas dans ses relations avec la communauté des bailleurs de fonds. Cela aurait pu être évité si les bailleurs de fonds avaient mieux coordonné et échelonné leur aide.

Renforcement des capacités dans les LICUS sortant d'un conflit

Les programmes de renforcement des capacités et d'amélioration de la gouvernance doivent être lancés rapidement, même dans les LICUS sortant d'un conflit. Au lendemain d'un conflit, la communauté internationale des bailleurs de fonds a tendance à concentrer son assistance sur la reconstruction de l'infrastructure. Vu les faibles capacités d'utilisation de l'aide et la mauvaise gestion des affaires publiques dans la plupart des LICUS sortant d'un conflit, la priorité initiale devrait être de renforcer les capacités et d'améliorer la gouvernance, pas seulement de reconstruire l'infrastructure matérielle. Cela pourrait passer par le renforcement des institutions publiques ou la création de nouvelles institutions, la réforme de la fonction publique et le recours aux compétences locales. Si on fait appel à des experts étrangers pour l'assistance technique, il faut veiller à ce que cela ne compromette pas le développement à long terme des capacités *locales*.

Coordination des bailleurs de fonds

La coordination des bailleurs de fonds ne peut être efficace sans une vision et un objectif communs. Lorsque les objectifs des bailleurs de fonds ne peuvent pas être pleinement harmonisés, il est important qu'ils soient au moins complémentaires. La démarche adoptée par la Banque n'a pas entièrement tenu compte des différentes motivations des bailleurs de fonds dans leurs opérations dans les LICUS. Bien que la notion globale de fragilité soit généralement comprise et acceptée, les pays jugés fragiles diffèrent selon les bailleurs de fonds. Les raisons de soutenir les États fragiles vont de la sécurité à la prévention des conflits, en passant par l'efficacité de l'aide, le développement équitable, la réduction de la pauvreté, l'édification de l'État et la consolidation de la paix.

En Afghanistan et au Tadjikistan, les enquêtes réalisées par l'IEG montrent que les principaux bailleurs de fonds n'ont pas le même objectif. En l'absence d'un objectif global commun, les politiques adoptées ne peuvent être cohérentes. L'ampleur et la nature des moyens déployés par la Banque pour coordonner l'action des bailleurs de fonds ne tiennent pas suffisamment compte des objectifs des différents acteurs dans chaque pays. Ceci étant, la coordination des bailleurs de fonds est une forme d'action collective qui demande que les autres bailleurs de fonds se montrent également solidaires de la

Banque et subordonnent leurs programmes bilatéraux aux objectifs multilatéraux convenus.

Coordination bien ordonnée commence par soi-même. La coordination n'est pas seulement importante entre les donateurs multilatéraux et bilatéraux. C'est également un impératif *au sein* de chaque bailleur de fonds. Les projets réalisés dans différents secteurs d'un même pays sont souvent exécutés parallèlement sans exploiter les synergies, comme dans le cas des projets d'autonomisation des populations locales et de promotion de l'agriculture parrainés par la Banque au Timor-Leste.

L'une des conséquences indirectes de la décentralisation des opérations de la Banque dans les bureaux extérieurs a été la concentration des données sur les pays entre les mains du personnel local et le manque de communication de ces données aux membres de l'équipe-pays, notamment ceux basés à Washington. Il est essentiel de régler les problèmes de coordination entre les différents services des bailleurs de fonds (tels que les services de la Banque chargés de la gestion du secteur public, de la prévention des conflits et de la reconstruction, des LICUS, du renforcement des capacités et des études) dans les LICUS, où les problèmes sont nombreux et complexes et nécessitent souvent des interventions multisectorielles.

Mesure et suivi des résultats

Le suivi et l'évaluation sont au moins aussi importants dans les LICUS que dans les autres pays. Le suivi et l'évaluation sont d'une importance cruciale pour plusieurs raisons :

- La Banque, comme les autres bailleurs de fonds, ne sait pas encore quelles démarches sont les plus efficaces dans les LICUS. Il est essentiel de suivre de près les résultats obtenus pour tirer les leçons de l'expérience, et il faut faire une plus grande place à l'apprentissage et au partage des données dans les travaux effectués au titre des LICUS.
- Sachant que les progrès sont souvent lents dans ces pays, il est important de réévaluer ré-

gulièrement le programme pour déterminer s'il a des chances de produire les résultats escomptés.
- L'instabilité et l'évolution constante de la situation dans les LICUS, où les progrès sont souvent en dents de scie, font qu'il est essentiel d'adapter les programmes : le suivi étroit des résultats aidera à déterminer quand des adaptations sont nécessaires et sous quelle forme.

L'apprentissage par l'action indispensable pour améliorer l'efficacité des opérations de la Banque dans les LICUS demande un rigoureux système de suivi et d'évaluation.

La Banque a indiqué que l'édification de l'État et la consolidation de la paix devraient être les critères utilisés pour évaluer le succès de l'initiative en faveur des LICUS. Mais elle n'a toujours pas défini d'indicateurs de performance à cet effet ni de critères d'évaluation des résultats. Lorsque le changement est plus souvent axé sur les processus, notamment dans les scénarios d'intervention en cas de détérioration et de crise prolongée ou d'impasse, les résultats et les impacts visés dans les autres scénarios ne sont pas forcément des critères de succès appropriés. Les objectifs devraient être adaptés au contexte particulier des LICUS, qui devrait lui-même déterminer les critères et garantir que les objectifs visés ne sont pas trop ambitieux.

Amélioration de l'appui fourni aux travaux sur les LICUS au niveau de l'organisation interne

La présence sur le terrain ne suffit pas à garantir la bonne mise en œuvre des stratégies-pays. Elle doit être assortie d'une communication adéquate entre les bureaux extérieurs et le siège des bailleurs de fonds. Il importe également de déployer un personnel de terrain suffisamment nombreux et doté des pouvoirs et des compétences voulus. La meilleure façon d'apprécier la situation dans un pays est souvent d'accroître la présence sur le terrain, mais cela ne suffit pas. Il est également important de procéder à une analyse interne dans tous les services compétents des bailleurs de fonds et d'appliquer les leçons tirées de cette analyse à toutes les interventions. Au Cambodge, par exemple, la présence de la Banque sur le terrain a permis de beaucoup mieux apprécier la situation politique, mais les entretiens menés avec les membres de l'équipe-pays et les autres parties prenantes montrent que ces données restent concentrées entre les mains de quelques responsables et leurs collaborateurs (principalement au sein de la représentation locale de la Banque et au centre de Bangkok), sans être systématiquement communiquées aux autres membres de l'équipe-pays.

Il s'agit moins aujourd'hui d'un problème d'appréciation des réalités politiques au Cambodge que de savoir qui détient ces informations au sein de l'équipe-pays de la Banque et comment elles sont utilisées pour éclairer les décisions concernant la mise en œuvre de la stratégie et du programme. Du fait que seuls quelques membres du personnel possèdent des données détaillées sur le pays, toutes les activités et interventions de la Banque ne peuvent pas en bénéficier. D'une manière générale, il faut accroître le transfert de connaissances entre les bureaux extérieurs des bailleurs de fonds et leurs équipes-pays et sectorielles basées au siège.

Bien que cela coûte cher, les bureaux extérieurs doivent être dotés du personnel voulu pour intervenir efficacement dans les pays clients. En Angola, la petite équipe locale initialement déployée a dû s'atteler à une multitude de tâches allant du dialogue stratégique avec le gouvernement et les bailleurs de fonds aux dispositions logistiques à prendre pour s'installer dans ses nouveaux locaux. La situation a été compliquée par le manque de personnel opérationnel présent sur place pour préparer les réunions de haut niveau entre les ministres et la Banque. Faute de personnel aux échelons inférieurs, les questions ont été adressées trop rapidement aux instances supérieures, ce qui a créé des tensions inutiles. Les bailleurs de fonds devraient déterminer les effectifs à déployer dans chaque LICUS en tenant compte de la portée et de la nature des opérations prévues ainsi que de leurs objectifs respectifs dans ces pays.

Outre la question des effectifs, les bureaux extérieurs doivent également jouir d'une autorité suffisante par rapport au siège pour faire en sorte que celui-ci ne doive pas approuver toutes les décisions. Pour avoir une véritable présence sur le terrain, il faut déployer un personnel compétent. Dans les entretiens semi-directifs organisés pour la présente étude, plusieurs bailleurs de fonds ont souligné que la coordination dépend tout particulièrement des forces et des faiblesses des individus concernés. En offrant une formation plus appropriée au personnel déployé dans des situations difficiles et en mettant en place des mesures pour l'encourager à collaborer avec les autres bailleurs de fonds, la Banque pourrait atténuer ces risques particuliers.

Dans un scénario de détérioration de la situation, où il pourrait y avoir une rupture du dialogue avec le gouvernement, le personnel des bailleurs de fonds devra déployer ses talents de négociation et de persuasion afin de poursuivre le dialogue tout en mobilisant des groupes non gouvernementaux, notamment la société civile.

Dans un scénario de crise prolongée ou d'impasse, où les problèmes sont chroniques et où la situation politique est bloquée, le personnel devra faire preuve d'une patience et d'une créativité exceptionnelles et chercher des solutions inédites pour sortir de l'impasse.

Dans un scénario de transition post-conflictuelle ou politique, le personnel devra disposer de connaissances techniques particulières pour savoir comment mettre en place des systèmes économiques valables, des institutions et des infrastructures de base. Il devra également être capable d'agir rapidement et résolument dans ces situations, avant que l'optimisme soulevé par le retour à la paix se dissipe et pour aider les pays à éviter une reprise des hostilités. Étant donné qu'une aide internationale massive est souvent mobilisée dans ces situations, le personnel des bailleurs de fonds doit posséder de solides aptitudes de coordination et de programmation pour organiser les partenaires du développement et leurs activités.

Dans un scénario d'amélioration graduelle de la situation, les principales compétences requises sont l'aptitude à fournir une assistance technique adaptée aux besoins et à travailler de pair avec un pays qui a déjà entrepris des réformes.

L'apprentissage passe par la mise en commun des données d'expérience – positives et négatives, mais cela demande un environnement institutionnel réceptif et l'appui de la direction. La mise en commun des données d'expérience sur les bonnes et les mauvaises solutions aux problèmes des LICUS peut promouvoir l'apprentissage, ce qui est particulièrement important pour les travaux effectués au titre des LICUS car les bailleurs de fonds continuent de s'interroger sur la meilleure façon d'aider ces pays en difficulté. Bien que la Banque ait partagé certains enseignements dégagés dans le cadre de la série de séminaires de son groupe de réflexion · sur les LICUS, il faut s'attacher davantage à faire régulièrement le point et à diffuser les nouvelles leçons tirées de l'expérience de ces pays, tant par la Banque que par les autres bailleurs de fonds.

Il est essentiel de créer un environnement institutionnel plus réceptif et d'obtenir l'appui de la direction pour partager les données d'expérience négatives. Jusqu'à présent, la Banque semble avoir surtout fait part des exemples positifs, comme on peut le constater dans ses derniers rapports sur les LICUS.

La communication est indispensable pour faire en sorte, d'une part, que les LICUS acceptent les démarches suivies par les bailleurs de fonds dans ces pays, et d'autre part, qu'ils n'attendent pas trop de ces efforts, surtout dans la période qui suit immédiatement la cessation des hostilités. Il importe de mieux informer les LICUS des objectifs et des démarches des bailleurs de fonds pour obtenir leur adhésion. Cela pourrait également éviter les déceptions en modérant les attentes des parties prenantes sur ce qui peut être accompli sur une période donnée.

Dans les scénarios de détérioration de la situation et de crise prolongée ou d'impasse, où la situation économique et sociale stagne ou se dégrade sur pratiquement tous les fronts, la stratégie de communication doit viser à promouvoir activement les avantages de la réforme auprès des autorités et de la société civile. Dans le modèle de transition post-conflictuelle ou politique établi par la Banque, il s'agit d'éviter les lendemains qui déchantent en tenant la population informée et en exposant clairement les tenants et les aboutissements de l'action des bailleurs de fonds, ainsi que les résultats visés. Dans un scénario d'amélioration graduelle de la situation, la stratégie de communication doit être davantage axée sur l'information en présentant les données de l'expérience dans différents pays et secteurs.

Dans la période immédiate qui suit la cessation des hostilités, la communauté internationale des bailleurs de fonds, y compris la Banque, a souvent engagé d'importants volumes d'aide assortis d'objectifs trop ambitieux. Cela crée généralement des attentes excessives dans la population et conduit au désenchantement lorsque ces attentes ne sont pas satisfaites et qu'il y eu peu d'améliorations tangibles dans la vie quotidienne. Il est essentiel d'éviter de poursuivre des objectifs trop ambitieux et de mieux utiliser la communication, et la Banque doit investir dans ces stratégies.

Des directives opérationnelles sont nécessaires pour adapter les démarches suivies par les bailleurs de fonds à la situation particulière des LICUS. L'initiative en faveur des LICUS a attiré l'attention sur la nécessité d'agir différemment dans les LICUS, mais la Banque et les autres bailleurs de fonds n'ont pas défini clairement la marche à suivre. Ils doivent également s'employer plus activement à déterminer dans quelle mesure les démarches adoptées dans les LICUS doivent, et peuvent, s'attaquer aux raisons pour lesquelles les pays sont ou deviennent des LICUS, et pas seulement aux symptômes. En adoptant des solutions qui considèrent les causes du mal comme un fait acquis, on risque d'ignorer des facteurs contextuels fondamentaux. Les directives opérationnelles des bailleurs de fonds doivent insister sur l'importance d'axer les efforts uniquement sur les domaines où ils ont un avantage relatif, de sorte que les travaux effectués par chaque bailleur de fonds prennent en compte et complètent ceux effectués par les autres.

Les plus grands défis à relever par la communauté des bailleurs de fonds se posent dans les situations de détérioration et de crise prolongée ou d'impasse, de même que dans les phases de transition et de développement qui suivent la phase de reconstruction dans le scénario de situation post-conflit ou de transition politique. Ce sont également des domaines dans lesquels il y a relativement peu d'idées nouvelles. Il est urgent de formuler des directives opérationnelles dans plusieurs domaines : comment organiser et échelonner les réformes selon les priorités tout en évitant les solutions partielles ; comment mettre rapidement en place des services sans compromettre le développement à long terme des capacités de l'État ; comment promouvoir la réconciliation politique tout en aidant à rétablir une gouvernance efficace et létigime ; comment intégrer les réalités politiques dans la conception et la mise en œuvre des stratégies-pays ; et comment tenir compte des liens entre politique, sécurité et développement.

Les récentes directives de la Banque sur la marche à suivre dans les LICUS portent davantage sur les instruments à utiliser que sur les différentes manières de procéder selon les catégories de LICUS. Il serait également bon que les équipes chargées des LICUS puissent se référer à des textes explicatifs, comme ceux présentés au chapitre 2 de la présente étude, ainsi qu'à des notes succinctes adaptées aux problèmes, au lieu des notes d'orientation officielles qui sont souvent trop condensées et sans rapport avec le contexte du pays.

Recommandations

- **Préciser la portée et la teneur du programme d'édification de l'État formulé par la Banque et renforcer la conception et la mise en place des mécanismes d'appui au renforcement des capacités et d'amélioration de la gouvernance dans les LICUS.**

Compte tenu de l'insuffisance des mesures prises dans le domaine du renforcement des capacités et de la gouvernance, et de la priorité accordée à l'objectif plus ambitieux d'édification de l'État dans les LICUS, la Banque doit préciser ses avantages relatifs par rapport aux autres bailleurs de fonds et adopter des démarches novatrices pour obtenir de meilleurs résultats sur le front du renforcement des capacités et de la gouvernance. Il y a trois impératifs à respecter : les interventions de la Banque doivent

mieux tenir compte de la capacité des LICUS d'assurer les fonctions centrales de l'État, elles doivent être bien échelonnées et adaptées à l'environnement des LICUS, où de grandes améliorations sont nécessaires dans pratiquement tous les aspects des capacités et de la gouvernance, et il faut mettre en place un système efficace de suivi dans ces domaines.

- **Définir des critères d'affectation de l'aide en faveur des LICUS pour faire en sorte que cette aide ne soit ni insuffisante ni excessive.**

La Banque doit effectuer un examen technique de l'effet cumulatif des différentes modifications du système d'affectation des fonds en fonction de la performance sur les volumes d'aide accordés aux LICUS. Il importe d'établir des critères d'affectation des fonds qui tiennent compte des objectifs de la Banque dans ces pays et de veiller à ce que l'aide fournie ne soit ni insuffisante ni excessive. Il convient également de déterminer dans quelle mesure ces critères devraient être basés sur des facteurs autres que l'efficacité des mesures prises par les pays (tels que les volumes d'aide des autres bailleurs de fonds, l'évaluation des risques et des résultats potentiels, et les retombées sur le plan régional et mondial), en tenant compte du fait que l'aide est limitée et qu'il y aura des choix à faire.

- **Renforcer l'appui interne de la Banque aux travaux accomplis au titre des LICUS au cours des trois prochaines années.**

L'appui interne de la Banque doit être renforcé dans deux domaines. Tout d'abord, il faut définir les priorités en ce qui concerne les effectifs, les compétences et les mesures à mettre en place pour encourager les travaux au titre des LICUS. Pour fournir des incitations à même d'attirer des individus qualifiés pour travailler sur les LICUS, au siège comme dans les bureaux extérieurs, il faut que les membres du personnel sachent clairement quels sont les critères de succès dans les LICUS, de quels résultats ils seront tenus comptables, quels risques ils peuvent raisonnablement prendre, comment les échecs seront évalués et comment ces résultats influenceront leur notation générale et leurs perspectives de carrière.

Tout comme dans les épreuves de plongeon aux Jeux olympiques, où la note finale tient compte de la qualité technique et de la difficulté du plongeon, la performance des membres du personnel dans les LICUS devrait être évaluée en utilisant un coefficient de pondération correspondant au degré de difficulté de l'environnement de chaque LICUS. Il convient également de signaler l'importance des travaux effectués au titre des LICUS à tous les niveaux de la direction.

En plus des mesures d'encouragement, la Banque doit faire en sorte que les membres du personnel travaillant sur les LICUS possèdent les compétences voulues, par exemple en gestion du secteur public, qu'ils soient capables d'obtenir les connaissances politiques nécessaires et de les utiliser, et qu'ils soient désireux et capables de travailler dans des équipes pluridisciplinaires. À noter une mesure positive, quoique tardive, à cet égard : il est prévu d'aborder ces questions dans le Rapport 2006 sur le renforcement des interventions dans les États fragiles.

Il importe de réfléchir plus systématiquement au personnel à affecter aux LICUS dans le contexte des effectifs globaux de la Banque, en tenant compte du fait que l'affectation d'un plus grand nombre d'individus plus qualifiés aux travaux à mener au titre des LICUS imposera probablement des arbitrages avec les autres équipes-pays de la Banque. La redistribution des effectifs en faveur des LICUS peut être justifiée ou non, selon les objectifs de la Banque dans ces pays et les besoins d'aide des autres pays clients.

Ensuite, il convient de simplifier la structure organisationnelle des travaux effectués au titre des LICUS et de la prévention des conflits. La Banque doit mettre en place une organisation efficace qui élimine les doubles emplois et la fragmentation de l'appui entre l'équipe chargée des LICUS et celle chargée de la prévention des conflits et de la reconstruction.

- ***Réexaminer la valeur ajoutée de la démarche suivie pour les LICUS au bout de trois ans.***

L'utilité d'une classification spéciale pour les LICUS et de la démarche adoptée pour ces pays, notamment l'intérêt opérationnel des modèles d'intervention, devra faire l'objet d'une évaluation indépendante au bout de trois ans, lorsqu'on disposera de suffisamment de données sur les résultats obtenus. Il sera alors possible de se poser la question plus fondamentale de savoir si l'aide fournie par la Banque contribue réellement à l'édification de l'État, et dans quelle mesure. La décision de la Banque de maintenir une classification et une démarche spéciales pour les LICUS devrait être basée sur les conclusions de cette réévaluation.

Principales mensajes de la evaluación

- Los países de ingreso bajo en dificultades (PIBD) experimentan algunas de las dificultades más severas en materia de desarrollo, y la comunidad de los donantes sigue batallando por hallar la manera más eficaz de ayudarlos. El Banco Mundial ha participado activamente en los debates internacionales de políticas referentes a los PIBD y desde que introdujo la Iniciativa para los PIBD, en 2002, se ha puesto en mejores condiciones operativas para darles respaldo.

- Antes de la Iniciativa para los PIBD, la mayor parte de los resultados de los programas del Banco en PIBD se situaban en la gama de lo insatisfactorio. La Iniciativa ha hecho que el Banco preste más atención a los PIBD, pero sería prematuro abrir juicio sobre los resultados. La experiencia en cuanto a ejecución de la Iniciativa ha sido despareja, y la mayoría de los resultados de las pocas estrategias para los países evaluadas por el Grupo de Evaluación Independiente (IEG) indican que los objetivos no se han alcanzado en la medida necesaria.

- Al adoptar como objetivo central el fortalecimiento del Estado, el Banco ha hecho de un ámbito de debilidad tradicional (creación de capacidad y gestión de los asuntos públicos) un componente de su enfoque principal en los PIBD. Para que la Iniciativa para los PIBD se centre en el complicado programa de fortalecimiento del Estado es necesario que el Banco establezca claramente sus ámbitos de ventajas comparativas y el alcance y el contenido del programa. Asimismo, debe identificar enfoques innovadores para lograr mejoras en el historial poco satisfactorio en materia de desarrollo de la capacidad y gestión de los asuntos públicos, así como indicadores de desempeño que permitan medir los resultados en cuanto a fortalecimiento del Estado.

- En los tres años transcurridos desde que se implementó el enfoque de la Iniciativa, poco se ha avanzado en la ejecución de reformas esenciales en la esfera de los recursos humanos relacionadas con número de funcionarios, calidad de sus aptitudes e incentivos para la realización de la labor referente a los PIBD.

- Aunque el Banco ha hecho hincapié recientemente en un necesario incremento de su presencia in situ en los PIBD, ello no basta para una eficaz ejecución de estrategias para los países. Se requiere, como complemento, una más sólida comunicación entre el personal del Banco in situ y en la sede, así como un número adecuado de funcionarios in situ poseedores de las facultades y aptitudes adecuadas.

- Podrían ser más selectivos los objetivos de reforma de los donantes en los PIBD. En los complicados entornos de los PIBD, en que se requieren reformas prácticamente en todos los sectores, es esencial establecer una apropiada secuencia de reformas y disponer de tiempo suficiente para llevarlas a cabo, a fin de lograr resultados sin hacer recaer una carga abrumadora sobre la escasa capacidad de los PIBD.

Resumen

Los países de ingreso bajo en dificultades (hasta recientementa conocidos en el Banco Mundial como PIBD), poblados por casi 500 millones de personas, aproximadamente la mitad de los cuales ganan menos de un dólar por día, suscitan cada vez más atención. Es causa de creciente preocupación la posibilidad de que esos países no logren alcanzar sus objetivos de desarrollo, así como los efectos económicos desfavorables que provoca su situación en países vecinos y la consiguiente posibilidad de que sus problemas se propaguen al resto del mundo.

Dada la multiplicidad de problemas crónicos que padecen, los PIBD plantean algunos de los desafíos más arduos en materia de desarrollo. En la mayor parte de ellos, la gestión de los asuntos públicos es insatisfactoria, y esos países están inmersos en amplios conflictos internos o se están debatiendo en el proceso de culminación de precarias transiciones en situaciones posteriores a conflictos. Todos tienen ante sí obstáculos similares: generalizada falta de seguridad, fractura de las relaciones sociales, significativos niveles de corrupción, desintegración del Estado de derecho y falta de mecanismos de generación de poder y autoridad legítimos, una enorme acumulación de necesidades de inversión insatisfechas, y limitados recursos públicos para el desarrollo. En general, la labor internacional llevada a cabo en el pasado en relación con esos países no ha generado mejoras significativas.

La comunidad de los donantes sigue batallando por hallar la manera más eficaz de ayudarlos. Dadas sus diferencias en cuanto a propósitos y objetivos, los donantes y los investigadores han optado por abordar diferentes aspectos de esos problemas, lo que los ha llevado a centrar la atención en grupos de países levemente distintos. Por ejemplo, en estudios recientes del Centro para el Desarrollo Mundial se centra la atención en los países de ingreso bajo en situación de estancamiento (definida por el producto nacional bruto per cápita y las tasas de crecimiento económico), y, en el Índice de Estados fallidos de *Foreign Policy,* la atención está centrada en las fallas del Estado y se identifica a los países según factores tales como nivel de deterioro económico, seguridad, sectores sociales predominantes organizados como facciones, personas desplazadas, violación de derechos humanos e intervención externa. La Agencia de los Estados Unidos para el Desarrollo Internacional procura hacer frente a problemas relativos a vulnerabilidad y crisis, muchos de los cuales pertenecen al entorno político. Las definiciones de Estados frágiles adoptadas por el Departamento del Reino Unido de Desarrollo Internacional (DFID) y por el Comité de Asistencia para el Desarrollo de la Organización de Cooperación y Desarrollo Económicos (CAD de la OCDE) son similares a las utilizadas por el Banco Mundial.

Tal como los define el Banco Mundial, todos los PIBD se caracterizan por lo inadecuado de sus políticas, instituciones y gestión de sus asuntos públicos. El Banco ha utilizado dos criterios para definir PIBD *básicos* y PIBD en situación *grave* (de aquí en adelante, por "PIBD" se entiende los de esas dos categorías, y no los *marginales*, que el Banco identifica tan sólo con fines de control): ingreso per cápita comprendido en el rango de admisibilidad de la Asociación Internacional de Fomento (AIF), y un desempeño de 3,0 puntos o menos (2,5 o menos en el caso de los PIBD en situación grave y entre 2,6 y 3,0 para la categoría básica) según la calificación global de la Evaluación de las políticas e instituciones nacionales (CPIA, por su sigla en inglés) y la calificación de la CPIA referente a gestión e instituciones del sector público.

También se incluyen algunos países de bajo ingreso sin datos de la CPIA. En el ejercicio de 2005, el Banco identificó 25 países como PIBD. Seis PIBD identificados en el ejercicio de 2005 —Afganistán, Liberia, Myanmar, Somalia, Timor-Leste y el territorio de Kosovo— carecían de puntajes de la CPIA. El presente examen basa su evaluación en la asistencia otorgada por el Banco a los 25 países clasificados como PIBD en el ejercicio de 2005.

El monto de los presupuestos para otorgamiento de préstamos y administrativo destinados a los PIBD se ha incrementado desde la puesta en marcha de la Iniciativa. El financiamiento otorgado a los PIBD aumentó de alrededor de US$2.500 millones en los ejercicios de 2000–02 (antes de la Iniciativa para los PIBD) a alrededor de US$4.100 millones en los ejercicios de 2003–05 (a partir de la puesta en marcha de la Iniciativa). En cifras per cápita, dicho financiamiento osciló entre US$0 y US$25,4 en los ejercicios de 2003–05. El monto de los presupuestos

administrativos para los PIBD se incrementó de aproximadamente US$104 millones en los ejercicios de 2000–02 a alrededor de US$161 millones en los de 2003–05. En cifras per cápita, dichos presupuestos oscilaron entre US$0,002 a US$4,5 en los ejercicios de 2003–05.

Gran parte del financiamiento otorgado a los PIBD en 2003-05 se destinó a PIBD en situaciones posteriores a conflictos (los países de esa categoría se identifican en función de indicadores de progreso en situaciones posteriores a conflictos, a los efectos determinar las donaciones excepcionales de la AIF), en tanto que los presupuestos administrativos se han distribuido en forma más pareja entre los distintos grupos de PIBD (siete PIBD en situaciones posteriores a conflictos de los 25 considerados recibieron un 64% del total del financiamiento para los PIBD y un 34% del total del presupuesto administrativo para este tipo de países).

Si bien la elevada proporción de financiamiento para PIBD en situaciones posteriores a conflictos pudo haberse alcanzado aunque no se hubiera creado la Iniciativa para los PIBD, dado que las asignaciones excepcionales de la AIF para países en situaciones posteriores a conflictos anteceden a la Iniciativa, es probable que ésta haya contribuido a una distribución más pareja de los recursos del presupuesto administrativo dentro del grupo (dado el incremento de no menos del 400% registrado por los presupuestos administrativos entre los ejercicios de 2000-02 y de 2003-05 en relación con tres PIBD —Liberia, Somalia y Sudán— que habrían recibido recursos administrativos ínfimos antes de la Iniciativa, dada su situación de excluidos del régimen de contabilidad en valores devengados).

El enfoque de la Iniciativa para los PIBD del Banco ha variado en relación con su estructura original, de 2002, que se basaba en seis principios fundamentales (véase el Cuadro R.1). El fundamento original de la Iniciativa consistía en dar más eficacia a la ayuda mediante la utilización de otros instrumentos, como la labor de análisis y las transferencias de conocimientos, complementados por transferencias financieras para promover reformas.

En 2005 los objetivos y el alcance de la Iniciativa para los PIBD pasaron de una eficacia general de la ayuda a objetivos de fortalecimiento del Estado y consecución de la paz. En la Iniciativa se introdujeron asimismo cuatro modelos (deterioro, crisis políticas o estancamiento prolongados, situaciones posteriores a conflictos o transición política, y mejora gradual) que dieron lugar a la aplicación de un tratamiento diferente a distintos tipos de PIBD. En 2005, se mantuvieron y se reforzaron los conceptos de aprendizaje práctico y atención a las cuestiones de organización contenidos en el enfoque de 2002.

A través del presente examen se procura dar respuesta a tres preguntas:

- ¿En qué medida ha sido eficaz el enfoque del Banco para los PIBD?
- ¿En qué medida son útiles desde el punto de vista operativo los criterios utilizados por el Banco para identificar y clasificar a los PIBD, y

en qué medida es útil el sistema de asignación de la asistencia que se les brinda?
- ¿En qué medida ha sido apropiado y adecuado el respaldo interno otorgado por el Banco a la labor referente a los PIBD?

Principales constataciones y conclusiones

Eficacia del enfoque del Banco para los PIBD

La experiencia obtenida en la aplicación de los principios básicos de la Iniciativa para los PIBD a nivel de países ha sido heterogénea (véase el Cuadro R.1). Los problemas de aplicación experimentados obedecen, en algunos casos, a la adopción de objetivos excesivamente ambiciosos por parte del Banco (se requieren objetivos más modestos) y, en otros casos, a que los esfuerzos del Banco o los aportes no han sido apropiados, como lo indican la labor sobre

Cuadro R.1: Experiencia en materia de aplicación de los principios básicos de la Iniciativa para los PIBD en los países

Principio de la Iniciativa para los PIBD	Calificación de la experiencia en materia de aplicación
Perseverancia en la participación	**Considerable**
Estrategias ancladas en un mejor análisis sociopolítico	**Mediana**
• Comprensión de la situación política	• Mediana-considerable
• Asimilación de esa comprensión de la situación política en el diseño y la ejecución de la estrategia	• Mediana-baja
Promoción de la demanda interna y la capacidad de realizar reformas positivas	**Baja**
Reformas sencillas y factibles en el nivel de ingreso	**Mediana-baja**
• Reformas macroeconómicas	• Considerable
• Creación de infraestructura física	• Considerable
• Transición de la fase de reconstrucción inmediata en situaciones posteriores a conflictos a la fase de desarrollo	• Baja
• Selectividad y priorización	• Baja
Examen de mecanismos innovadores para la prestación de servicios sociales	**Mediana**
Colaboración de los donantes	**Mediana**
• A nivel de políticas internacionales	• Considerable
• A nivel de países	• Mediana-baja
Medición y seguimiento de los resultados[a]	**Baja**

Fuentes: Labor sobre el terreno y análisis temático de antecedentes realizados para este examen, IEG, 2005.

a. El Banco no lo menciona específicamente como principio básico autónomo, pero el IEG lo incluyó porque es un puntal de los objetivos de aprendizaje práctico de la Iniciativa para los PIBD.

el terreno del IEG y las revisiones de los informes de terminación de las estrategias de asistencia a los países (deben intensificarse los esfuerzos).

La mayoría de los entrevistados en la encuesta de interesados realizada por el IEG dijeron que la contribución positiva al desarrollo que implica el programa global del Banco para los PIBD ha sido escasa, opinión que se refiere al respaldo otorgado por el Banco en general, no al enfoque mismo de la Iniciativa para los PIBD.

En relación con los principios de la Iniciativa para los PIBD, se han logrado algunos notables éxitos iniciales. La Iniciativa ha hecho posible una mayor participación del Banco en países en que probablemente habría sido menor. Recientemente, el Banco atendió la situación de varios PIBD desde los primeros días de paz o de transición política, y ha contribuido a la estabilidad macroeconómica y al suministro de un volumen significativo de infraestructura física, especialmente en PIBD en situaciones posteriores a conflictos. Se han logrado avances sustanciales en materia de coordinación de los donantes a nivel de políticas internacionales, como lo pone de manifiesto la reciente aceptación, por un amplio espectro de donantes, incluido el Banco, de los 12 principios de participación internacional del CAD del OCDE.

El Banco ha cumplido repetidamente un papel orientador como copresidente de reuniones internacionales de donantes y coautor de documentos de políticas conjuntos. Recientemente introdujo modelos en que se establecen diferencias entre distintos tipos de PIBD, lo que probablemente permita atender mejor las necesidades específicas de los PIBD. El porcentaje de proyectos de PIBD cerrados y clasificados por el IEG como satisfactorios desde el punto de vista de los resultados aumentó desde el 50% en el ejercicio de 2002, antes de que se estableciera la Iniciativa para los PIBD, hasta el 58% en 2003, 65% en 2004 y 82% en 2005. Las cifras correspondientes de proyectos ejecutados en países de ingreso bajo que no eran PIBD oscilaron entre 70% y 79%.

No obstante, subsisten considerables dificultades. La participación inicial del Banco en relación con algunos PIBD no siempre ha sido seguida por un programa de reforma debidamente focalizado y dotado de una adecuada secuencia de etapas. Además el Banco aún no ha asimilado suficientes conocimientos políticos en el diseño y la ejecución de estrategias de países. También es necesario que la institución coordine mejor sus actividades en los países con otros donantes, especialmente en cuanto al seguimiento de todas las etapas de la ejecución, que van más allá de los acuerdos de políticas.

Además el Banco ha hecho de un ámbito de debilidad tradicional (creación de capacidad y gestión de los asuntos públicos) un aspecto cardinal de su enfoque, al adoptar el objetivo de fortalecimiento del Estado, que es más complejo. Para ello debe identificar con mayor precisión su ventaja comparativa; mejorar su desempeño, incluso a través de la creación de enfoques innovadores, e identificar asociados que puedan complementar su labor para hacer efectivo el logro de los resultados deseados. Finalmente, el propio término *fortalecimiento del Estado* puede ser inapropiado, dadas sus connotaciones políticas e ideológicas.

Es necesario que el Banco elabore sus enfoques operacionales en el marco de la Iniciativa para los PIBD, especialmente en relación con los modelos de *deterioro* y *crisis o estancamiento prolongados*. Es necesario, asimismo, perfeccionar aún más los modelos, teniendo en cuenta en forma más explícita las diferencias de capacidad para el cumplimiento de funciones estatales fundamentales (por ejemplo, generación de recursos, asignación de recursos, suministro de infraestructura y servicios sociales básicos, y admisión de la discrepancia y la seguridad en la esfera política), para que el Banco pueda hacer coincidir mejor sus enfoques operacionales con los diversos entornos institucionales de los PIBD.

La labor del Banco en los países en situaciones posteriores a conflictos antecede al enfoque de la Iniciativa para los PIBD, por lo cual el modelo que corresponde a los PIBD en situaciones posteriores a conflictos tiene una estructura más diáfana que la de los restantes modelos. No obstante, presenta imperfecciones y es necesario desarrollarlo mejor para orientar las fases de transición y desarrollo que siguen a la fase de reconstrucción inmediata posterior a conflictos. Por otra parte, aunque el Banco ha venido prestando cada vez mayor atención a la prevención de conflictos, poco se sabe sobre la eficacia de los esfuerzos realizados en ese ámbito.

Aún no se han establecido claramente el papel y la ventaja comparativa del Banco en materia de prevención de conflictos, en especial porque, para cumplir esa labor, la institución debe prestar mayor atención a las *causas profundas* de los conflictos y tener en cuenta factores étnicos, sociológicos y políticos. El Banco debe definir mejor el contenido del objetivo de consecución de la paz y lo que es ajeno a éste, así como la manera de alcanzarlo.

Utilidad operativa de los mecanismos de identificación, clasificación y asignación de asistencia para los PIBD que aplica el Banco

A pesar del énfasis en los objetivos de fortalecimiento del Estado y consecución de la paz, el Banco sigue basándose casi exclusivamente en la CPIA para identificar a los PIBD. Esas evaluaciones, sin embargo, no permiten captar algunos aspectos esenciales de fragilidad del Estado (como la admisión de las discrepancias políticas) y conflictos (por ejemplo, inestabilidad política y seguridad, o susceptibilidad a conflictos), lo que puede requerir mecanismos complementarios. Para reforzar el método de identificación de los PIBD se requeriría un marco analítico centrado en forma más explícita en los objetivos de la Iniciativa para los PIBD.

A lo largo de los años, el sistema utilizado por el Banco para asignar recursos de la AIF (denominado asignación basada en el desempeño) se ha ido haciendo más selectivo con respecto a las políticas, y se ha reducido el financiamiento de la AIF disponible para países con políticas e instituciones más débiles y una gestión pública menos satisfactoria. Esto ha llevado a preguntarse si los PIBD están recibiendo de la AIF un volumen apropiado de asistencia. Los ajustes a la asignación basada en el desempeño han dado lugar a un aumento del financiamiento de la AIF, incluido el otorgado a algunos PIBD en situaciones posteriores a conflictos y a PIBD que realizan transiciones políticas. No obstante, dista mucho de ser claro si los actuales niveles de financiamiento de la AIF permiten afirmar que los PIBD no reciben menos ni más ayuda de la necesaria.

La cuestión de la asignación de la ayuda ha vuelto a primer plano, y en algunos estudios se ponen en tela de juicio las pruebas empíricas referentes a la existencia de un vínculo positivo entre políticas y eficacia de la ayuda (en que se basa el sistema de asignación basado en el desempeño). En otros estudios se sostiene que la ayuda puede promover un cambio sostenible de las políticas en los Estados en descomposición, al crear y reforzar las condiciones previas de la reforma o al aumentar la probabilidad de que ésta, una vez establecida, se mantenga. En esos últimos estudios se concluye que conceder asistencia a los PIBD puede ser extremadamente beneficioso, aunque los riesgos de fracaso sean sustanciales.

Por su parte, el Banco aún no ha abordado la cuestión de la asignación de la ayuda para los PIBD a través de un método que refleje los objetivos correspondientes a esos países e impida que esa asistencia sea insuficiente o excesiva.

Pertinencia y suficiencia del respaldo interno del Banco a la labor referente a los PIBD

El respaldo interno otorgado por el Banco a la labor referente a los PIBD ha avanzado en varios ámbitos:

- Ampliación de la labor de análisis, gracias a que se desvinculan, de los volúmenes de financiamiento, los presupuestos administrativos destinados a financiar los estudios económicos y sectoriales y la asistencia técnica
- Utilización de las notas provisionales sobre la estrategia, que permiten diseñar estrategias que abarcan un período más breve para dar cabida a las condiciones inestables de los PIBD
- Acceso a la administración superior del Banco para los administradores de la Iniciativa
- Creación de un Fondo Fiduciario de los PIBD para otorgar financiamiento a países excluidos del régimen de contabilidad en valores devengados (en relación con los cuales el Banco carecía anteriormente de instrumentos).

De la experiencia en los países, la Unidad de PIBD ha extraído orientaciones sobre algunos temas importantes y las ha hecho gravitar en el asesoramiento operativo a los grupos a cargo de los países y en más amplios debates externos sobre políticas.

No obstante, tres años después que el Banco reconociera la necesidad de una modificación cultural interna tendiente a una eficaz aplicación del enfoque de PIBD, poco se ha logrado en cuanto al otorgamiento de respaldo interno del Banco para la labor de la Iniciativa. Sigue siendo insatisfactorio el avance de reformas esenciales sobre recursos humanos relativas a número de funcionarios, calidad de sus aptitudes e incentivos para la realización de la labor relativa a los PIBD. Los comentarios del personal del Banco sobre la importancia que reviste trabajar tanto en países pertenecientes a la Iniciativa como en otros países revelan que dentro del Banco no se reconoce en la medida apropiada la labor referente a los PIBD, e indican la necesidad de reformar el sistema de incentivos.

El personal señaló como un problema el desigual nivel de atención que prestan al tema los diferentes directores a cargo de países, en especial cuando se ocupan de un país mayor, más "exitoso" o más destacado. Puso también de manifiesto la necesidad de que, en toda la jerarquía de la administración se preste atención sistemática a la labor referente a los PIBD. En la mayor parte de las respuestas del personal del Banco a la encuesta de interesados realizada por el IEG, se señala que trabajar en el área de los PIBD no ha producido cambio alguno en relación con varias cuestiones de recursos humanos (véase el gráfico R.1).

Existe considerable duplicación de esfuerzos y confusión en torno a las funciones y responsabilidades de la Unidad de PIBD y la Unidad de prevención de conflictos y de reconstrucción. Preocupan al personal las cuestiones prácticas de saber a qué unidad hay que acudir para obtener determinados tipos de asesoramiento y qué tipos de apoyo cabe esperar de cada unidad. En la encuesta de interesados del IEG, alrededor de los dos tercios de los funcionarios del Banco que respondieron mencionó algún problema de la actual estructura institucional: un 37% señaló

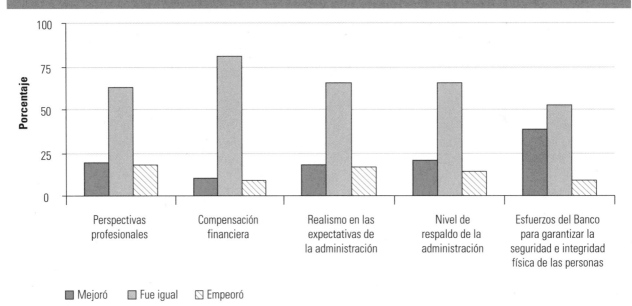

Gráfico R.1: En la mayor parte de las respuestas del personal del Banco se sostiene trabajar en el área de los PIBD no produjo cambio alguno en varias esferas (que a continuación se mencionan)

Fuente: Apéndice Z (Resultados de la encuesta de interesados).

Nota: El número de respuestas válidas está comprendido entre 213 y 238. En la pregunta formulada en la encuesta no se distinguió entre los funcionarios que, en su cometido anterior, habían trabajado con un PIBD y los que lo habían hecho con un país que no pertenecía a dicha categoría.

cierta duplicación de esfuerzos entre el respaldo de la Unidad de PIBD y el de la Unidad de prevención de conflictos y de reconstrucción del Banco; el 15% mencionó un alto grado de duplicación y el 12%, la existencia de conflictos o contradicciones.

Enseñanzas de la experiencia para Banco y otros donantes

De este examen de la experiencia recogida por el Banco en la aplicación de los principios básicos del enfoque de la Iniciativa para los PIBD se extraen varias enseñanzas. Muchos de los problemas a los que se refieren esas enseñanzas se percibieron como ámbitos que requerían mejoras en el Informe del grupo de estudio de los PIBD de 2002 (Banco Mundial 2002) —por ejemplo, la necesidad de anclar las estrategias en mejores análisis sociopolíticos o respaldar objetivos de reforma muy focalizados— y también se hizo hincapié en ellos en los informes del Banco de 2005 sobre los PIBD. Las enseñanzas emanan de la experiencia del Banco en materia de ejecución, pero también pueden ser útiles para orientar otra asistencia de donantes en países de la Iniciativa.

Presencia en los PIBD

Perseverar en la participación no es más que un medio encaminado a un fin, por lo cual, en la Iniciativa para los PIBD, esa presencia debe ser seguida sin tardanza por un programa de reforma claro y pertinente. Si no se cuenta con un programa de reforma claro y pertinente, los éxitos iniciales suscitados por la presencia de los donantes pueden ser fugaces y no contribuir más que en escasa medida al logro de los objetivos de la estrategia para el país. Los ejemplos de la República Centroafricana y Haití muestran que varios obstáculos pueden dificultar la continuación de una participación inicial exitosa en un PIBD. Como los éxitos políticos no contaron con suficiente respaldo económico, el Gobierno de la República Centroafricana se ve ahora confrontado con una crisis presupuestaria potencialmente desastrosa. En Haití, la comunidad de los donantes parece no haber prestado adecuada atención al logro de un nivel mínimo de seguridad. En ambos casos, los resultados iniciales satisfactorios de la Iniciativa para los PIBD corren el riesgo de deteriorarse.

En ciertos casos puede requerirse, al menos por ciertos períodos, una salida estratégica, salvo en lo referente a la labor interna de análisis. Se trata de una estrategia especialmente apropiada cuando se considera que una labor en común con el Banco confiere, inadecuadamente, legitimidad al gobierno de un PIBD o reduce la presión interna en procura de reformas y, por lo tanto, dificulta el surgimiento de las condiciones necesarias para suscitar reformas políticas serias y sostenibles.

En los modelos de deterioro y crisis o estancamiento prolongados, en que suele haber limitado consenso entre los donantes y el gobierno con respecto a la estrategia de desarrollo, es necesario que la participación comprenda un diálogo de políticas encaminado a dar cabida a la reforma a la vez que se trabaja en un programa de reforma, por si surgiera una ventana de oportunidad. En los modelos de situación posterior a conflictos o transición política y mejora gradual, la participación deberá tener un carácter más pronunciadamente técnico y centrarse en mayor medida en la ejecución del programa de reforma, dado el mayor consenso entre los donantes y el gobierno al respecto.

La directriz del Banco para relacionarse con países con conflictos o impases políticos prolongados establece que "temas de desarrollo relativamente no polémicos pueden ser un punto de partida para un diálogo constructivo entre las partes en conflicto". Para aquellos países donde hay un deterioro en su gobernabilidad, la directriz establece que el Banco debe aportar "ideas sobre cuestiones económicas específicas que sean importantes para la mediación y que puedan ayudar a reiniciar el diálogo" (Banco Mundial 2005e).

Los problemas de identificación y capacidad de absorción de los países afectan tanto a los productos del conocimiento como a los productos financieros. La participación de contrapartes nacionales en la labor de análisis del Banco sigue estando limitada a los aspectos administrativos; mucho menor es la participación de los países clientes en la selección de temas y la realización de análisis, lo que va en detrimento del interés de los países en el programa. No obstante, la participación de contrapartes nacionales es esencial para lograr la identificación de los clientes y mejorar el impacto de la labor de análisis.

En Tayikistán, la falta de participación del gobierno en la selección y preparación de la labor de análisis del Banco redujo el interés del gobierno en los resultados, lo que fue en detrimento de una eficaz ejecución. En Angola, altas autoridades públicas percibieron ciertos aspectos de la labor de análisis orientada por el Banco (por ejemplo, el reciente memorando económico sobre el país) como una imposición de los puntos de vista del Banco en los asuntos internos de su país, lo que fue en detrimento de la identificación del país y del desarrollo de su capacidad. Sin esa identificación, es poco probable que la labor de análisis influya sobre la política pública.

Las dificultades de capacidad de absorción de los gobiernos de los PIBD a los efectos de utilizar la labor de análisis pueden también reducir una posible transferencia de conocimientos. El gobierno angoleño, por ejemplo, se manifestó de acuerdo con la nota provisional sobre la estrategia del Banco, pero expresó preocupación con respecto al volumen de actividades de análisis y asesoramiento previstos, lo que generó dudas acerca de la plena utilización de los productos analíticos por parte del gobierno. La capacidad de absorción del gobierno está sujeta a severos límites, y las actividades de análisis y asesoramiento realizadas principalmente por el Banco crean el riesgo de generar tensiones en las relaciones con el gobierno, sea cual fuere su calidad técnica. En Camboya, los planes de prestación de servicios de análisis y asesoramiento en el marco de la Estrategia de asistencia al país (EAP) de 2005 —con un total de 30 tareas que han de completarse a lo largo de los ejercicios económicos de 2005-07— parecen excesivamente ambiciosos, dada la escasa capacidad institucional del país.

Conocimiento de la situación política y su utilización en la estrategia para el país

Encargar y aprovechar —no necesariamente producir— análisis políticos acertados es esencial para los donantes en los PIBD. El objetivo de un grupo a cargo de un país debería consistir en encargar o utilizar (no necesariamente producir) análisis directamente pertinentes para la preparación de una estrategia, que puedan utilizarse en el curso de esa labor. En los PIBD, especialmente en entornos en que sea esencial actuar con celeridad, los donantes, antes de encomendar nuevos análisis políticos, deben comprobar que se aprovechan los existentes.

En la República Democrática Popular Lao, el Banco aprovechó eficazmente análisis políticos existentes e invitó a un especialista en Ciencia Política que había realizado amplias publicaciones sobre Laos a efectuar una exposición sobre política y reforma ante el equipo a cargo del país. Esto permitió preparar un resumen independiente de análisis políticos pertinentes (adaptados a las necesidades de la comunidad de los donantes en general y del Banco en particular) y difundirlo entre un grupo pertinente de funcionarios del Banco y otros donantes. Se evitó así el elevado costo que suponía preparar un análisis "del Banco", así como una posible tensión con el gobierno, dado que permitió evitar que el Banco se viera trabado por algunos de los problemas de susceptibilidad que rodeaban el análisis. Para el Banco, en este caso, la adquisición de conocimientos existentes, así como su difusión, resultaron más importantes y eficaces que la creación de conocimientos.

Los esfuerzos de los donantes deben centrarse en ayudar al personal a asimilar análisis políticos al diseñar y aplicar estrategias. Aunque en algunos PIBD el Banco ha realizado o ha tenido acceso a acertados análisis políticos, éstos no se han reflejado adecuadamente en la estrategia de la institución. Por ejemplo, la estrategia provisional para Papua Nueva Guinea contiene un adecuado análisis del sistema político y en ella se reconocen problemas tales como lealtades de clanes, clientelismo político, corrupción y falta de capacidad. No obstante, la estrategia trata esos problemas como cuestiones técnicas; no las utiliza adecuadamente como pilares del enfoque global.

Programa de reforma centrado en objetivos

En entornos complejos de PIBD, en que prácticamente todos los sectores requieren reformas, es esencial establecer una adecuada secuencia de reformas y disponer de tiempo suficiente para aplicarlas, a fin de lograr resultados sin hacer recaer una carga abrumadora sobre la escasa capacidad de los PIBD. Aunque los donantes deben esforzarse en lograr una selectividad colectiva, esto dista mucho de haberse alcanzado, como lo indican los ejemplos del programa de reforma de Afganistán, respaldado por donantes, y el Marco de Cooperación Provisional de Haití, que más abajo aparecen. No obstante, aunque no se logre de inmediato dicho objetivo, es preciso que el Banco, basándose en sus competencias esenciales, aplique un enfoque apropiado y el principio de selectividad en su propio programa de asistencia. En los últimos años, esa selectividad del Banco ha ido en aumento, pero la dificultad persiste.

En Afganistán, las reformas realizadas por donantes ocupan una amplia gama; sus prioridades no se han desarrollado en forma suficiente y han dado lugar a 120 proyectos de leyes. Es necesario establecer cuidadosamente el orden de prelación y la secuencia de esas reformas, que abarcan prácticamente todos los aspectos económicos y sociales del país, pero los donantes aún no lo han hecho. En Haití, el Marco de Cooperación Provisional está destinado a orientar la asistencia y cooperación internacionales con ese país hasta septiembre de 2006. El programa comprende prácticamente todas las funciones estatales básicas, tales como seguridad, diálogo nacional, buen gobierno en la esfera económica, recuperación económica y servicios básicos. Cada uno de esos ámbitos, tomados separadamente, parece importante, pero en conjunto constituyen un programa de enormes proporciones.

Con respecto al programa de asistencia del propio Banco, en la revisión del informe de terminación de la estrategia de asistencia al país realizado por el IEG con respecto a los ejercicios 2001–05, referente a Santo Tomé y Príncipe, se concluyó que el Banco era excesivamente ambicioso en relación con los recursos asignados al país. Muchos de los objetivos de la EAP siguieron sin alcanzarse, o sólo se lograron en parte.

Aparte de la cuestión de la selectividad en las EAP, es esencial centrar y priorizar adecuadamente los programas actuales de reforma sobre el terreno. Sin estos pasos, surgen dudas acerca de la eficacia, en especial porque la capacidad de los PIBD es limitada. Aunque es difícil actuar selectivamente en un país que padece la urgente necesidad de arreglar muchas cosas, es esencial diseñar una adecuada secuencia de reformas, para no gravar excesivamente la reducida capacidad de los PIBD y evitar soluciones parciales. Será fundamental establecer reformas en una secuencia adecuada, que abarquen un número suficiente de años, y lograr que los donantes se comprometan a seguir su evolución.

En Timor-Leste, quizá los donantes se retiraron antes de tiempo, sin ocuparse en medida suficiente de las apremiantes necesidades de capacidad que experimenta el país. En Haití, la asistencia para el desarrollo ha fluctuado pronunciadamente a lo largo de los años. El país ha atravesado varios ciclos "de abundancia o hambruna" en sus relaciones con la comunidad de los donantes, lo que podría haberse evitado si diversos donantes hubieran establecido un adecuado cronograma y secuencia para su ayuda.

Desarrollo de la capacidad en PIBD en situaciones posteriores a conflictos

La ejecución de los programas de desarrollo de la capacidad y buena gestión de los asuntos públicos debe iniciarse tempranamente, aun en PIBD en situaciones posteriores a conflictos. Inmediatamente después de la cesación de un conflicto, la comunidad internacional de los donantes tiende a centrar su asistencia en obras físicas de reconstrucción. Como los PIBD en situaciones posteriores a conflictos tienen escasa capacidad de utilizar eficazmente la ayuda, y como la gestión pública suele ser insatisfactoria, es necesario centrar la atención, desde el inicio, en la creación de capacidad y una mejor gestión de los asuntos públicos, y no tan sólo en la reconstrucción de la infraestructura física. Para ello puede ser necesario crear o reforzar instituciones públicas, realizar la reforma del servicio civil y recurrir a expertos técnicos locales. Si se utilizan los servicios de expertos extranjeros para obtener asistencia técnica, ello no debe comprometer el desarrollo a largo plazo de la capacidad *local*.

Coordinación de los donantes

No puede lograrse la coordinación de los donantes si éstos no adoptan una visión común y persiguen una misma finalidad; cuando los objetivos de los donantes no puedan armonizarse plenamente, es importante que, por lo menos, sean complementarios. En su enfoque, el Banco no ha reconocido plenamente las diferentes razones que llevan a los donantes a ocuparse de los PIBD. Aunque el amplio concepto de fragilidad se conoce y acepta en forma generalizada, varían los criterios de los donantes para calificar como frágil la situación un país. Se otorga respaldo a los Estados frágiles por diversos motivos: seguridad, eficacia de la ayuda, desarrollo equitativo, reducción de la pobreza, fortalecimiento del Estado, consecución de la paz, prevención de conflictos, etc.

Tanto en Afganistán como en Tayikistán, el IEG concluyó, a través de su labor sobre el terreno, que los principales donantes no perseguían un objetivo único y claro. A falta de un objetivo global común, es improbable lograr coherencia de políticas. En los esfuerzos y modalidades de coordinación de los donantes del Banco, no se tienen en cuenta en medida suficiente los objetivos de los distintos protagonistas que actúan en un país. Pero la coordinación de los donantes es una modalidad de acción colectiva que requiere que otros donantes, análogamente, tengan un contacto más estrecho con el Banco y subordinen sus programas bilaterales a objetivos multilaterales adoptados de común acuerdo.

La coordinación debe iniciarse dentro de cada entidad donante. No basta con coordinar la labor de las entidades multilaterales y bilaterales donantes. Se trata también de una cuestión esencial *dentro de* cada uno de los organismos donantes. Los proyectos realizados en diferentes sectores de un mismo país suelen operar en forma paralela, sin aprovechar sinergias. Así sucedió en Timor-Leste con los proyectos agrícolas y de potenciación comunitaria del Banco.

Un efecto secundario de los esfuerzos de descentralización del Banco hacia sus oficinas en los países ha sido la concentración de los conocimientos sobre los países en los funcionarios locales y una inadecuada difusión de ese saber entre los grupos a cargo de los países, en especial los que tienen su centro de operaciones en la ciudad de Washington. Hacer frente a los problemas de coordinación entre los diversos departamentos de las entidades donantes (por ejemplo entre los departamentos del Banco que se ocupan de la gestión del sector público, la prevención de conflictos y la reconstrucción, los PIBD, la creación de capacidad y la investigación) reviste especial importancia en los PIBD, cuyos problemas, complejos y generalizados, suelen requerir soluciones multisectoriales.

Medición y seguimiento de resultados

El seguimiento y la evaluación no son menos importantes en el caso de los PIBD que en el de cualquier otro país. Varias razones hacen esencial la labor de seguimiento y evaluación en los PIBD:

- Primero, el Banco, al igual que otros donantes, aún se encuentra en el proceso de comprender qué enfoques son apropiados en contextos de PIBD. Es esencial realizar un seguimiento de las experiencias para extraer enseñanzas, y el aprendizaje y el intercambio de información deben convertirse en un componente más destacado de la labor referente a los PIBD.
- Segundo, como en esos países el avance suele ser lento, es importante evaluar continuamente la cuestión de si el programa sigue estando encaminado hacia el logro de los resultados deseados.

- Tercero, un entorno de PIBD constantemente cambiante e inestable, en que el avance suele no ser lineal, hace esencial la adaptación del programa, por lo cual un estrecho seguimiento del desempeño contribuirá a establecer cuándo se requiere adaptación y qué tipo de adaptación es necesaria.

Sólo a través de una firme labor de seguimiento y evaluación puede lograrse un aprendizaje práctico eficaz para aumentar la eficacia de la futura labor del Banco en los PIBD.

El Banco ha declarado que el fortalecimiento del Estado y la consecución de la paz deben ser los objetivos utilizados para medir el éxito de la Iniciativa para los PIBD. No obstante, el Banco aún no ha identificado indicadores de desempeño a esos efectos ni patrones de medición del desempeño. En un contexto en que el cambio está orientado más bien por procesos, especialmente en los modelos de deterioro y crisis o estancamiento prolongados, los resultados que pueden esperarse en otros modelos quizá no sean patrones de éxito apropiados. Los objetivos deberían adaptarse al contexto especial de cada PIBD, lo que, a su vez, determinaría patrones de medición y garantizaría que los valores para medir el éxito se establecieran en los niveles apropiados.

Mejor respaldo institucional interno para la labor referente a los PIBD

La presencia sobre el terreno no basta para una eficaz ejecución de la estrategia para el país; es preciso complementarla a través de una adecuada comunicación entre el personal en el terreno y el de las oficinas centrales de las entidades donantes, y de un adecuado número de funcionarios en el terreno, poseedores de las atribuciones y aptitudes apropiadas. La mejor manera de comprender las circunstancias de los países suele consistir en una significativa presencia sobre el terreno, aunque esto de por sí no basta. No menos importante resulta que todos los departamentos de las entidades donantes participantes asimilen los resultados de los análisis y apliquen las enseñanzas emanadas de ellos a todas las intervenciones. En Camboya, por ejemplo, la

presencia del Banco sobre el terreno ha permitido mejorar significativamente el conocimiento de la situación política. Pero los debates con los miembros del grupo a cargo del país y otros participantes indican que ese conocimiento quizá sigue estando sumamente concentrado en unos pocos administradores y funcionarios (en su mayor parte en la oficina en el país y en el centro de actividades de Bangkok), y que es relativamente limitada la difusión en resto del grupo a cargo del país.

El problema parece haber variado: de un conocimiento parcial de las realidades políticas de Camboya a la cuestión de quién posee ese conocimiento dentro del grupo del Banco a cargo del país y la manera en que se lo utiliza para orientar la adopción de decisiones en materia de ejecución de programas y estrategias. El hecho de que el conocimiento en profundidad de un país se concentre en tan sólo unos pocos funcionarios implica que sólo beneficia a algunas actividades e intervenciones del Banco. En general se requiere una mayor transferencia de conocimientos entre las oficinas de los donantes en los países y su personal de países y sectores que opera en la sede.

Pese a su costo, las oficinas fuera de la sede deben estar adecuadamente dotadas de personal para que puedan trabar eficaces relaciones con los clientes. En Angola, el inicialmente reducido grupo de funcionarios en el terreno se vio confrontado con múltiples tareas: desde el diálogo estratégico con gobiernos y donantes hasta actividades de logística, como el traslado de la oficina a nuevas instalaciones. La situación se hizo aún más difícil por la falta de personal de nivel operativo en la oficina en el país que, en consulta con funcionarios del ministerio, pudiera preparar el terreno antes de que los ministros y el Banco celebraran reuniones de alto nivel. Una tramitación demasiado acelerada hacia los niveles jerárquicos superiores —provocada por el hecho de que los niveles inferiores carecían de personal— provocó innecesarias tensiones. Las decisiones de los donantes con respecto al número de funcionarios en cada PIBD deberían reflejar la escala y las características de la participación deseada, a la luz de los objetivos perseguidos por los respectivos donantes en esos países.

Es necesario que el personal en el terreno, además de ser suficiente, posea adecuadas potestades, en relación con la sede, para que no todas las decisiones deban ser aprobadas por la sede. Una eficaz presencia sobre el terreno requiere la actuación en el país del tipo de funcionarios apropiado. En entrevistas semiestructuradas realizadas para el presente estudio, varios donantes hicieron hincapié en que las virtudes y defectos de las personas cuya actividad haya de coordinarse influyen poderosamente sobre la coordinación. Podrían mitigarse esos riesgos de idiosincrasia a través de una capacitación más apropiada para los funcionarios a quienes se encomienden difíciles cometidos de campo, y de mejores incentivos dentro del Banco para que el personal colabore con otros donantes.

En el modelo de deterioro, en que el diálogo con el gobierno puede interrumpirse, el personal de las entidades donantes deberá poseer firmes aptitudes diplomáticas y de persuasión que garanticen que se mantenga abierta la puerta para un diálogo con el gobierno, a la vez que se movilizan grupos no gubernamentales, incluida la sociedad civil.

En el modelo de crisis o estancamiento prolongados, en que los problemas son crónicos o se produce una parálisis política, el personal, entre otras aptitudes, deberá poseer extraordinaria paciencia, así como creatividad, con constantes innovaciones para despejar atascos persistentes.

En el modelo de situaciones posteriores a conflictos o de transición política, el personal, entre otras cosas, deberá contar con conocimientos técnicos específicos para desarrollar una infraestructura esencial, instituciones y sistemas económicos sólidos. Además deberá estar en condiciones de actuar rápida y enérgicamente en esos contextos, antes de que se disipe el optimismo que sigue a la paz, y de contribuir a evitar que los países vuelvan a sumirse en conflictos. Como esas situaciones suelen atraer una asistencia internacional en gran escala, el personal de los donantes debe poseer sólidas aptitudes de coordinación y establecimiento de secuencias de actividades para organizar a los asociados para el desarrollo y a sus actividades.

En el modelo de mejora gradual, la principal de las aptitudes que requiere el personal consiste en la capacidad de proporcionar asistencia técnica adaptada a las necesidades del caso y de trabajar en estrecha relación con un cliente que ya ha emprendido reformas.

El intercambio de experiencias —positivas y negativas— es esencial para el aprendizaje, pero requiere respaldo de la administración y un entorno institucional favorable. Se puede promover el aprendizaje a través del intercambio de experiencias sobre éxitos y fracasos en diferentes situaciones de PIBD. El aprendizaje reviste especial importancia en la labor relativa a los PIBD porque la comunidad de los donantes sigue batallando por hallar la manera más eficaz de ayudar a esos países, cuya situación representa un desafío. Aunque el Banco ha difundido ciertas enseñanzas a través de la serie de seminarios del grupo de estudio sobre PIBD, es mucho mayor la atención necesaria para evaluar y difundir sistemáticamente experiencias emergentes relativas a los PIBD, recogidas por el Banco y otros donantes.

Será esencial crear un entorno institucional más receptivo y lograr el respaldo de la administración para el intercambio de experiencias negativas. Hasta ahora el Banco parece estar principalmente dispuesto a intercambiar ejemplos positivos, como ocurre en sus recientes informes sobre la Iniciativa para los PIBD.

Una comunicación eficaz es esencial para lograr la aceptación, por parte de los países, de los enfoques de los donantes referentes a PIBD y para atemperar las expectativas poco realistas de los países sobre lo que puede lograrse, en especial inmediatamente después que cesa el conflicto. Será preciso dar a conocer mejor los objetivos y enfoques de los donantes en los PIBD, para que éstos se identifiquen con el programa. Con ello se podrá además prevenir desilusiones, moderando las expectativas poco realistas de los interesados acerca de lo que puede lograrse en determinado período.

En los modelos del Banco sobre deterioro y crisis o estancamiento prolongados, en que la situación económica y social en su mayor parte está empeorando o se ha estancado, sería necesario que a través de la estrategia de comunicación se dieran a conocer activamente al gobierno y a la sociedad civil los beneficios de la reforma. En el modelo del Banco sobre situaciones posteriores a conflictos o transición política, para prevenir la disolución que sigue a las expectativas faltas de realismo, la estrategia de comunicación debería estar orientada hacia la totalidad de la población y establecer expresamente lo que han de hacer los donantes, cuándo y cómo deberían hacerlo, y qué resultado cabría prever. La estrategia de comunicación correspondiente al modelo de mejoramiento gradual deberá tener un carácter más informativo, y en ella deberían presentarse experiencias comparadas de países o de sectores.

En muchos casos, inmediatamente después de la cesación del conflicto los donantes internacionales, incluido el Banco, han comprometido un gran volumen de asistencia aunado a objetivos excesivamente ambiciosos. Ello ha creado a menudo grandes expectativas en la población y ha conducido a desilusiones cuando esas expectativas han quedado insatisfechas y los resultados tangibles cotidianos han sido limitados. Evitar los programas demasiado ambiciosos y utilizar mejores procedimientos de comunicación son factores esenciales, por lo cual es necesario que el Banco invierta en estrategias de ese género.

Se requiere una mejor orientación operativa para adaptar los enfoques de los donantes a las condiciones especiales de los PIBD. La Iniciativa para los PIBD ha creado conciencia sobre la necesidad de tratar en forma diferente a esos países, pero el Banco y otros donantes aún no han determinado con precisión la manera de hacerlo. También es preciso establecer con mayor certeza la medida en que, en los enfoques de los donantes frente a los PIBD, deben y pueden tenerse en cuenta en forma eficiente las causas —y no simplemente los síntomas— que hacen que los países se conviertan en PIBD o mantengan la condición de tales. Una solución que considere las causas como datos inmutables puede no tener en cuenta factores contextuales extremadamente

importantes. La orientación operativa de los donantes debe garantizar que los ámbitos ajenos a la ventaja comparativa de determinados donantes se dejen en manos de otros, en tanto que en su propia labor se tenga en cuenta y se complemente adecuadamente la labor realizada por otros.

En los modelos de deterioro y crisis o estancamiento prolongados preparados por el Banco, y en las fases de transición y desarrollo que siguen a la fase inmediatamente posterior a la reconstrucción en el modelo de situaciones posteriores a conflictos o transición política, se plantean algunos de los mayores desafíos que tiene ante sí la comunidad de los donantes. Se trata asimismo de ámbitos en que el pensamiento innovador ha sido relativamente limitado. Existe una apremiante necesidad de orientación operativa en varias esferas, incluida la de hallar mecanismos para priorizar y establecer la secuencia de las reformas y a la vez evitar soluciones parciales; mecanismos que permitan una rápida prestación de servicios que no vaya en detrimento de la creación de capacidad a largo plazo del sector público; mecanismos tendientes a promover la reconciliación política y al mismo tiempo contribuir a una labor pública eficaz y legítima; mecanismos que permitan aprovechar los conocimientos políticos en el diseño y la ejecución de las estrategias, y mecanismos que permitan abordar eficazmente los vínculos entre política, seguridad y desarrollo.

La orientación reciente del Banco con respecto a los PIBD se concentra más en la determinación de los instrumentos que deben utilizarse que en la formulación de enfoques operacionales con respecto a lo que es necesario hacer en forma diferente —y la manera de hacerlo— en distintos grupos de PIBD. Además, los grupos a cargo de los países de la Iniciativa se beneficiarían de una mayor cantidad de orientaciones expositivas, como la que se presenta en el capítulo 2 del presente examen, así como notas breves, orientadas por problemas, en lugar de las notas de orientación más formales, que suelen ser excesivamente concentradas, y en las cuales no se describe en forma suficiente el contexto del país.

Recomendaciones

- **Establecer claramente el alcance y contenido de los objetivos de fortalecimiento del Estado que persigue el Banco y reforzar el diseño y el suministro de respaldo en materia de desarrollo de la capacidad y gestión de los asuntos públicos en los PIBD.**

Dado su historial insatisfactorio en materia de desarrollo de la capacidad y gestión de los asuntos públicos, así como el hecho de que actualmente centra la atención en el objetivo, más ambicioso y complejo, de fortalecer el Estado en su labor referente a los PIBD, es necesario que el Banco delimite claramente sus ámbitos de ventajas comparativas en relación con los demás donantes y adopte enfoques innovadores que garanticen mejores resultados en materia de capacidad y gestión de los asuntos públicos. Es preciso elaborar enfoques innovadores para establecer una correspondencia más estrecha entre las intervenciones del Banco y la capacidad de un PIBD de cumplir funciones estatales básicas; hacer efectiva la aplicación de intervenciones centradas con precisión y en adecuada secuencia en contextos de PIBD —en que prácticamente todos los aspectos relativos a la capacidad y al buen gobierno pueden requerir considerables mejoras—, y realizar un efectivo seguimiento de los resultados en materia de capacidad y buen gobierno.

- **Elaborar criterios de asignación de la ayuda para que los PIBD no reciban menos ni más ayuda de la necesaria.**

Es necesario que el Banco lleve a cabo un examen técnico del efecto acumulativo que tienen, sobre los volúmenes de ayuda a los PIBD, los diversos ajustes introducidos al sistema de asignación basada en el desempeño. Deben elaborarse criterios de asignación de asistencia que reflejen los objetivos del Banco en esos países y hagan que la asistencia que se les conceda a éstos no sea insuficiente ni excesiva. Es preciso establecer si los criterios deben basarse en factores distintos de los resultados de políticas (por ejemplo, los niveles de la asistencia de otros donantes, la evaluación de potenciales riesgos y premios, y los efectos

secundarios regionales y mundiales), y en qué medida corresponde hacerlo, teniendo en cuenta que la ayuda es limitada, por lo cual habrá que adoptar soluciones de compromiso.

- **Reforzar el apoyo interno, en el Banco, para la labor referente a los PIBD en los próximos tres años.**

Es necesario prestar atención a dos aspectos del respaldo interno en el Banco. En primer lugar debe priorizarse el objetivo de establecer adecuadas cifras de funcionarios dotados de aptitudes e incentivos apropiados para que se ocupen de los PIBD. Para establecer adecuados incentivos que atraigan a personal calificado —en la sede y en las oficinas fuera de la sede— que se ocupe de los PIBD habrá que impartir claras señales sobre lo que se considera éxito en los PIBD, de qué resultados se hará responsable al personal, en qué medida es razonable asumir riesgos, cómo se juzgarán los fracasos y cómo se tendrán en cuenta los puntajes de las evaluaciones globales de desempeño y el desarrollo profesional de los funcionarios.

Al igual que en las zambullidas olímpicas, en que en el puntaje depende de la perfección técnica y de la dificultad de la zambullida, el desempeño del personal en los PIBD debería evaluarse asignando apropiada ponderación a la magnitud de las dificultades que presentan los distintos entornos de los PIBD. También será preciso poner de manifiesto la importancia de la labor referente a los PIBD en toda la línea jerárquica de la administración.

Además de esos incentivos es necesario que el Banco se asegure de que el personal que se ocupa de los PIBD posea aptitudes adecuadas para su tarea, por ejemplo en materia de administración del sector público; sea capaz de buscar y utilizar conocimientos políticos, y quiera y pueda realizar una labor basada en equipos interdisciplinarios. Merecen plácemes, aunque sean tardíos, los planes actuales encaminados a atender esos temas en el estudio de 2006 sobre fortalecimiento de la respuesta orgánica a los Estados frágiles.

Se requiere un pensamiento más sistemático con respecto a las decisiones sobre dotación de personal para la labor referente a los PIBD en el contexto de los planes globales de dotación de personal del Banco, dado que, para asignar personal más numeroso y más capacitado a la labor que se realice en beneficio de esos países, probablemente habrá que llegar a soluciones de compromiso con otros grupos del Banco a cargo de países, lo que se justificará o no según los objetivos que adopte el Banco en relación con esos países y las necesidades de asistencia que experimenten otros clientes de la institución.

Segundo, es necesario simplificar la estructura orgánica de la labor relativa a los PIBD y a los conflictos. Es preciso que el Banco establezca una eficiente estructura orgánica que elimine la duplicación y fragmentación del apoyo entre la Unidad de PIBD y la Unidad de prevención de conflictos y de reconstrucción.

- *Al cabo de tres años, volver a evaluar el valor agregado del enfoque de la Iniciativa para los PIBD.*

Transcurridos tres años, cuando se disponga de experiencia suficiente con respecto a los resultados del enfoque de los PIBD, será necesario someter a una evaluación independiente el valor de la categoría PIBD y el enfoque correspondiente, incluida la utilidad, para las operaciones, de los modelos. A esa altura podrá abordarse la cuestión, más fundamental, de si la asistencia del Banco puede respaldar eficazmente una labor sostenible de fortalecimiento del Estado, y en qué medida puede hacerlo. El continuo respaldo del Banco para la categoría de los PIBD y para el enfoque debería basarse en las conclusiones de esa nueva evaluación.

ACRONYMS AND ABBREVIATIONS

AAA	Analytical and advisory activities
ADB	Asian Development Bank
ARPP	Annual Report on Portfolio Performance
BP	Bank procedure
CAS	Country Assistance Strategy
CASCR	Country Assistance Strategy Completion Report
CDD	Community-driven development
CDF	Comprehensive Development Framework
CEM	Country Economic Memorandum
CEP	Community Empowerment Project
CFAA	Country Financial Accountability Assessment
CPAR	Country Procurement Assessment Report
CPIA	Country Policy and Institutional Assessment
CPR	Conflict Prevention and Reconstruction Unit
CRN	Country Reengagement Note
CSO	Civil society organization
DEC	Development Economics Vice Presidency
DFID	Department for International Development (United Kingdom)
DO	Development objective
DPL	Development Policy Lending
DPR	Development Policy Review
EA	Environmental assessment
ESW	Economic and sector work
EU	European Union
FRM	Financial Resource Mobilization Department
FSG	Fragile States Group
GDP	Gross domestic product
GEMAP	Governance and Economic Management Assistance Program
GNI	Gross national income
HDI	Human Development Index
HIPC	Heavily indebted poor country
IBRD	International Bank for Reconstruction and Development
ICF	Interim Cooperation Framework (Haiti)
ICR	Implementation Completion Report
IDA	International Development Association
IDF	Institutional Development Funds
IEG	Independent Evaluation Group (formerly Operations Evaluation Department, OED)
IFA	Integrative Fiduciary Assessment
IGR	Institutional and Governance Review
ISN	Interim Strategy Note

ISR	Implementation Status and Results Report (formerly Project Status Report, PSR)
JAM	Joint Assessment Mission
KKZ	Kaufmann, Kraay, and Mastruzzi indicators
LIC	Low-income country
LICUS	Low-Income Countries Under Stress
MDGs	Millennium Development Goals
NGO	Nongovernmental organization
Norad	Norwegian Agency for International Development
ODA	Official development assistance
OECD-DAC	Organisation for Economic Co-operation and Development's Development Assistance Committee
OP	Operational policy
OPCS	Operations Policy and Country Services Department
PA	Poverty Assessment
PBA	Performance-based allocation
PCF	Post-Conflict Fund
PCPI	Post-Conflict Progress Indicator
PEFA	Public Expenditure and Financial Accountability
PER	Public Expenditure Review
PIU	Project Implementation Unit
PREM	Poverty Reduction and Economic Management Network
PRSC	Poverty Reduction Support Credit
PRSP	Poverty Reduction Strategy Paper
PSR	Project Status Report (now ISR)
QAG	Quality Assurance Group
QEA	Quality at entry
SVP	Rural medical centers (Uzbekistan)
SWAp	Sectorwide approach
TFET	Trust Fund for East Timor
TRM	Transitional Results Matrix
TSS	Transitional Support Strategy
UN	United Nations
UNDG	United Nations Development Group
UNDP	United Nations Development Programme
UNTAET	United Nations Transitional Administration in East Timor
USAID	U.S. Agency for International Development
VDC	Village development committee
WAEMU	West African Economic and Monetary Union
WBI	World Bank Institute

OED changed its official name to the Independent Evaluation Group (IEG) in December 2005. The new designation "IEG" will be inserted in all IEG's publications, review forms, databases, and Web sites.

Chapter 1: Evaluation Highlights

- Plagued by a multitude of chronic problems, LICUS pose some of the toughest development challenges.
- Donors and researchers are grappling with how best to respond to LICUS and have chosen to focus on different aspects of the problem.
- Bank lending and administrative budgets to LICUS have increased since the start of the LICUS Initiative and have amounted to about $4.1 billion and $161 million, respectively, during fiscal 2003–05.
- Post-conflict LICUS absorbed a large share of LICUS lending during fiscal 2003–05; administrative budgets were more evenly distributed across the LICUS group.
- General aid effectiveness concerns in LICUS have been replaced by state-building and peace-building objectives that remain inadequately defined.
- The Bank has yet to identify appropriate performance indicators for its state- and peace-building objectives.

Background

T he ongoing debates on aid effectiveness as well as international events, especially the attacks of September 11, 2001,[1] have attracted increasing attention to the problems facing Low-Income Countries Under Stress (LICUS).

Concern is growing about the ability of these countries to reach the Millennium Development Goals (MDGs), as well as about the adverse economic effects they have on neighboring countries and the global spillovers that may follow.[2]

With their multiplicity of chronic problems, LICUS pose some of the toughest development challenges (box 1.1). Most have poor governance; are embroiled in extended internal conflicts or are struggling through tenuous post-conflict transitions; and face similar hurdles of widespread lack of security, fractured relations among societal groups, significant corruption, breakdown in the rule of law, absence of mechanisms for generating legitimate power and authority, a huge backlog of investment needs, and limited government resources for development. Past international engagement with these countries has generally failed to yield significant improvements.[3]

The donor community is grappling with the question of how best to assist countries faced with such challenging problems. With their differing motivations and objectives, donors and researchers have chosen to address varying aspects of these problems, which has led them to focus on slightly different groups of countries.

For instance, recent research by the Center for Global Development focuses on stagnant low-income countries (defined by gross national product per capita and growth rates), and *Foreign Policy*'s Failed States Index focuses on state failure. It identifies countries based on such factors as the level of economic decline, security, factionalized elites, displaced persons, human rights breaches, and external intervention. The U.S. Agency for International Development (USAID) aims to address issues surrounding vulnerability and crisis. Many of these issues pertain to the political environment. The U.K. Department for International Development (DFID) and the Organisation for Economic Co-operation and Development's (OECD) definitions of fragile states are similar to that used by the Bank.[4]

As defined by the Bank, all LICUS are characterized by weak policies, institutions, and governance. The World Bank has used two criteria to define *core* and *severe* LICUS: per capita income within the threshold of International Development Association (IDA) eligibility, and performance of 3.0 or less on both the overall Country Policy and Institutional Assessment (CPIA) rating and on the CPIA rating for Public Sector Management and Institutions.[5] Some low-income countries without CPIA data are also included.[6] Depending on the income level and CPIA rating, a LICUS country is classified in one of three subgroups: *severe, core,* or *marginal.*[7] Marginal LICUS score on the edge of what is considered LICUS, and hence are identified by the Bank only for monitoring purposes (henceforth, *LICUS* refers to core and severe LICUS, not marginal LICUS).

In fiscal 2005, the Bank characterized 25 countries as LICUS (see table 1.1 and figure 1.2). This review focuses on these 25 countries. Appendix B presents the list of core, severe, and marginal LICUS for fiscal 2003–06, and illustrates which countries have moved in and out of the

Dismal social indicators and poor prospects for achieving the MDGs are common to LICUS.

LICUS category over time. The Bank has recently replaced the term LICUS with *fragile states,* while retaining the same criteria to identify these countries.[8]

LICUS share a number of similarities. They have dismal economic and social indicators (figures 1.3–1.7). Besides being home to almost 500 million people, roughly half of whom earn less than a dollar a day, they have an infant mortality rate a third higher than that of other low-income countries, a life expectancy that is 12 years lower, and a maternal mortality rate that is about 20 percent higher.[9] If the trend continues, most LICUS will be unable to meet the MDGs (appendix C). A vast majority of LICUS are conflict-affected.

Despite their similarities, there are also important differences among LICUS. While some LICUS, such as Angola and Cambodia, grew at around 4 percent a year during 1995–2003, others, such as the Solomon Islands, the Democratic Republic of Congo, and Guinea-Bissau, experienced negative growth rates of

Box 1.1: The LICUS Challenge: Views from the Field

Haiti

"Preval's task is colossal," said a Haitian-born professor and author. "Everything has to be built . . . There are no institutions in Haiti. The challenge is really monumental." Preval will be forced to confront the problems of a nation with almost no functioning judicial system, corrupt and inept law enforcement, deep poverty, and abominable public sanitation. Then there are the violent gangs that rule urban slums, the kidnapping rings and a flourishing drug and money-laundering trade. There are also tens of thousands of children who do not attend school, hundreds of miles of unpaved or poorly maintained highways, and a national budget kept afloat primarily by the largess of international aid groups and foreign countries.

Afghanistan

Despite many accomplishments, the general perception among the Afghans more than three years into the reconstruction program is that there has been only minimal improvement in their lives. Many in Kabul complain about the persistent unreliability of the power supply, poor condition of the roads, and a lack of jobs.

The rural economy has suffered from prolonged drought and also because donors have had little success in supporting projects in rural areas because of concerns about security. Donors are under growing criticism for not having delivered on their much-publicized aid pledges, and for having channeled a large part of what they did deliver into the high fees and salaries of consultants and nongovernmental organizations.

Kosovo

"Out of all our non-luck came luck," said the owner of a highly popular Thai restaurant in Pristina, referring to the vast amount of international aid that has been poured into the province since its liberation following the 1999 war. "It is as though we have been given a second chance to rebuild our own home." Constructing the peace has, however, proved to be far from easy. Although life has demonstrably improved under the UN's guardianship, Kosovo's transformation into a modern, multiethnic society—the international community's much-vaunted aim—continues to remain elusive.

Sources: For Haiti, *The Washington Post,* "Challenges Loom for Preval in Haiti," February 21, 2006. For Afghanistan, work undertaken for this review, IEG, 2005. For Kosovo, *The Guardian,* "A Second Chance to Rebuild Our Home," October 31, 2003.

Table 1.1: Twenty-five LICUS, Fiscal 2005

Severe LICUS	Core LICUS
Afghanistan[a,b]	Burundi[a,b]
Angola[a,b]	Cambodia[a]
Central African Republic[a,c]	Comoros[a]
Haiti[a]	Democratic Republic of Congo[a,b]
Liberia[a,c]	Guinea-Bissau[a,b]
Myanmar[a,c]	Kosovo (territory)
Solomon Islands[a]	Lao People's Democratic Republic
Somalia[a,c]	Nigeria[a]
Sudan[a,c]	Papua New Guinea
Zimbabwe[c]	Republic of Congo[a,b]
	São Tomé and Príncipe
	Tajikistan[a]
	Timor-Leste[a,b]
	Togo[c]
	Uzbekistan

Source: OPCS, World Bank.

Note: The countries classified as LICUS change slightly from year to year (appendix B).

a. Conflict-affected countries in fiscal 2005.

b. Post-conflict countries in fiscal 2005.

c. Countries in non-accrual in fiscal 2005. Loans to, or guaranteed by, a sovereign are placed in non-accrual status when the oldest payment arrears are six months overdue—that is, when the second consecutive payment is missed on the loans with the oldest arrears.

similar magnitudes. Vastly higher levels of external debt as a percentage of gross national income prevail in Liberia and São Tomé and Principe than in Uzbekistan and Haiti.

A number of LICUS have abundant natural resources, including Angola, the Democratic Republic of Congo, Nigeria, and Papua New Guinea, but not Burundi or Haiti. Furthermore, the LICUS group includes countries such as São Tomé and Principe, the Solomon Islands, Tajikistan, and Uzbekistan, where the Human Development Index (HDI) is above the low-income country (LIC) average, as well as countries such as Burundi, the Central African Republic, and Guinea-Bissau, where the HDI is considerably below the LIC average (figures 1.4–1.6).

During fiscal 2003–05 (the period after the launch of the LICUS Initiative), the Bank provided about $4.1 billion in lending to the 25 LICUS, compared with about $2.5 billion during fiscal 2000–02 (the period before the initiative). Sixty-four percent of the total LICUS lending dur-ing fiscal 2003–05 went to 7 post-conflict LICUS (28 percent of the total number of LICUS)[10] (figure 1.1 and table 2.1).

During fiscal 2000–02, the Sector Boards that received the most Bank LICUS lending were Economic Policy (25 percent); Health, Nutrition, and Population (12 percent); and Private Sector Development (11 percent). During fiscal 2003–05, the Sector Boards with the greatest LICUS lending were Transport (22 percent), Rural Development (13 percent), and Economic Policy (10 percent). Comparing the two time periods, 2000–02 and 2003–05, the Sector Boards with increases in LICUS lending were Transport and Rural Develop-ment; and those with a decline in lending were Private Sector Develop-ment and Economic Policy.

With respect to ad-

But LICUS are otherwise a heterogeneous group.

Lending to LICUS has increased, with a large share of lending going to post-conflict LICUS.

Figure 1.1: A Larger Share of LICUS Lending during Fiscal 2003–05 Went to Post-Conflict LICUS, While Administrative Budgets Were More Evenly Distributed across the LICUS Group

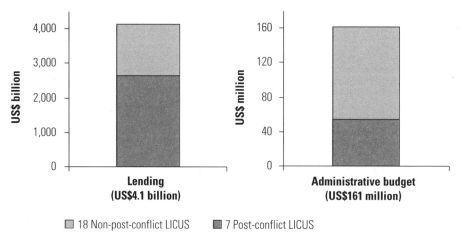

Source: World Bank database.

Note: For definitions of LICUS, post-conflict LICUS, lending, and administrative budgets, see "Definitions and Data Sources" in appendix A.

ministrative budgets, the Bank allocated about $161 million during fiscal 2003–05, compared with about $104 million during fiscal 2000–02. Sixty-six percent of the total administrative budget to LICUS during 2003–05 went to 18 non-post-conflict LICUS (72 percent of the total number of LICUS), and was thus more evenly distributed across the LICUS group than lending (figure 1.1 and table 2.1).[11]

Administrative budgets to LICUS have also increased.

While the large proportion of lending to post-conflict LICUS might have occurred even without the LICUS Initiative (given that IDA's exceptional post-conflict allocations predate it), the initiative likely contributed to the more even distribution of administrative budgets across the LICUS group (given an increase of 400 percent or more in administrative budgets between fiscal 2000–02 and 2003–05 for three LICUS—Liberia, Somalia, and Sudan—which would have received minuscule amounts of administrative budgets before the initiative because of their non-accrual status).

The share of administrative budgets is more evenly distributed across the LICUS group than lending is.

The LICUS Approach

The Bank first articulated its LICUS approach in 2002. The approach has since evolved and was rearticulated in 2005. Key elements of both these stages in the development of the initiative are presented below, and the main differences between them highlighted.

The 2002 LICUS approach

The Bank coined the term LICUS and established the LICUS Task Force in November 2001. The initiative thus both reflected and contributed to broader concerns in the donor community about aid effectiveness in difficult countries. The Task Force Report, published in 2002 (henceforth called the 2002 LICUS Task Force Report, World Bank 2002), aimed to describe how the Bank could best help chronically weak-performing countries get onto a path leading to sustained growth, development, and poverty reduction.

The rationale provided for the LICUS Initiative, as stated in the 2002 LICUS Task Force Report, was that:

Aid does not work well in these [LICUS] environments because governments lack the capacity or inclination to use finance effectively for poverty reduction. Yet neglect of such countries perpetuates poverty in some of the world's poorest countries and may contribute to the collapse of the state, with adverse regional and even global consequences. The challenge of aid effectiveness in LICUS is thus to use other instruments, supplemented by financial transfers where necessary, to promote change (World Bank 2002, p. 1).

The "other instruments" referred to by the Task Force included analytical work and knowledge transfer (which were to receive much more emphasis than financial transfers, although precisely *how much more* was not defined).

The LICUS approach was also to include greater management attention and support of LICUS work within the Bank. The approach outlined in the LICUS Task Force Report was subsequently summarized as core country-level and Bank-level principles (box 1.2). Implementation of the approach began following discussion of the Task Force Report by the Bank's Board of Executive Directors in June 2002, thus launching the LICUS Initiative. In October 2002, the Bank established the LICUS Unit in the Operations Policy and Country Services (OPCS) Vice Presidency to coordinate LICUS implementation. The LICUS Initiative was meant to be a learning-by-doing initiative.

The 2005 LICUS approach

Taking stock of experience since the LICUS Task Force Report, the Bank elaborated its LICUS approach (reaffirming some aspects, changing the emphasis of others, and adding some new elements) in the 2005 Fragile States Good Practices in Country Assistance Strategies Report (henceforth called the 2005 Fragile States Report, World Bank 2005e) and the 2005 Low-Income Countries Under Stress Update (henceforth called the 2005 LICUS Update, World Bank 2005h). Since the 2002 LICUS Task Force, the objectives and scope of the LICUS Initiative have shifted from general aid effectiveness concerns to state-building and peace-building objectives (World Bank 2005e).

State building and peace building have not been well defined, however, and remain somewhat abstract, especially from an operational point of view. This leaves several questions insufficiently answered. For example, what precise balance between state and non-state capacity does state building imply? To what extent are the common political and ideological connotations of the terms state building and peace building intended? What is the exact role of the Bank in the security

General aid effectiveness concerns have been replaced by state-building and peace-building objectives that have not yet been well defined.

LICUS is intended to be a learning-by-doing initiative.

Box 1.2: The 2002 LICUS Approach: Core Principles

Country level
- Stay engaged.
- Anchor strategies in stronger sociopolitical analysis.
- Promote domestic demand and capacity for positive change.
- Support simple and feasible entry-level reforms.
- Explore innovative mechanisms for social service delivery.
- Work closely with other donors.

Bank level
- Give much more attention to analytical work and transferring knowledge, and much less to transferring financial resources.
- Ensure high-quality staff in LICUS.
- Further clarify, disseminate, and revise operational policies and procedures for LICUS work to enable a faster and more effective response.
- Support a more balanced approach to LICUS country programs, underpinned by enhanced institutional support and management attention.

Source: World Bank 2004b.

sector? Furthermore, LICUS-specific approaches to achieve state-building and peace-building objectives have not been adequately articulated—how will these approaches differ from past approaches and ensure a higher chance of success than in the past?

According to the Bank, state building and peace building should be the goals by which to measure the LICUS Initiative's success. However, the Bank has yet to identify performance indicators that would permit this to be done, beyond stating that the "logical corollary of a central focus on peace-building and state-building in the Bank's assistance strategy for fragile states is that short-term results measurement should also emphasize these dimensions while continuing to focus on growth, poverty reduction, and the Millennium Development Goals within the long-term vision for recovery" (World Bank 2005h, p. 7).

Recognizing the diversity among LICUS, the 2005 Fragile States Report distinguishes among four types of LICUS: those experiencing deterioration; those facing prolonged political crisis or impasse; those that are post-conflict or in political transition; and those experiencing gradual improvement. The Bank has proposed a different business model for intervening in each of the four types (appendix D). The Bank does not intend to maintain a list of LICUS that fall under each business model, but instead to use the business models as an aid to planning scenarios when country teams are designing assistance strategies. The expectation is that a country could fall under more than one business model and move in or out of given models over time.

The Bank's recent business models aim to address the diversity of LICUS.

The 12 Principles for International Engagement in Fragile States, agreed to by the OECD's Development Assistance Committee (OECD-DAC) at the January 2005 London Forum (appendix E), also inform the Bank's LICUS approach.[12] The Bank has clustered the 12 principles into 4 main themes to structure its own work: building state capacity and accountability; peace, security, and development linkages; donor coordination for results; and institutional flexibility and responsiveness (appendix F).

Learning by doing and the focus on organizational issues in the 2002 approach were retained and further reinforced in the 2005 approach. The 2005 approach is based on a two-way knowledge flow: global knowledge is to inform staff guidance and country operations, and country experiences are to be distilled into staff guidance and global knowledge.

Differences between the 2002 and 2005 LICUS approaches

There are four main differences between the Bank's LICUS approach as articulated in the 2002 LICUS Task Force Report and recent elaborations of the approach in the 2005 Fragile States Report and the 2005 LICUS Update:

- The 2005 approach emphasizes state building and puts greater focus on building state than non-state capacity compared with the 2002 approach.
- Compared with the 2002 approach, which focused on capacity building,[13] the 2005 approach adopts the more expansive state-building objective.
- Peace building is one of the key objectives of the 2005 approach, and greater prominence is given to conflict prevention. The 2002 approach did not mention peace building or conflict prevention among its core principles.
- The 2005 LICUS approach distinguishes among LICUS and recommends a separate business model for each of the four groups of LICUS; the 2002 approach was presented in terms of core principles applicable across all LICUS.

Objectives, Purpose, and Organization of the Review

The review responds to the interest of the World Bank's Board of Executive Directors in ensuring the effectiveness of Bank support to LICUS. This review aims to answer three questions:

- How effective has the Bank's LICUS approach been?
- How operationally useful are the Bank's criteria for identifying and classifying LICUS and the aid-allocation system for them?

- How appropriate and adequate has the Bank's internal support for LICUS work been?

Given the relative newness of the LICUS Initiative, this review assesses implementation experience rather than outcomes. It uses the Bank's stated LICUS approach as the benchmark—how well or badly the Bank followed its core country-level LICUS principles (chapter 2). The review also assesses the Bank's criteria for identifying and classifying LICUS and for determining lending allocations for them (chapter 3), as well as the appropriateness and adequacy of the Bank's internal support for LICUS work (chapter 4). The final chapter presents the conclusions and recommendations (chapter 5).

It is beyond the scope of this review to assess the effectiveness of the Bank's fiduciary controls in LICUS or the extent of fraud and corruption associated with Bank projects in LICUS. This is a topic that needs careful review, especially in light of the Quality Assurance Group's finding that "fraud and corruption problems affect some projects as demonstrated by detailed implementation reviews in several risky countries" (World Bank 2006b, p. iv).

The Independent Evaluation Group's (IEG's) forthcoming evaluation of the effectiveness of the Bank's fiduciary work examines Country Financial Accountability Assessments (CFAAs) and Country Procurement Assessment Reports (CPARs) with a view to assessing how these instruments influenced Bank assistance and strengthened public financial management reform in client countries, including some LICUS.

Because the Bank's LICUS business models were introduced in December 2005, it was found to be premature to assess their implementation experience. Efforts to examine retrospectively the extent to which the Bank followed the guidance contained in the business models in different groups of LICUS yielded little insight, given the still broad and general nature of the business model guidance.

During fiscal 2000–05, the Bank approved 26 Regional (multicountry) programs, amounting to about $2.9 billion, that included one or more of the 25 LICUS.[14] This review does not, however, address Regional programs in LICUS. A forthcoming IEG evaluation of the Bank's support to Regional programs will shed light on the performance of multicountry projects and partnership programs.

Finally, this review does not, at this early stage, question the need for the LICUS Initiative itself, rather deferring that judgment to the follow-up review recommended in three years, when sufficient evidence on outcomes will be available. The focus of this review is on how the Bank's stated LICUS approach has been implemented, what has been learned about effectiveness, and how the Bank can do better in the future (which may or may not be good enough to merit the existence and continuation of the LICUS Initiative).

In three years' time, based on the outcomes achieved, it will be opportune to ask—and answer—the question of whether the Bank should have a LICUS category and approach at all. At that time, it should be possible to address the more fundamental question of whether and to what extent Bank assistance can effectively support sustainable state building. In academic debates about state reconstruction, two main views prevail. One view questions "the dominant idea that failing states should always be rebuilt [consistent with the liberal democratic model] as most state reconstruction efforts have failed and bred new problems. . . . Until very recently, failing states were dismantled, not rebuilt," (Carnegie Endowment for International Peace 2004).

The second view recognizes the difficulties and imperfections in rebuilding states following this model, but stresses that the rebuilding of states is necessary to improve the social and economic viability of failing states and to prevent conflicts from spilling over (Carnegie Endowment for International Peace 2004).

The recent approach emphasizes state capacity over non-state capacity.

Peace building and conflict prevention are more prominent in the 2005 approach.

Review Instruments and Methods

Several instruments were used to conduct this review:

- Literature review
- Portfolio assessment
- Thematic reviews
- Fieldwork in 10 LICUS—Afghanistan, Angola, Cambodia, the Central African Republic, Haiti, Lao People's Democratic Republic, Sudan, Tajikistan, Timor-Leste, and Zimbabwe (chosen to ensure Regional representation, representation of post-conflict and other LICUS, and inclusion of countries of interest to the IEG-Norad partnership)
- Semistructured interviews of Bank staff
- A survey of 455 persons, including in-country stakeholders, Bank staff, and other donor staff (henceforth referred to as the Stakeholder Survey), with response rates of 16 percent (24 respondents), 31 percent (382 respondents), and 35 percent (49 respondents), respectively (appendix Z). The survey data presented in this

review should be treated with caution because the response rates, especially for in-country stakeholders, are very low.

The 25 countries classified by the Bank as severe and core LICUS in fiscal 2005 constitute the population for this review. The review focuses on the effectiveness of the Bank's LICUS approach, but where possible, comments are made on the effectiveness of the Bank's overall program in LICUS, noting that the two are not synonymous. Specific aspects of the Bank's engagement in LICUS are compared with those in various other groups of LICUS and non-LICUS: post-conflict LICUS and non-LICUS low-income countries (non-LICUS LICs). Appendix A contains the definitions of these groups of LICUS and non-LICUS, other concepts used in the review, and the respective data sources.

Twenty-Five Fiscal 2005 LICUS at a Glance

Figure 1.2: LICUS Population Concentrated in Africa

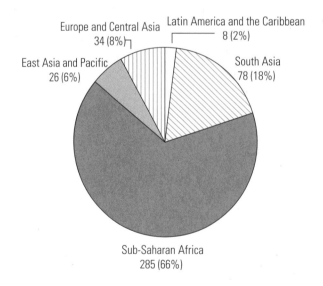

Source: World Bank 2005j.

Note: Number indicates population in millions (percentages in parentheses). Total population in the 25 LICUS = 432 million.

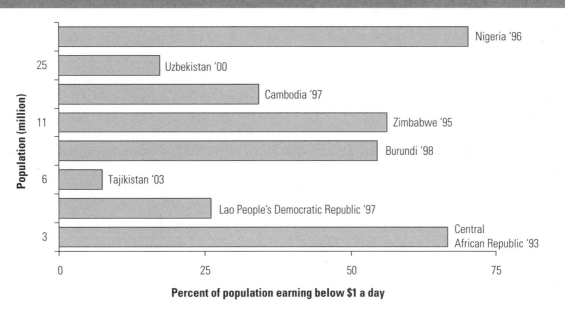

Figure 1.3: More than Half the Population of Four LICUS (of Eight with Data) Earns Less than $1 a Day

Source: World Bank 2005j.

Note: Data not available for 17 of the 25 LICUS. Year for which data were available is indicated along with the name of the country.

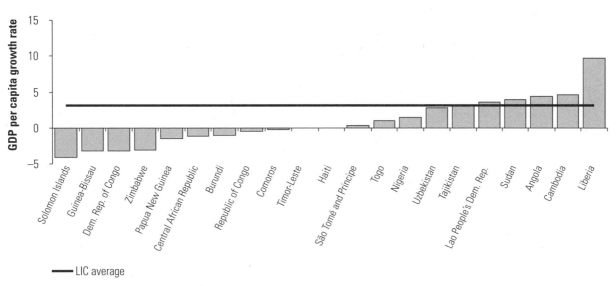

Figure 1.4: Negative Growth Rate in about Half of LICUS, Lower Growth Rate in Most LICUS Compared with Low-Income Country Average (1995–2004)

Source: World Development Indicators 2006.

Note: Data not available for Afghanistan, Kosovo, Myanmar, and Somalia. For Haiti, growth rate represented is during 1998–2004. GDP = gross domestic product; LIC = low-income country.

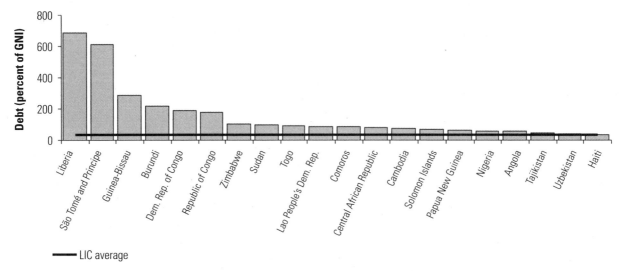

Figure 1.5: External Debt More than 175 Percent of GNI for Six LICUS and Higher than Low-Income Country Average for All LICUS in 2004

— LIC average

Source: World Development Indicators 2006.

Note: Data not available for Afghanistan, Kosovo, Myanmar, Somalia, and Timor-Leste. GNI = gross national income; LIC = low-income country.

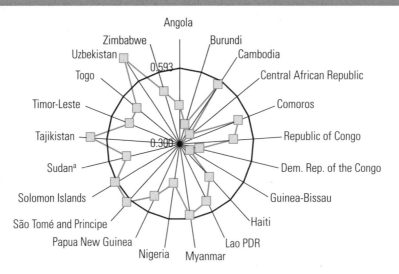

Figure 1.6: Human Development Index for LICUS Worse than for Low-Income Countries in 2003

Source: UNDP 2005.

Note: Dark circle indicates HDI (Human Development Index) of LICs (low-income countries).

LICs include all low-income countries (including LICUS) as defined by UNDP.

HDI is a composite index produced by the United Nations and measures average achievement in three basic dimensions of human development—a long and healthy life (measured by life expectancy at birth), knowledge (measured by adult literacy rate and gross enrollment ratio), and a decent standard of living (measured by GDP per capita [purchasing power parity U.S.]). Countries with a value greater than 0.593 (outside the circle) are, on average, doing better than LICs; and countries with values smaller than 0.593 (inside the circle) are, on average, doing worse than LICs.

a. Based on an estimate for northern Sudan.

Figure 1.7: Kaufmann, Kraay, and Mastruzzi (KKZ) Governance Indicators Worse for LICUS than for Non-LICUS Low-Income Countries

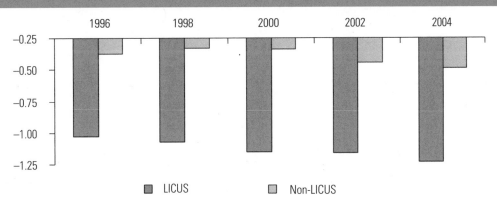

Source: http://www.worldbank.org/wbi/governance/data.html.

Note: Graph presents the aggregate of: (i) control of corruption, (ii) governance effectiveness, (iii) political stability, (iv) rule of law, (v) regulatory quality, and (vi) voice and accountability. Unweighted average excludes Kosovo.

The KKZ scale ranges from −2.5 to + 2.5. The KKZ indicators are a statistical compilation of responses on the quality of governance, given by a large number of enterprise, citizen, and expert survey respondents in industrial and developing countries, as reported by a number of survey institutes, think tanks, nongovernmental organizations, and international organizations (including the World Bank and its CPIA). The KKZ results should be interpreted with caution, because even the most recent aggregate indicators, for 2004, have substantial margins of error. The margins of error are not unique to perception data—measurement error is pervasive among all measures of governance and institutional quality. An advantage of KKZ measures of governance is that they are able to be explicit about the accompanying margins of error, whereas these are most often left implicit with objective measures of governance. Aggregation of separate sources of data, the six indicators and over countries, on average, reduces the margin of error compared with an individual data source. At an individual country and indicator level, very few countries would show significant change over 2000–04.

Chapter 2: Evaluation Highlights

- The Bank's implementation experience in LICUS has been mixed.
- Its operational readiness to engage in LICUS has improved.
- The Bank has contributed to macroeconomic stability and the delivery of significant amounts of infrastructure, especially in post-conflict countries.
- The Bank's effectiveness needs to be improved after the immediate post-conflict phase, when structural change is needed.
- The Bank has not yet sufficiently internalized political understanding in its country strategies.
- Its reform agenda in LICUS has lacked selectivity and prioritization.
- The strong donor coordination at the international policy level needs to be replicated at the country level.
- State building has been made a central objective, despite the weak record in capacity development and governance.

Effectiveness of the Bank's LICUS Approach

This chapter assesses the effectiveness of the Bank's LICUS approach based on implementation experience since adoption of the initiative in June 2002. The main reason for the focus on implementation experience rather than on outcomes is that the LICUS Initiative is relatively new, and most available outcome data pertains to the period before 2002. The implementation narratives presented in this chapter are intended to determine early on what is working and what is not and to provide lessons for the future.

The effectiveness of the approach is first assessed against the Bank's stated approach for each of the country-level LICUS principles and their subsequent elaborations. An additional aspect of the approach is also discussed—measuring and monitoring results—that is not specifically mentioned as a separate principle by the Bank, but that is pivotal to the Bank's learning-by-doing LICUS agenda. Aggregate data on the overall LICUS approach are then presented in the last section of this chapter.

Stay Engaged

Stated approach
The 2002 LICUS Task Force Report (World Bank 2002) noted that Bank disengagement from LICUS could put these countries at risk of state failure and discourage other donor support. The report recognized that the nature of engagement with LICUS would be somewhat different from that with a typical LIC. It re-commended that much more attention be given in LICUS to analytical work and transferring knowledge than to transferring financial resources, and to grants rather than to loans. The 2005 Fragile States Report and the 2005 LICUS Update continued to emphasize the importance of staying engaged.

Implementation experience
The Bank has made substantial progress on this principle. Since 2002, the Bank has improved its operational readiness to support LICUS and has been more likely to engage, be it in the Central African Republic, Haiti, Somalia, Sudan, or Zimbabwe. The Bank has engaged with LICUS in a number of ways over fiscal 2003–05: preparation of country strategies with shorter time frames; provision of lending; provision of trust funds, including through the LICUS Trust Fund (appendix A); and provision of administrative budgets. The LICUS Trust Funds are specific to LICUS.

Interim Strategy Notes have allowed continued strategy design in LICUS.

The Bank's work on strategy design in LICUS continued during fiscal 2003–05 through the preparation of Interim Strategy Notes (ISNs).[1] The use of ISNs for LICUS has allowed the design of strategies that cover a shorter period (up to 24 months), which is more appropriate to the generally volatile conditions prevailing in LICUS. During fiscal 2003–05, the Bank prepared an increasing number of ISNs or Country Assistance Strategies (CASs) to stay engaged in LICUS—7 in fiscal 2003, 4 in 2004, and 13 in 2005 (appendix G).

The Bank's lending to LICUS increased by 67 percent between fiscal 2000–02 and 2003–05, compared with a 10 percent increase in lending to non-LICUS LICs. Lending to LICUS increased from $2.0 per capita in fiscal 2000–02 to $3.2 in fiscal 2003–05, compared with an increase for non-LICUS LICs (excluding India) from $5.2 in fiscal 2000–02 to $6.0 in fiscal 2003–05[2]

Lending to LICUS has increased compared with lending to non-LICUS LICs.

(appendix I). Post-conflict LICUS absorbed a large share of lending during fiscal 2003–05 (with 7 post-conflict LICUS, comprising 28 percent of the total number of LICUS, receiving 64 percent of total LICUS lending) (table 2.1). Lending to post-conflict LICUS averaged $8.2 per capita yearly compared with $1.5 to non-post-conflict LICUS (appendix I).

At the same time, there was a 70 percent increase in trust fund financing to LICUS between fiscal 2000–02 and 2003–05, compared with a decline of 87 percent in trust fund financing to non-LICUS LICs. As with lending, post-conflict LICUS absorbed a large share of trust fund resources going to LICUS during fiscal 2003–05 (table 2.1).

Post-conflict LICUS have absorbed a large share of LICUS lending.

The LICUS Trust Fund was introduced by the Bank in 2004, mainly to finance engagement in LICUS that were in non-accrual.[3] The Trust Fund accounted for 1.3 percent of trust funds going to LICUS during fiscal 2003–05. A full evaluation of the extent and nature of benefits resulting from the projects financed by the LICUS Trust Fund, the sustainability of their benefits, and consistency with activities financed by other trust funds, including the Post-Conflict Fund, is still pending.

Based on stakeholder perceptions, the early experience with the Trust Fund seems to have been generally positive, although there have been significant delays in disbursing funds. In Haiti, the Trust Fund facilitated Bank reengagement with the country and has been instrumental in supporting the implementation of the Interim Cooperation Framework, which was established to guide international assistance and cooperation with the government. In the Central African Republic, the Trust Fund helped finance activities in the Transitional Results Matrix (TRM) and helped intensify the reengagement process by multiplying the contacts and exchanges among all parties. In Liberia, the LICUS Trust Fund facilitated enactment of public procurement legislation and implementation of government-wide procurement procedures, and contributed to donor coordination through support for implementation of the multidonor results framework.

The proportion of grants relative to loans going to LICUS has increased. Consistent with the recommendation of the 2002 LICUS Task Force Report that a greater proportion of grants relative to loans be used in LICUS, the grant component of total project lending to LICUS has increased from less than 20 percent in fiscal 2003 to about 50 percent in fiscal 2005, while the grant component of total project lending to non-LICUS LICs stayed around 15 percent. If grants from trust funds are included, LICUS would show an even higher proportion of grant financing. Moreover, during the discussions to replenish IDA funding in 2004 (IDA 14), it was agreed that debt sustainability will be the basis for the allocation of grants to IDA-only countries under which all LICUS are expected to qualify for 100 percent grant financing.[4] Five LICUS are currently between the decision and completion points for debt relief through the Highly Indebted Poor Country (HIPC) Initiative, and eight additional countries may qualify in the

Table 2.1: Lending, Trust Funds, and Administrative Budgets Going to LICUS and Non-LICUS Low-Income Countries during Fiscal 2000–02 and 2003–05

	Fiscal 2000–02	Fiscal 2003–05	Percentage change, fiscal 2000–02 to fiscal 2003–05	Fiscal 2003–05 share of total LICUS (%)
Lending (million US$)				
Post-conflict LICUS	—	2,664	—	64
Non-post-conflict LICUS	—	1,473	—	36
Total LICUS	2,480	4,137	67	
Non-LICUS LICs	18,557	20,400	10	
Trust fund (million US$)				
Post-conflict LICUS	—	1,816	—	92
Non-post-conflict LICUS	—	159	—	8
Total LICUS	1,159	1,974	70	
Non-LICUS LICs	11,090	1,485	−87	
Administrative budget (million US$)				
Post-conflict LICUS	—	54	—	34
Non-post-conflict LICUS	—	107	—	66
Total LICUS	104	161	55	
Non-LICUS LICs	380	450	18	

Sources: Appendix I; Trust Fund Database.

Note: For definitions of LICUS, post-conflict LICUS, non-LICUS LICs, lending, trust funds, and administrative budgets, see "Definitions and Data Sources" in appendix A.

The share of lending to the post-conflict LICUS is further exaggerated on a per capita basis because only a quarter of the total LICUS population resides in the seven post-conflict LICUS.

For every dollar lent per capita in non-post-conflict LICUS, $5.4 is lent in post-conflict LICUS.

future, but no LICUS has yet reached the completion point and received HIPC grants (appendix H; IEG 2006b).

Administrative budgets going to LICUS also increased by 55 percent between fiscal 2000–02 and 2003–05, compared with an 18 percent increase in non-LICUS LICs.[5] Unlike lending and trust funds that have gone mostly to post-conflict countries, administrative budgets during fiscal 2003–05 have been distributed more evenly across the LICUS group (with 18 non-post-conflict LICUS, comprising 72 percent of the total number of LICUS, receiving 66 percent of total LICUS administrative budgets; table 2.1). In Cambodia, a higher administrative budget for the country office (97 percent increase between fiscal 2000 and 2004) has helped to deepen the Bank's understanding of the political underpinnings of the Cambodian state and improve donor coordination.

Determining whether the increased overall LICUS administrative budgets are adequate for LICUS work requires assessing the efficiency of resource use and is beyond the scope of this review. Instead, staff views on the adequacy of the administrative budgets are presented here.

The Liberia team noted the challenges for staff of working on a reengagement strategy and the added time cost of working in a volatile institutional and political environment. It found that requests for further staff support could not be met by the existing Bank budget, while the strategy of

Proportion of grants to LICUS relative to loans has increased.

Administrative budgets have increased and have been more evenly distributed across the LICUS group than has lending.

minimum engagement itself made it difficult to justify further increases in the Bank budget.

In LICUS with no lending program, staff pointed out that they must claim additional Bank budget as a special dispensation, which can also add to the state of uncertainty—in the Africa Region, a part of the Bank budget is held back during the year, and LICUS country teams need to reapply for budget based on milestones achieved. With respect to supervision budgets, staff noted that country norms tended to apply, irrespective of whether the country was LICUS or not, despite the much higher supervision intensity of projects in LICUS.

The appropriate levels of administrative budget for LICUS need to be determined in the broader context of the allocation of administrative budgets across all Bank departments. The above-average increase in LICUS administrative budgets for fiscal 2003–05 meant that non-LICUS LICs received a below-average increase. Non-LICs, in contrast, received their share of the increase in the administrative budget. The Bank needs to determine whether this is an appropriate distribution of the Bank's administrative budget.

But Bank staff in some LICUS say that administrative budgets are still inadequate.

While six LICUS show a decline in the administrative budget for analytical work in fiscal 2003–05 compared with fiscal 2000–02, the Bank has nearly doubled the administrative budget for analytical work in aggregate in LICUS, from about $25 million in fiscal 2000–02 to about $50 million in fiscal 2003–05. The administrative budget for analytical work in non-LICUS LICs has also increased, from about $69 million in fiscal 2000–02 to about $110 million in fiscal 2003–05, a 59 percent increase over the two time periods (appendix I). The increase may partly be explained by the delinking of administrative budgets for economic and sector work and technical assistance (the two main components of analytical work) from lending volumes by the Bank, in recognition of the importance of maintaining analytical

Budgets for analytical work have increased for all but six LICUS.

and capacity-building work in LICUS, even when lending is low.

While the administrative budget for economic and sector work in LICUS has more than doubled since the start of the LICUS Initiative, one-fourth or more of LICUS do not have any economic and sector work (ESW) being conducted in Sector Boards such as Education; Environment; Health, Nutrition and Population; Social Development; Social Protection; Transport; Urban Development; and Water Supply and Sanitation. This lack of ESW in important Sector Boards raises some questions about the effectiveness of future Bank assistance (appendix O).

Although there is some variability, the quality of economic and sector work seems to be satisfactory overall in LICUS, and the analytical work has enabled the Bank to maintain operational readiness in a number of LICUS. Quality Assurance Group (QAG) assessments show that the quality of economic and sector work in LICUS is improving over time. There also do not appear to be systematic differences between the quality of economic and sector work based on CPIA status in fiscal 2001 and 2002. No comparable figures are available for later years. QAG assessments of analytical and advisory activities (AAA) rated "internal quality" as satisfactory for Angola and marginally satisfactory for Uzbekistan.

Improvements in the *process* aspects of the Bank's ESW would help enhance country-level effectiveness. The involvement of country counterparts in the Bank's analytical work remains limited to administrative aspects, with much less country-client participation in selecting topics and undertaking analysis, which has reduced national buy-in.

This was the case in Tajikistan, where lack of government involvement in the selection and preparation of analytical work limited its interest in the results, which hindered implementation. In Angola, some Bank-led analytical work (for instance, relating to the recent Country Economic Memorandum) was perceived by senior government officials as an imposition of Bank views on internal affairs, which led to limited ownership and capacity development. In the Stakeholder Survey, over 40 percent of in-country, Bank, and other donor respondents said that analytical work has achieved intended results only to a slight extent or not at all (figure 2.1).

Analytical work done in collaboration with other donors can also improve the Bank's policy influence. For example, Sudan's Joint Assessment Mission—which involved multiple donors and culminated in the preparation of a needs assessment report—helped the Bank to gain the confidence of the government and to increase its own policy influence. This highlights the importance of designing programs of analytical work as part of a coordinated process with other donors, rather than by the Bank alone. Principles of donor coordination should apply as much to analytical work and policy capacity development as to other areas of donor programs.

Absorptive capacity constraints apply at least as much to knowledge products as to financial products, so the amount of knowledge transfer that can be usefully undertaken will differ across LICUS. In Angola, the government endorsed the Interim Strategy Note but expressed concern about the amount of foreseen analytical and advisory activities. This has raised doubt about whether the analytical products would be fully

used by the government. The absorptive capacity of the government is severely limited, and analytical and advisory activities done mostly by the Bank risk straining relations with the government, no matter what their technical quality. In Cambodia, plans for analytical and advisory services in the 2005 CAS—a total of 30 tasks to be completed over fiscal 2005–07—appear excessive.

ESW quality seems to be satisfactory overall in LICUS.

Anchor Strategies in Stronger Sociopolitical Analysis

Stated approach

The 2002 LICUS Task Force Report (World Bank 2002) emphasized the importance of sociopolitical analysis to help identify feasible reforms and the best ways to promote them. The rationale was that understanding local dynamics, perceptions, and circumstances allows clearer understanding of the effects of proposed reforms on various societal groups, their likely response to them, and thus the likely success of the reform agenda.

Collaboration with other donors can increase the Bank's policy influence.

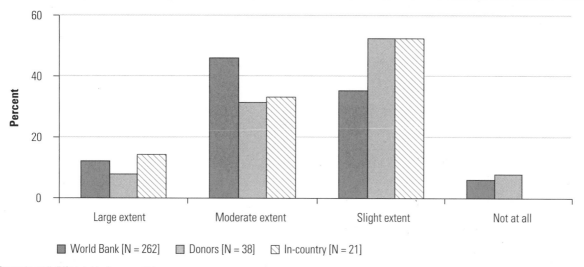

Figure 2.1: Over 40 Percent of Respondents Said That the Bank's Analytical Work Has Achieved Its Intended Results Only to a Slight Extent or Not at All

Legend: ■ World Bank [N = 262]   ■ Donors [N = 38]   ▨ In-country [N = 21]

Source: Appendix Z (Stakeholder Survey results).

Note: N indicates the number of valid responses.

Absorptive capacity constraints apply as much to knowledge products as to financial products produced.

The Fragile States Report (World Bank 2005e) and the 2005 LICUS Update (World Bank 2005h) have continued to emphasize the importance of political factors, including the need to complement invisible reforms with more visible ones that show tangible changes, thereby enhancing popular support.

Implementation experience

The understanding of Bank staff of the political environment in which they work has been mixed. Even where such understanding exists, it has not necessarily influenced strategy design and implementation. Political analysis is all the more important in LICUS, where decision-making processes are not institutionalized and may be influenced by personal and political interests. The Bank has increasingly encouraged more open discussion and treatment of political issues in its activities, including through guidance from the LICUS Unit. However, the Bank has yet to internalize political understanding sufficiently in LICUS country strategy design and implementation.

Examples of good political understanding. IEG's fieldwork for Sudan found that Bank staff have demonstrated good understanding of the country's political environment and been tactful in a complex environment. Overall, the Bank has managed to avoid being seen as siding with any one of the parties to the conflict, as other international actors have been perceived to be doing, although serious challenges remain for the Bank with the ongoing situation in Darfur.

Bank staff understanding of the political environment in which they work has been mixed.

Similarly, a useful internal piece of political analysis of Haiti's communication demonstrated that Bank staff are aware of the importance of the political environment and are drawing some practical conclusions from such insights. Focusing on the inadequate information

strategy in the government's Interim Cooperation Framework (ICF), the piece analyzes what media Haitians are using as the source of their information and offers recommendations on how to improve the information policy and practices of the transitional government.[6]

The risk sections in the Bank's strategy documents for the Central African Republic highlight the country's political instability, lack of reform commitment and champions, weak capacity to implement reforms, and inadequate external support as major dangers that could thwart the success of the Bank's operations. They also seem to suggest an appreciation by Bank staff of the country's political situation.

Sensitivity to day-to-day politics in Timor-Leste, specifically unrest among military veterans, led the Bank to start a small program to deal with their grievances before the issue could become a factor of destabilization in a still-fragile country.

Examples of inadequate attention to political issues. In other countries, the Bank could have improved its strategy by better reflecting the political situation. For example, in Zimbabwe, the limited political analysis is apparent in the focus of the Bank's 2005 ISN on what Zimbabwe has to do on economic reforms, reestablishing social service delivery, and rebuilding infrastructure, rather than on the more difficult question of how such a process can be encouraged and initiated to balance the political and technical aspects of a future reform process.

In Haiti, a number of donors see the lack of more thorough political analysis as the reason for what they consider a key shortcoming in the execution of donor strategy—that is, the dangerous neglect by the donor community of the need to provide adequate resources for dealing with the current security problems.

While the Bank's political understanding of Cambodia has improved recently, it has been a voyage of slow and gradual discovery. Progress has been punctuated by successive over-estimations of the role of the formal government institutions in relation to that of informal institutions based on patronage and political and military power. The Bank did not appear to have internalized such understanding sufficiently (for example, in its treatment of demobilization, including the subsequent IDA-financed project), nor of the role of institutionalized corruption in supporting these less formal institutions (for example, in its approach to forestry).

The forestry project in Cambodia foundered, at least in part, because of insufficient attention by the Bank to the problem of corruption. Many non-Bank stakeholders cited this project as an example of the Bank's neglect of the political reality of the country, arguing that the outcome of the project was entirely predictable.

Respondents to the Stakeholder Survey noted an improvement over time in the grounding of the Bank's work in an understanding of a country's politics (appendix Z). However, only about a third of Bank respondents, and a quarter of both other donor and in-country respondents, said the Bank's work is largely grounded in an understanding of the country's politics. About a quarter of in-country respondents, Bank respondents, and other donor respondents said it is so only to a slight extent or not at all (figure 2.2).

Commissioning and consuming—not necessarily producing—good political analysis is critical for the Bank in LICUS. In Lao PDR, the Bank effectively tapped existing political analysis (box

2.1), but this has not always been the case. The Bank should commission such analysis only in cases where good political analysis does not already exist.

Critical to the Bank's effectiveness is its ability to adequately reflect sound political analysis in its strategy. This has been an area of weakness in the Bank. For example, the Interim Strategy in Papua New Guinea has a good discussion of the political system. It recognizes the problems of clan loyalties, political patronage, corruption, lack of capacity, and other factors, but the Strategy then goes on to disregard some of this vital knowledge and treat these issues as technical problems. The political analysis and reasons for past failures should have underpinned the Bank's strategy in the country.

While in Lao PDR the Bank effectively tapped

Sound political understanding and its appropriate distillation into Bank strategy remains a function of specific personalities rather than something that can be expected more commonly.

Commissioning and consuming—not necessarily producing— good political analysis is critical for the Bank in LICUS.

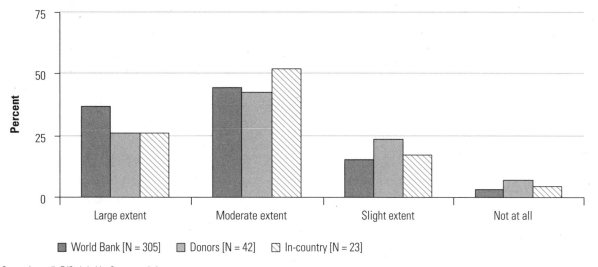

Figure 2.2: Bank Respondents Somewhat More Likely than Other Respondents to Say That the Bank's Work Has Been Grounded Largely in an Understanding of the Country's Politics

World Bank [N = 305]   Donors [N = 42]   In-country [N = 23]

Source: Appendix Z (Stakeholder Survey results).

Note: N indicates the number of valid responses.

Box 2.1: Lao People's Democratic Republic: Good Practice Example of Using Existing Political Knowledge

The Bank invited a political scientist who had published extensively on the Lao People's Democratic Republic to make a presentation to the country team on politics and reform in the country. This allowed for preparation of an independent summary of relevant political analysis (tailored to the needs of the donor community in general and to the Bank in particular) and dissemination of this information to relevant Bank staff and other donors. It also avoided the higher costs of preparing a "Bank" analysis, as well as potential tension with the government. In other words, acquisition of existing knowledge as well as its dissemination proved more important and effective than knowledge creation.

Source: Fieldwork undertaken for this review in Lao People's Democratic Republic, IEG, 2005.

existing political analysis, as noted above; even in that case the internalization of the knowledge gained in Bank strategy remained insufficient.

The main focus of the Bank's efforts to improve attention to political factors needs to be on helping staff internalize political analysis in strategy design and implementation. Appendix J outlines the many types and layers of political analysis that are useful in strategy development.

The Bank has not yet sufficiently internalized political understanding in strategy design and implementation.

The operational aspects of the Bank's LICUS approach do not fully reflect the *conflict-prevention* goal, which was given more prominence in the 2005 LICUS approach than in the 2002 iteration. The 2005 Fragile States Report includes conflict prevention as part of the peace-building objective, and more specifically under its deterioration business model, where it emphasizes the importance of contributing to multidonor and community-level conflict-prevention efforts.

The conflict-prevention goal will require the Bank to address root causes, but its role in this area is yet to be clearly established.

Addressing conflict prevention will require the Bank to give much greater attention to the root causes of conflict—conflict prevention "necessarily entails address-

ing the political dynamics that shaped the conflict and that will determine the course of the peace process" (Rogier 2005). This will inevitably take the Bank into addressing ethnic, sociological, and political factors. Although the Bank has given more attention to preventive aspects recently,[7] there is limited knowledge about the effectiveness of these efforts, and the Bank's role and comparative advantage in these areas have yet to be clearly established.

Promote Domestic Demand and Capacity for Positive Change

Stated approach
The 2002 LICUS Task Force Report argued that donors should work strategically to build capacity for reform both inside and outside government. Shifting the emphasis, the 2005 Fragile States Report stresses the centrality of building capacity inside the state. With respect to non-state actors, it recommends balancing state capacity-building efforts with support for civil society and the private sector.

Implementation experience
There has been a marked jump in the Bank's lending and trust funds devoted to capacity development in LICUS (see definition of capacity development in the note to table 2.2). The level has increased from less than $90 million in fiscal 2002 to over $366 million in 2005 (table 2.2, appendix K). Capacity development, however, has not historically been an area of strength for the Bank. Continuing problems with the design and implementation of its capacity development work in LICUS suggest that its effectiveness is likely to remain limited.

According to the 2005 Comprehensive Development Framework (CDF) Progress Report (World Bank 2005c), capacity-building support in most LICUS tends to consist of isolated interventions in specific areas, and it is not always responsive to country priorities. Of 39 countries where this was found to be the case, 18 (46 percent) were LICUS.

IEG's 2005 review of the Bank's capacity-building interventions in Sub-Saharan Africa

Table 2.2: Capacity Development Lending and Trust Funds in LICUS (US$ million)

| | Fiscal year | | | | | | |
	2000	2001	2002	2003	2004	2005	2000–05
Total	122	22	87	55	16	366	669
Percentage of total resources	23	5	6	4	1	30	10

Sources: For IBRD, IDA, and Social Fund data—World Bank database; for LICUS Trust Fund, Institutional Development Fund, and Post-Conflict Fund data—LICUS Unit, OPCS.

Note: Capacity development is defined broadly to include Bank interventions dealing with, for example, state capacity development, accountability, and private sector development. Capacity-development financing here includes financing for all Bank-supported projects that were either free-standing capacity-development projects or where capacity development accounted for at least 80 percent of the project cost. The list of capacity-development projects includes those financed through IBRD, Global Environment Facility (GEF), Special Financing (country-specific trust funds), IDA, LICUS Trust Fund, Post-Conflict Fund (PCF), and Institutional Development Fund (IDF)—they were identified by IEG and cleared by the LICUS Unit and are presented in appendix K.

noted that country programs generally do not address—systematically and in an integrated way—the issue of countries' ability to build capacity. In the majority of country programs, capacity-building support remains fragmented—designed and managed operation-by-operation. Fiduciary and other ESW products still involve clients mainly in organizational tasks and data collection, and only to a limited extent in data analysis, report writing, and dissemination.

Despite the severity of governance and institutional problems in LICUS and limited past success in these areas, the Bank has continued to rely on traditional approaches to capacity development. In Tajikistan, the Bank identified highly relevant areas for capacity development, but the approach used a Project Implementation Unit (PIU). The PIU was distant from the government and had little impact on broader governmental capacity development. The recent Country Partnership Strategy in Tajikistan aims to link interventions to various levels of government, but there is little implementation experience so far. In Timor-Leste, while some capacity development has been accomplished in the health sector, capacity development in other key areas (education, agriculture, and growth) has been limited.

IEG's fieldwork for Afghanistan found that the Bank has provided a significant amount of technical assistance (over $135 million in the past three years). This was useful in the early stages to start critical government functions, but has not been effective in developing capacity, because it was provided with few Afghan counterparts, resulting in little transfer of knowledge. Government capacity remains weak nearly four years after the formation of the first government.

Continuing weaknesses in the design and implementation of capacity-development work suggest that the Bank's effectiveness will remain limited in this area.

The "buying of capacity" through massive technical assistance has not delivered capacity development, and some evidence suggests that it detracted from this objective. The amount of technical assistance provided to date is well beyond the country's absorptive capacity. Massive technical assistance has not only meant wasted resources that could have been used more productively elsewhere, but also a diversion of scarce institutional capacity toward lower-priority tasks. Some government officials also pointed out that open-ended consultant contracts create perverse incentives to provide unnecessary technical assistance.

Fresh approaches for enhancing capacity and accountability are needed.

In the Stakeholder Survey, Bank respondents were more positive than other donor respondents in their views on the extent to which the Bank's technical assistance has achieved its intended results. Despite that, 45 percent of Bank respondents said that the results were achieved to only a slight extent or not at all, compared with 65 percent of other donor respondents and 47 percent of in-country respondents (appendix Z).

Reliance on massive technical assistance has not helped to develop capacity.

In the absence of capacity development in the central administration, the Bank's capacity development efforts in Timor-Leste have been "inevitably ad hoc and uneven" (Schiavo-Campo 2003), lacking a strategic approach. While capacity development was not within the Bank's mandate according to the agreement made at the Tokyo meeting, which entrusted the United Nations Transitional Administration in East Timor (UNTAET) with this responsibility, the Bank took on the objective of developing capacity at the community level and setting up a local governance structure through the Community Empowerment Projects.

As noted by a 2004 European Union evaluation, given the importance of capacity building, there should have been discussion and agreement between the Bank and UNTAET to address the issue jointly (IEG 2006c). The assumption that capacity would be developed in the government through on-the-job transfer of expertise from international advisors and training was flawed in an environment of very weak country capacity. The international advisors ended up focusing on project implementation and had little time for ensuring the transfer of capacity (IEG 2006c).

In general, the Bank has had more success in contributing to long-term capacity when it has worked through governments rather than through PIUs (IEG 2000) or when a longer-term plan for the transfer of relevant functions from the PIU to government agencies has been instituted and executed from early days (IEG 2002, 2005b).

The contribution to long-term capacity has been greater when working through government agencies or when making an early effort to transfer functions from the PIU to government agencies.

For example, in the Bank's Road Maintenance Program in Lao PDR—which relied on the relevant ministry to lead program prepara-tion and contributed to enhancement of the government's capacity to design and implement transport investments—the lack of a specialized PIU did not result in major delays or complications in implementation.[8] But even in that country, this institutional arrangement was an exception rather than the general practice.

Similarly, in Afghanistan, the capacity development effort through the Priority Restructuring and Reform process, which aimed directly at ministries and their incentive structures rather than at creating PIUs, is an example of a promising approach (box 2.2). Nevertheless, capacity development efforts in the country at large still face significant hurdles.

In Cambodia, a number of recent Bank reports assessing capacity development from 2000–05 similarly concluded that achievements were extremely limited because of a combination of governance problems and poor donor coordination[9] and the insufficient level of resources (particularly human resources in the field) provided by the Bank in the early years of the CAS period. Cambodia's 2000 CAS called for sector-wide approaches (SWAps) to reduce the transaction costs of multiple projects and multiple PIUs and to develop capacity by supporting government programs in a joint effort financed by several donors, and implemented by the responsible government agency.

Two years after the end of the CAS period, no SWAp had yet been approved.[10] Several of the IDA-funded operations more directly geared to capacity development also did not take place (Public Sector Reform, Legal Reform) or encountered substantial problems (Forestry Learning and Innovation Loan, which was rated unsatisfactory, and the Economic Capacity Building Project, which was rated unsatisfactory but upgraded to satisfactory in June 2005).

Although the LICUS Initiative has sought to increase the Bank's emphasis on improving governance in LICUS, the Bank has yet to address sufficiently the basic governance problems that plague some of its own projects. Recently, the Bank's Integrity Department investigated seven projects in Cambodia, and problems such as misuse of funds, misprocure-

Box 2.2: Afghanistan Priority Restructuring and Reform Process: Developing State Capacity through the Direct Restructuring of the Civil Service

The Priority Restructuring and Reform process (PRR) in Afghanistan allows individual ministries and government organizations to award higher salaries (up to $300 a month compared with current monthly salaries of about $30) in return for implementing a reform program as approved by the Civil Service Commission. Units concerned are required to define their objectives, plans for rationalization/downsizing, job specifications, selection criteria for each position, and a competitive process of recruitment.

This approach seeks to draw out existing skills in the civil service, while weeding out unqualified recruits previously brought into the government. In 2004, the PRR process was supplemented with a program of "lateral entry" that brought qualified Afghans in the country or greater region into the civil service on a contract basis, as well as with a recruitment program that provided even higher salaries to attract highly qualified expatriate Afghans living in Western countries ($800–1,500 a month for lateral entry and $4,000–7,000 for Afghan expatriates).

The PRR is expected to build a pyramid structure in the civil service, placing civil servants at the base, and successively fewer lateral-entry and expatriate Afghans toward the top. Foreign consultants to develop capacity would only be recruited once necessary Afghan staff was in place.

Source: Fieldwork undertaken for this review in Afghanistan.

ment, fraud, collusion, and corruption were found in certain contracts in each of the projects (World Bank 2006c).

The Bank's operational approaches do not sufficiently address issues of instrument choice for capacity development, or discuss which instruments—technical assistance, SWaps, capacity development as part of investment projects, or a totally new instrument—are effective under which LICUS situations. The Bank also has not defined its capacity-development strategy to achieve its state-building objective, and has thus far insufficiently monitored its work in the area of capacity development and governance.

Furthermore, the operational approaches have not been differentiated enough to fit the varying institutional environments of different LICUS. In some LICUS, the state is exclusionary or represents only the interests of particular groups. How does the Bank intend to approach state building in these circumstances? Similarly, what would its approach be in LICUS where engaging with non-state actors may not be feasible given strong negative reactions of the government to such contact? The complexities of addressing state building in LICUS are outlined in box 2.3.

To address capacity constraints effectively, a distillation of experience that would indicate the right entry points, as well as approaches to determine them in countries with weak overall capacity (in the balance between immediate and longer-term needs, or different levels of administration or government functions) would be beneficial for strategy development. Entry points will necessarily differ across LICUS, and the Bank has not sufficiently developed operational approaches to distinguish between situations where it is justified in developing state capacity directly, where it is justified in doing so indirectly through non-state actors, and where the capacity of non-state actors themselves needs to be developed.

The 2005 LICUS approach made state building its central objective, despite the Bank's weak record in capacity development and governance. In taking on the complex and more ambitious state-building agenda, the Bank has the responsibility to indicate what this agenda does and does not include, demonstrate that it has identified its role and comparative advantage in state building, and develop operational approaches to ensure a higher chance of success than in the past.

Some other donors have similarly adopted the state-building terminology. The Bank is working with them to articulate a state-building

Operational approaches need to be further differentiated to fit the varying institutional environments of different LICUS.

Box 2.3: The Complexities of State Building in LICUS: Is the Bank Ready?

In Sudan, both the government and the Sudan People's Liberation Movement welcome the focus on capacity development implicit in the Bank's activities, including in the LICUS Trust Fund. But the Bank faces tough choices. For example:
- Whose capacity should be built, particularly in North Sudan?
- To what extent should the Bank strengthen and transform existing structures and chains of command?
- To what extent should it circumvent or replace structures considered too heavily influenced by political patronage interests?
- What is the moral responsibility of the Bank in the difficult circumstances presented by the genocide in Darfur?

In Papua New Guinea, the Bank faces another set of tough questions:
- Is the concept of a "central" government applicable?
- Does the country need more decentralization, especially if the center is weak?
- Should the Bank's capacity development efforts reinforce clan structures or supplant them?

In Timor-Leste, some key questions are:
- How far should donors go in promoting plans for long-term development and local capacity development for a country without a sovereign government (as was the case in Timor-Leste before 2002)?
- How can foreign expertise be delivered in a way that promotes local capacity development?

Sources: For Sudan, fieldwork undertaken for this review, IEG 2006c; for Papua New Guinea, background work undertaken for this review; for Timor-Leste, IEG 2006c.

agenda and to identify its own role within it, and the Bank has introduced some relevant capacity-development measures (such as leadership support, anti-corruption work, political economy of reform, development policy operations, transitional results matrixes, and demand-side measures). These measures do not, however, amount to the jump in thinking and approach required to address effectively the tough capacity development and governance challenges in LICUS.

A deeper approach to capacity development and governance than what we see in the Bank's 2005 LICUS Update and LICUS country strategies seems warranted. While state fragility is often associated with weak institutions and poor governance, the more operationally relevant question is why such problems exist in LICUS. Any approach that does not sufficiently address this deeper question is unlikely to help LICUS transition out of their fragility in a sustainable manner.

The state-building agenda needs to be unpacked and the Bank's specific role and comparative advantage identified.

Building stronger state institutions and governance requires social transformations, including those of civil society and in the relationship between the state and civil society. While the Bank's 2002 LICUS approach noted the importance of these issues and its 2005 approach reaffirmed their importance, the Bank has yet to develop specific guidance on, for example, what the appropriate balance is between state and non-state capacity development in different LICUS situations and how it can be achieved effectively. Country strategies and the Bank's assistance in the field also have yet to be adequately informed by such considerations.

Leadership training will bring limited benefits unless it is complemented by measures that simultaneously foster a broader political debate and discourse, including one stimulated by the media. The inherently political nature of such activities cannot be ignored. The Bank needs to be explicit about what aspects of the problem it will include in its assistance program, as well as which donors it will work with to ensure that its own efforts are adequately complemented and supported.

Furthermore, while the Bank's approach to state building emphasizes the development of basic systems of public administration, public finance, and macroeconomic management in LICUS, their prioritization will be key, but remains inadequately addressed thus far. Finally, with respect to social service delivery, guidance is lacking on how much and to whom to deliver these services. Given the inevitable resource and capacity constraints in LICUS, how will the Bank strike a balance between catering to elite interests (which may be necessary to stabilize power) and catering to those of the poor (which will be necessary to equitably improve living conditions and avoid negative spillovers)?

The question remains whether the Bank should have adopted state building as a central LICUS objective without first fully understanding what it entails and how it can be achieved, especially given the Bank's traditional weakness in the area of capacity development and governance. Does the Bank have convincing approaches to bring about accountable governance? Where demand for capacity development is low (as is likely to be the case in LICUS), what approaches will the Bank adopt? How will the Bank ensure that alternative delivery mechanisms do not detract from the state-building agenda?

The focus on state building in LICUS also raises questions about the adequacy of staff with the relevant public sector management skills. In addition, the Bank has yet to develop an appropriate set of performance indicators against which state-building outcomes can be measured. And finally, the choice of the term "state building" may itself be inappropriate given its political and ideological connotations.

The Bank's *World Development Report 1997: The State in a Changing World* recommended matching the state's role to its capability, while at the same time raising state capability by reinvigorating public institutions. The Bank has not given enough attention to developing approaches that address both these aspects of state capacity in LICUS. The idea of "good enough governance" would seem to be relevant to matching the state's role to its capability in LICUS (Grindle 2004). It emphasizes selectivity in a world in which all good things cannot be pursued at once. Instead, the task is to determine what is essential and what is not, what should come first and what should follow, what can be achieved in the short term and what can only be achieved over the longer term, and what is feasible and what is not.

IEG comments on the Bank's Action Plan to implement the recommendations of the Bank's 2005 Task Force on Capacity Development in Africa have also identified several areas for further development of the Bank's approach (box 2.4). In terms of measuring governance and accountability performance, the Bank's 2006 *Global Monitoring Report* identifies specific CPIA indicators;[11] Kaufmann, Kraay, and Mastruzzi (KKZ) indicators; Doing Business[12] and Investment Climate Survey indicators;[13] Public Expenditure and Financial Accountability (PEFA) indicators;[14] Global Integrity Index indicators;[15] Polity indicators;[16] and Transparency International indicators as good measures.[17]

Resource-rich LICUS pose special problems of accountability and rent-seeking. While country strategy design has emphasized issues of governance in natural resource management in recent years, the Bank's implementation arrangements have been inadequate. For example, in the Central African Republic, necessary actions for the forestry and mining sectors are outlined in Bank's country strategy, but it is unclear how they will be implemented, or what happens if they are not implemented (appendix L).

Support Simple and Feasible Entry-Level Reforms

Stated approach

The 2002 LICUS Task Force Report emphasized the importance of a highly focused reform agenda in LICUS. It explained that this would consist of two or three reforms that are important in economic terms and are likely to result in a rapid and substantial payoff, but that

---

Box 2.4: Areas for Further Development in the Bank's Approach to Capacity Development

The Bank's Africa Action Plan (World Bank 2005i) needs to indicate how the Bank will act on the broad and general observations of the Bank's 2005 Africa Capacity Development Report. The Action Plan should aim to answer the following specific questions:

How will the CAS be improved to reflect capacity building as a core country program objective? The report's first building block for the Bank is to use the CAS better. What changes will be made to ensure that capacity-building objectives are clearly articulated in the CAS results matrix and tracked during CAS implementation?

How will the Bank and borrowers take account of the sectoral characteristics that affect capacity needs? The health sector, for example, has different capacity issues than the roads sector. What roles will networks and sector boards play in developing sector-specific analysis and benchmarking? A single corporate focal point, as proposed by the 2005 Africa Capacity Development Task Force, is unlikely to be able to provide deep enough sectoral knowledge to meet these needs.

In which areas will the Bank concentrate, and how will it support capacity building more effectively than in the past? The 2005 Africa Capacity Development Report proposes, as its second building block, a long list of substantive areas—ranging from public expenditure management and health service delivery to empowering the press and parliaments. The capacity development record to date in some of these areas is weak, so it will be important for the Action Plan to identify the areas of the Bank's comparative advantage and what will be done to achieve better results.

How can lending instruments be made more effective? What actual activities—training, technical assistance, and other interventions—have proved effective for building capacity within lending operations? The Task Force recommends a continued shift to programmatic lending. Although there are potential advantages to programmatic lending, this instrument has not automatically led to better results. How should programmatic loans be designed to establish clear objectives and effective actions for capacity building?

How should World Bank Institute (WBI) activities change to support country programs more effectively? The 2005 Africa Capacity Development Report calls for a "more focused" working relationship for WBI in country programs, but describes a WBI role that appears quite similar to its present one. What changes are planned?

Source: IEG comments on World Bank 2005i.

Note: The 2005 Africa Capacity Development Report refers to the report of the Bank's 2005 Task Force on Capacity Development in Africa (World Bank 2005a).

---

are also feasible in sociopolitical terms, tending to unite a broad coalition for reform. The 2005 Fragile States Report noted that political, security, and development linkages are particularly important in fragile state contexts.

Implementation experience

Implementation progress on this principle has been modest, with good progress on some reform aspects (such as contributing to macroeconomic stability, including controlling inflation or delivery of physical infrastructure), but less progress on others (such as prioritizing and sequencing reforms, building institutions, or strengthening governance).

The Bank has generally contributed to macroeconomic stability, including the control of inflation, through, for example, currency and banking reforms, especially in post-conflict countries. It also has often contributed to the delivery of significant amounts of physical infrastructure.

Helping to move a country through the immediate post-conflict reconstruction phase and into the development phase presents major challenges, especially for institution building and employment creation (for example, mass protests broke out in Dili, Timor-Leste, first in 2002 and again in mid-2005, partly as a result of people seeking jobs), where the Bank has been less successful. Areas that are less technocratic and where the cultural content of institutions is greater—governance, corruption, conflict of interest between public and private interests—have proven to be tough.

IEG's fieldwork in Timor-Leste found that there should have been a more deliberate process of transition from the immediate post-conflict reconstruction phase to the development phase, and that longer-term development challenges should have been more thoroughly considered. A more timely CAS (originally scheduled for 2002 but not completed until 2005) might have helped stimulate discussion about a relevant development strategy.

While the Trust Fund for East Timor (TFET) provided much-needed immediate reconstruction support, and did so reasonably quickly, it has not been as successful in policy development in some important areas (education, agriculture, economic growth). Although the process surrounding the Bank's three budget support loans, the Transitional Support Programs (TSPI-III), drew government and donor attention to the broad policy agenda, including the issue of expenditure management, it involved several hundred individual actions and insufficiently focused on the core issues of institutional capacity and the future direction of the economy. The general use of Development Policy Loans (DPLs) and other forms of budget support in LICUS is discussed in appendix M.

IEG's fieldwork for the Central African Republic also raises the question of whether the LICUS approach and its instruments are adequate for meeting all the challenges facing the Bank's strategy in the next, post-political transition phase of its engagement with the country. That challenge is to build on the success of the election process and use it to consolidate and amplify the reform effort.

While the Bank has played an important early engagement role in several LICUS, staying engaged is only a means to an end. In some instances, strategic disengagement—with the exception of in-house analytical work—may be needed, at least for periods of time, especially when involvement with the Bank is seen as inappropriately giving legitimacy to the LICUS government or when it dampens internal pressure for reform. Where engagement is appropriate, effective follow-up through a clear and relevant reform agenda will be important, or else the early successes of engagement may be short-lived and may contribute little to the achievement of CAS objectives.

As the examples of the Central African Republic and Haiti show, all sorts of obstacles may make the follow-through on a successful LICUS engagement difficult. The Central African Republic is now faced with a potentially disastrous budget crisis just at the moment when its political success needs to be backed up on the economic side. In Haiti, the donor community seems to have given inadequate attention to ensuring a minimum level of security. In both cases, a good initial result of the LICUS Initiative is now at risk of being diminished.

The Bank needs to improve its effectiveness in the period that follows post-conflict reconstruction, when easy reforms have been exhausted and structural change (in institutions or governance, for example) is needed. In some ways the Bank appears to have moved from emergency reconstruction to development without discussion of the process and the implications for Bank strategy in post-conflict situations. Box 2.5 presents three lessons from the Bank's post-conflict experience.

The Bank's approach in post-conflict LICUS also has other shortcomings. For example, immediately following the cessation of conflict, international donors, including the Bank, have often committed large amounts of aid coupled with overly ambitious agendas. This has frequently created high expectations among the population and led to disillusionment when expectations remained unfulfilled and few tangible improvements are seen in day-to-day living.

This disillusionment has been further aggravated by the perception of a "foreign footprint" created by the infusion of

The Bank has succeeded in contributing to macroeconomic stability, especially in post-conflict situations.

Staying engaged is only a means to an end and needs to be followed up with an effective reform agenda.

Effectiveness needs to improve in the phase following reconstruction, when structural change is needed.

Box 2.5: Three Lessons from Post-Conflict Countries

Domestic political processes, however slow, are necessary to prevent a relapse into conflict. The hard work of building a strong domestic base and engaging civil society in an organized manner is unavoidable, but highly time consuming.

Often the post-conflict period sees a continuation of strife, but by nonviolent means. The principal instrument for the continuation of the conflict can be economic. Constructing artificial barriers to flows of commerce and transport; severing of normal economic linkages across ethnic groups; refusal to harmonize taxes and customs; regulations that impede the creation of a common economic and trade space; and fracturing of institutions or mechanisms that process economic conflict (courts, arbitration mechanisms, chambers of commerce) have all been used to keep differences alive. Where the organizers of separateness have access to quasi-state resources, and the means to extract the allegiance of the population through force or loyalty, creating a coherent national unit will be a long process.

Institutional development and state capacity formation need to start from the first days of a post-conflict program. A post-conflict society's capacity to use aid efficiently is low, yet both donor and country expectations of the peace dividend are high. The need to reinforce capacity is thus a high priority.

This requires the early formation of the basic public institutions, adequate salaries for staff (and hence the imperative of donor budget support in the first years of post-conflict assistance), training of staff, and making good use of existing institutions and individuals. External capacity will have to be bought, but should be contracted only with sunset provisions to maintain the incentives to develop local capacity.

Economic instruments (aid, policy advice, technical assistance) work best when kept in line with the absorptive capacity of the country and with the willingness and the appetite of representative governments to reform. This calls for scaling down the ambitions of rapid state building.

Early expectations in a number of post-conflict countries of a very large physical reconstruction program—initially through donor grants and rapidly thereafter by the country—leading to self-sufficiency within a decade or so have often been vitiated by security problems and inadequate local engagement in the vision. Donor involvement has turned out to be of greater duration than initially thought, with disbursements stretched out and much more modest in the initial years than planned.

Source: Mitra 2004.

large amounts of international funds and personnel in the country. According to a 2005 Reuters estimate, up to 60 cents of each dollar of an aid project in Afghanistan goes into overhead, including payment to donor staff (Francois and Sud 2006). Better communication is critical to lower expectations to realistic levels and is something that the Bank needs to invest in.

Speed should not be prioritized over the achievement of longer-term objectives, especially when the objectives relate to difficult institutional issues that require a learning-by-doing approach by stakeholders. An excessive focus on speed in the initial phases may compromise laying the groundwork necessary for sustainable future outcomes.

Given the limited capacity in LICUS, the Bank's currently broad reform agendas in several

A large infusion of external funds increases the "foreign footprint" in the country and can cause resentment.

countries (as opposed to the "highly focused reform agenda" recommended by the 2002 LICUS Task Force) do not augur well for effectiveness. Nicolas van de Walle (2005) notes, "although [the] LICUS [Initiative] voices all of the right concerns for ownership and selectivity, it is terribly vague about how the Bank will avoid the past pitfalls in this strategy's implementation" (Van de Walle 2005, p. 80).

While donors must strive for collective donor selectivity, this is far from being achieved, as Afghanistan's donor-endorsed reform agenda and Haiti's ICF (discussed below) show. However, even if this collective donor selectivity is not immediately achieved, the Bank itself needs to ensure focus and selectivity in its own assistance program, based on its core competences. Such Bank selectivity has been increasing in recent years, but remains a challenge, as the example of São Tomé and Principe (discussed below) seems to suggest.

In Afghanistan, the reforms covered by donors are wide-ranging, show lack of sufficient priority, and have led to 120 pieces of pending legislation. These reforms, dealing with virtually every economic and social aspect of the country, need to be carefully prioritized and sequenced, but donors have yet to do so. In Haiti, the ICF, which is meant to guide international assistance and cooperation with Haiti through September 2006, covers practically all basic state functions, ranging from security, to national dialogue, to economic governance, to economic recovery, to basic services. Individually, all these areas seem important, but together they add up to a formidable program.

With respect to the Bank's own assistance program, São Tomé and Principe is an example where the Bank was far too ambitious in relation to the resources allocated to the country, with the result that many of the CAS objectives were not achieved or were only partially achieved.

Beyond selectivity in CASs, it is critical to ensure that actual reform agendas in the field are focused and well-prioritized. While it is difficult to be selective in complex LICUS environments where reforms are needed in virtually every area, greater effort must be made to prioritize and sequence reforms to avoid overtaxing limited capacity, while at the same time rejecting partial solutions.

In Timor-Leste, donors may have pulled out too quickly, without sufficiently dealing with the country's pressing capacity needs (box 2.6). In Haiti, development assistance has greatly fluctuated over the years. The country has gone through several "feast or famine" cycles in its relations with the donor community. This may have been avoided had various donors better coordinated the sequencing of their aid.

Overall, the Bank has been overly optimistic about what it can achieve in LICUS, as indicated by some wide-ranging country strategy objectives and the mostly unsatisfactory or moderately unsatisfactory outcome ratings given by in IEG in its CAS Completion Report (CASCR) Reviews for LICUS. In the Stakeholder Survey, a fifth of in-country and Bank respondents and a third of other donor respondents said that the Bank supported a focused reform agenda consisting of key actions and reforms in the LICUS country to a slight extent or not at all.

Appropriate sequencing of reforms is key to ensuring selectivity while avoiding partial solutions.

Explore Innovative Mechanisms for Social Service Delivery

Stated approach
The 2002 LICUS Task Force Report emphasized the importance of exploring alternative mechanisms for social service delivery. The report argues that the strategy for improving basic social outcomes is to supplement weak central government delivery by strengthening multiple alternative channels. Compared with the 2002 LICUS Task Force Report, the 2005 Fragile States Report plays down the importance of alternative service-delivery mechanisms.

Box 2.6: Timor-Leste: Excessive Optimism, Impatience, and Partial Solutions?

From 1999 to 2002, the United Nations (UN) lent enthusiastic support to an ambitious nation-building project in Timor-Leste. The project, however, did not work out as many had envisioned. An economic uptick during the three years of UN rule in Timor-Leste collapsed after many of the foreign advisors departed. Recent donor reports state that little headway has been made in improving basic services in the country.

A Timorese country official expressed concern that, below the ministerial level, the country lacked people with adequate experience to fill essential jobs and run things on a day-to-day basis. He complained that "we have ministers but no middle managers" and that a good deal of the nation's mess is the result of actions taken by the foreign donors.

The Timorese government has asserted that more than half the foreign assistance to their country was spent on salaries and consultancy fees for the foreign advisors. The country official explained that, in essence, the foreigners were too impatient. They came, spread their money around, and left. "They all had a time frame—one year, two years, four years," the country official said. "You can't build a country from nothing in that amount of time."

Source: Perlez 2006. Quotes from Sidonio Freitas, Senior Manager, Timor Sea Designated Authority.

Implementation experience

Alternative service delivery mechanisms have succeeded in the quick and effective delivery of substantial infrastructure, but there is less evidence of success in meeting other objectives, such as empowering communities or developing government capacity. Implementation progress on this principle has thus been modest.

Alternative delivery mechanisms have provided substantial infrastructure.

Alternative service delivery mechanisms have included social funds, community-driven development (CDD) projects, and projects with nongovernmental organization (NGO) or private sector involvement. A number of these projects, such as the Angola Social Action Fund, Cambodia Social Fund, and Timor-Leste Community Empowerment Projects, have succeeded in quickly disbursing significant amounts of resources and delivering substantial amounts of infrastructure. But other benefits have been more elusive.

In Timor-Leste, the breakdown of institutions, poor governance, widespread suffering, and massive displacement of the population put pressure on the donor community to respond speedily. The Bank met the challenge through three Community Empowerment Projects (CEP-I, II, and III) that quickly transferred resources to communities and delivered massive amounts of infrastructure. But speed came at the cost of the other project objectives, particularly community empowerment and the development of local institutions. CEP-established project councils, which bypassed local traditional leaders, were seen by communities primarily as conduits for channeling donor money and were not able to take on the larger role envisaged for them as development agents in their communities (IEG 2006c).

But they have had less success in empowering communities or developing government capacity.

In Tajikistan, while the 2003 CAS built strongly on the CDD approach, the CASCR acknowledged that CDD did not take root as planned because it was seen as an NGO-driven agenda, disconnected from the pressing concerns of state building and enhancing central government capacity. The 2005 CAS has a very limited discussion of CDD, and instead relies on developing state capacity for service delivery. More than eight years after the end of the civil war, donors have made little headway in developing government capacity.

In the Stakeholder Survey, the majority of in-country and Bank respondents said that the use of nongovernmental or semi-autonomous arrangements made a small positive contribution to both service delivery and the development of long-term government capacity in LICUS. About 40 percent of other donor respondents said that the contribution to service delivery was large, while 40 percent also said that there was no contribution to development of long-term government capacity (figure 2.3).

When alternative delivery mechanisms are used, there needs to be a clear transition plan for moving the functions back to the government. In Afghanistan, more than three years after the start of post-conflict reconstruction, none of the donors has a strategy for doing so.

Alternative delivery mechanisms may not be feasible in some LICUS. For instance, in Lao PDR, where there is a single-party system and a very limited role for civil society, alternative mechanisms would make unlikely candidates for service delivery. Similarly, in Zimbabwe, the government's sensitivity to the Bank engaging with nongovernmental actors limits the extent to which the Bank can follow this principle. In Timor-Leste, an otherwise democratic and open government has begun to adopt an increasingly hostile attitude toward civil society organizations. The Bank has recently attempted to understand how to engage with civil society in LICUS effectively (appendix N).

Work Closely with Other Donors

Stated approach

The 2002 LICUS Task Force Report noted that partnership with other agencies is central to Bank Group activities, particularly in LICUS. The 2005 Fragile States Report emphasizes higher levels of

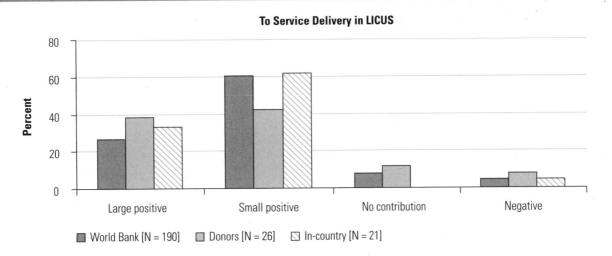

Figure 2.3: Most Respondents Said That the Use of Nongovernmental or Semi-Autonomous Arrangements Has Made a Small Positive Contribution

To Service Delivery in LICUS

■ World Bank [N = 190]   ■ Donors [N = 26]   ◫ In-country [N = 21]

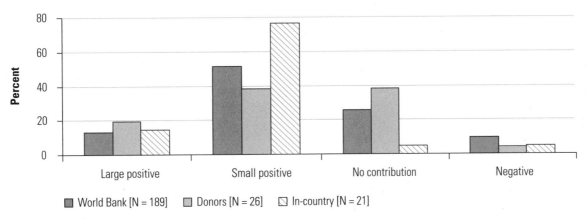

To the Development of Long-Term Government Capacity in LICUS

■ World Bank [N = 189]   ■ Donors [N = 26]   ◫ In-country [N = 21]

Source: Appendix Z (Stakeholder Survey results).

Note: N indicates the number of valid responses.

partnership, such as donor alignment, policy coherence, and harmonization, and also highlights the importance of addressing capacity constraints through donor collaboration.

Implementation experience
The quality of donor coordination, with strong Bank participation, has been substantial at the international policy level, as exemplified by the recent donor agreement on the 12 OECD-DAC principles of engagement. But the quality of donor coordination at the country level has been medium to low. While country-level policy agreements among donors have been increasing in a

number of LICUS, there are still instances of basic disagreements among donors on critical strategies, and implementation follow-through on agreed policies has typically been weak.[18] Implementation progress on donor coordination in LICUS is thus rated medium overall.

Alternative delivery mechanisms may not be feasible in some LICUS.

Donor coordination at the international policy level.
The Bank has long been active in international policy debates on fragile states, often playing a leading role as co-chair of donor events and co-

author of joint policy papers (appendix Y). An important element in the Bank's drive for partnership and cooperation at the international policy level is the Fragile States Group (FSG).[19] The FSG, supported by the DAC Secretariat in the OECD, is motivated by the understanding that all donors recognized the importance of more emphasis on fragile states, the need to stay engaged and find ways of working effectively, and the importance of acting together in these difficult circumstances at about the same time. The FSG's work is uniformly well regarded among donors.[20] Most believe it has been instrumental in elevating the issue of fragile states to the international level and in laying a foundation for coordinated action.[21] The best-known result of this is the recently promulgated principles of international engagement in fragile states (appendix E) (OECD 2005c).

The strength of donor coordination will be tested during implementation of the 12 OECD-DAC principles through pilots. This process is likely to present several coordination challenges. Many solutions have been identified to address these challenges in a concept note prepared by the FSG (OECD 2005b). However, implementing these solutions will require significant effort. For example, comparable actions by 12 donors in 10 pilot countries that represent a wide range of views will have to be agreed and translated into concrete actions.[22] Close interaction with ongoing security and humanitarian missions will be needed. The likelihood that the pilots will result in effective ways of implementing the design embodied in the principles is far from certain and should be monitored.

Implementation of the OECD-DAC principles needs to be monitored.

From the outset, the LICUS Initiative has sought to build relevant partnerships with key players—UN agencies such as the UN Development Program (UNDP) and UN Development Group (UNDG),[23] and some bilateral donors, such as the United Kingdom and Australia. The Bank has had a number of successful partnerships with the UN at the policy level. The recent UNDG-Bank Operational Note on Transitional Results Matrices (World Bank and UNDP 2005)

builds on and complements earlier joint work by the UNDP and the Bank's Conflict Prevention and Reconstruction Unit on multilateral needs assessments in post-conflict situations (UNDG, UNDP, and World Bank 2004).

The Bank and UN have also collaborated on developing the Joint Assessment Missions (JAM) tool, and donors have recently completed joint country strategies in Cambodia, Nigeria, Somalia, and Togo, and they are under way for the Central African Republic and the Democratic Republic of Congo. Furthermore, the Bank has collaborated with the UN Department of Peace-keeping on a joint staff training program and is developing a joint state-building program with UNDP.

In Timor-Leste, while significant problems between some donors emerged later (for example, between the Bank and the UN, as discussed below), the immediate donor response following the referendum for independence was well executed. A JAM of experts from five donor countries, the European Commission, UN agencies, the Asian Development Bank (ADB), and the World Bank visited Timor-Leste in late 1999. A subsequent donors' meeting in Tokyo endorsed the establishment of two multidonor trust funds, one of which was under the trusteeship of the Bank with the ADB as co-implementer. It moved quickly to commit funds to cover virtually every sector in its sphere of responsibility.

In a number of instances, however, Bank-UN relations have encountered significant problems. In Timor-Leste, the Bank and the UN could not agree on a common approach to community development. The UN favored close alignment with the emerging district administration, while the Bank argued for bypassing the weak district level. The end result, as noted by the joint government–civil society study of development projects, was that the Bank's community empowerment program developed in parallel with UN local government grant agreements. In Sudan, the Bank and UN worked on the JAM process without any formal agreement between them.

Among the Bank's bilateral partnerships, that with the DFID stands out, especially because of agreement on many aspects of how development in fragile states might be undertaken. Some donors view DFID as providing the intellectual leadership on fragile states, while the Bank provides a systematic approach. The partnership with Australia is also strong. Cooperation is growing with several other bilateral donors, including Canada, Denmark, France, the Netherlands, Norway, and the United States.

Donor coordination at the country level. The quality of donor coordination experience at the country level has been medium to low. While there are a number of examples of good aid coordination at the country level, in far too many cases coordination is unsatisfactory. Donors have pointed out that the Bank's current tendency—to get approval first up the management line (often at headquarters), and then to seek collaboration with other donors, asking them to harmonize with the Bank—is against the spirit of donor coordination.

Examples of good country-level aid coordination. In Liberia, close donor coordination resulted in agreement on the Governance and Economic Management Assistance Program (GEMAP) between the National Transitional Government and various bilateral and multilateral donors. The GEMAP was developed to help improve financial and fiscal administration, transparency, and accountability in Liberia and received the recognition and support of the UN Security Council.

Despite a poor earlier donor coordination experience, Cambodia has made progress recently. The 2005 CAS is the product of close coordination between donors, with large parts of it common to the ADB, DFID, and the UN development system.

Examples of weak country-level donor coordination. It is not uncommon to find multiple donors providing capacity development to the same organization using different procedures, further burdening overloaded ministries. In Afghanistan, for example, the Ministry of Finance receives technical assistance for customs modernization from the Bank, USAID, the European Union (EU), and DFID. The ADB has spread its technical assistance for capacity development (about $15.2 million) over 18 tasks in various ministries. Similarly, large missions can overload the government, and in the absence of early warning and sustained follow-up can be counterproductive.

The Bank has made a strong effort to coordinate with the UN from the outset.

In Angola, several development partners noted that the Bank could have done more to foster partnership and coordination, and the Bank has only lately emphasized this aspect. The Bank was perceived as giving priority to establishing its own credentials with the government at the expense of a joint approach and as giving insufficient attention to the crucial details of partnership, increasing the risk of duplication of effort.

In semistructured interviews, some complained that the Bank was unwilling to listen to donors with many years of experience in Angola and that partners were being informed ex post rather than consulted ex ante. Incoming missions from the Bank did not seek close collaboration with other partners, who then concluded that decision making in the Bank was strongly centralized in Washington. Although the difficult overall environment in Angola created many challenges, the Bank's particular engagement contributed to donors and the government inadequately coordinating the policy dialogue relating to governance and transparency issues.

It has similarly made a strong effort to coordinate with bilaterals.

As noted earlier, country-level donor coordination in Timor-Leste experienced significant problems. The experience of Timor-Leste highlights the critical importance of coordination among donors supporting reconstruction in a newly independent post-conflict country. While the inter-

The Bank needs to replicate its success at the international policy level by raising its game at the country level.

national community was able to raise a large amount of resources for development of Timor-Leste, the general lack of coordination between the major players in the country worked to the detriment of both the donors and the country and led to less effective and efficient utilization of resources (IEG 2006c).

IEG's Stakeholder Survey did not specifically ask respondents about country-level donor coordination. With respect to overall donor coordination, the majority of in-country respondents said that the Bank has pursued collaboration with other donors to a large or moderate extent. Other donor respondents were about equally divided among the large, moderate, and slight choices. The majority of all respondents said that there has been a positive change in the Bank's effectiveness in pursuing donor collaboration, comparing the period before and after the adoption of the LICUS Initiative (figures 2.4 and 2.5).

Capacity building was identified as an area for donor coordination in the 2002 LICUS Task Force Report, but the Bank has not provided much of an operational approach to achieve it effectively. Given that the Bank is not likely to have compar-

ative advantage over other donors in all (or even many) aspects of capacity development, the identification of capacity development as an area for donor coordination in the 2002 LICUS Task Force Report was useful. Subsequent LICUS documents, including the 2005 Fragile States Report, do not elaborate on specific areas of the Bank's comparative advantage and how donor coordination for capacity building could be effectively pursued. From an operational perspective, this is an important omission, especially given that state building is now a central focus of the LICUS Initiative.

Borrower governments could contribute to, and learn from, the debates and discussions among donor agencies, but their participation so far has been scant. Representatives from recipient countries (or from key NGOs) are rarely drawn into contributing to and learning from the debates and discussions among donor agencies and associated institutions. Indeed, the discussion in forums such as the FSG seems quite removed and does not adequately reflect country circumstances, although the recent piloting of the principles of engagement is likely to address this problem, at least in part.

Figure 2.4: The Majority of Bank Respondents Said the Bank Has Pursued Collaboration with Donors to a Large Extent; the Majority of In-Country Respondents Said It Has Done So to a Large or Moderate Extent

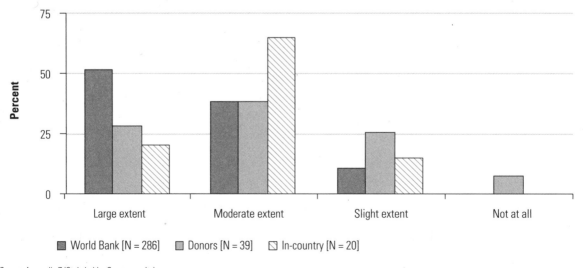

■ World Bank [N = 286]   ■ Donors [N = 39]   ▧ In-country [N = 20]

Source: Appendix Z (Stakeholder Survey results).

Note: N indicates the number of valid responses.

Figure 2.5: The Majority of Respondents Noted a Positive Change in the Bank's Effectiveness with Donor Collaboration

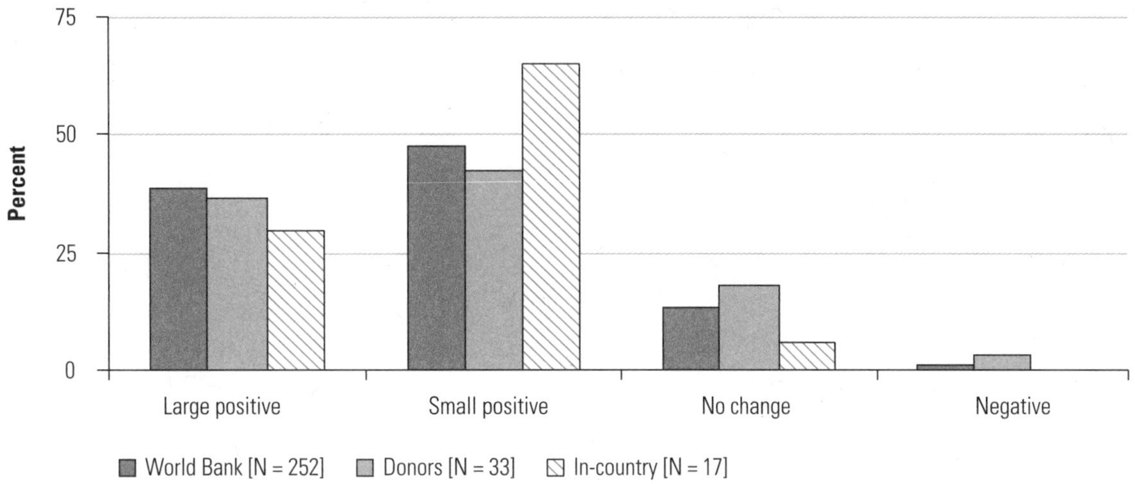

Source: Appendix Z (Stakeholder Survey results).

Note: N indicates the number of valid responses.

Increased inclusion of credible participants from fragile states in forums such as the FSG can help to ground discussions in LICUS country circumstances further, thus producing more customized strategies for varying fragile environments.

Donors may not have invested enough in confidence-building measures among borrower governments before introducing fully coordinated or joint strategies. In Papua New Guinea, the government did not take kindly to the proposed joint strategy by the three biggest donors (Australia, World Bank, and Asian Development Bank), fearing this to be an attempt by donors to "gang up."

The Bank's approach has not fully recognized the differing motivations of donors for engaging with LICUS. Although the broad concept of fragility is widely understood and accepted, the countries identified by donors as fragile vary. The motivations for supporting fragile states range from security, to aid effectiveness, to equitable development, to poverty reduction, to state building, to peace building and conflict prevention.

In Afghanistan and Tajikistan, IEG's fieldwork revealed that major donors did not subscribe to a single clear objective. Without a common overall objective, policy coherence is unlikely. Varying donor visions in Afghanistan were also reported by country officials (box 2.7). The Bank's donor coordination efforts and modalities are insufficiently informed by the objectives of the different players in a country. Donor coordination, however, is a form of collective action and requires that other donors also improve their outreach to the Bank and subordinate bilateral agendas to agreed multilateral objectives.

Coordination is not only important among different multilateral and bilateral donor agencies, but it is also a vital issue within the Bank itself. Bank projects in different sectors in the same LICUS country still often work in parallel and do not tap synergies—an example is the Community Empowerment and Agricultural Projects in Timor-Leste (IEG 2006c).

A side effect of the Bank's decentralization to country offices has been the concentration of country knowledge among local staff and its inadequate dissemination across the country

Borrower governments have participated little in donor agency debates.

Gaining government confidence is necessary for effective donor coordination.

Box 2.7: Afghanistan: Lack of a Common Vision among Donors Works against Effective Action

Interviewer: The American government and international community have said Afghanistan is at the center of the war on terrorism and have poured in billions of dollars. Do they have a vision?

Ali Jalali: They all have different visions. You see this clearly in the development of the security sector. The main pillars of reform—army, police, justice, counter-narcotics, and disarmament—are interconnected, but they were each supported by one "lead nation" from the G-7 group, and their approaches can be very different. For example, even if you built a very good police force, the criminal justice sector being developed very weakly by the Italians wouldn't support it. When you arrest a suspect, the police can legally hold him for 24 hours, and then he goes to the judicial sector. Often the suspects buy their way out.

Source: Interview with Ali Jalali, former interior minister in the Karzai government, Afghanistan. Conducted by Marc Kaufman, *The Washington Post*, May 28, 2006.

> *The Bank's donor coordination efforts and modalities need to be informed by the objectives of the different players in a country.*

team, especially those based in Washington. Addressing the problems of coordination across the departments of the Bank (such as among those dealing with public sector management, conflict prevention and reconstruction, LICUS, capacity development, and research) is particularly important in LICUS, where problems are complex and widespread, and often require multisectoral solutions.

Measure and Monitor Results

Stated approach

The 2002 LICUS Task Force emphasized that the Bank's programs in LICUS should identify expected outcomes and indicators to measure success. The 2005 LICUS Update recognized that the "logical corollary of a central focus on peace-building and state-building in the Bank's assistance strategy for fragile states is that short-term results measurement should also emphasize these dimensions, while continuing to focus on growth, poverty reduction, and the Millennium Development Goals within the long-

term vision for recovery" (World Bank 2005h, p. 7). The 2005 LICUS Update did not, however, spell out the indicators that would be used for such measurement.

Implementation experience

The LICUS Initiative's intended emphasis on monitoring and evaluation has not yet made its way into country strategies, and the focus on results monitoring across LICUS remains negligible. An assessment of 16 strategy documents in LICUS[24] carried out as part of this review found that in only 5 countries does the Bank's strategy build on a clear articulation of expected outcomes of the financed activities, including clearly defined strategic objectives, well-measured baselines, a clear definition of outcomes from the Bank's interventions, reasonable timelines of outcomes, and objective and monitorable milestones and indicators. In the Stakeholder Survey, a quarter of in-country respondents, 35 percent of Bank respondents, and 42 percent of other donor respondents said that the Bank has defined clear and monitorable indicators to measure "success" in LICUS only to a slight extent or not at all (appendix Z).

Two main problems can be identified in effective monitoring and evaluation at the country-strategy level. One is insufficient clarity and measurability of expected results. The Transitional Support Strategy in Afghanistan and the ISN in Papua New Guinea, for example, lack a results matrix, and progress indicators are either not defined or not quantified.

In Sudan, capacity development is one of the main themes of the Bank's Country Reengagement Note, but indicators against which progress would be assessed are not specified, making assessment difficult. In Zimbabwe, the Results Summary Matrix in the ISN is presented in general terms, such as "enhanced knowledge base" or "enhanced in-country partnerships," with nonspecific indicators such as "progress toward" and "improved response and implementation capacity," which are impossible to monitor properly.[25]

The second problem is insufficient selectivity and prioritization of objectives and indicators. Few Bank strategies are adequately prioritized, which hinders effective monitoring. For example, while the Liberian Results-Focused Transitional Framework Matrix made some contributions in monitoring, it is almost 40 pages long—hardly the simple planning tool envisioned by the 2005 Senior-Level Forum on Development Effectiveness in Fragile States.

Transitional results matrixes can potentially prove to be useful tools for donor coordination, prioritizing actions, and monitoring country-level progress. While it is too soon to judge their ultimate impact, some examples point to the need for closer attention to their implementation. For example, in Haiti a comprehensive transitional results matrix was prepared, but by May 2005 (some 10 months after its adoption), the reporting system on matrix results had not yet started functioning. That made it difficult to address problems encountered and to assess actual implementation.

Monitoring and evaluation are a necessity in LICUS. First, the Bank, like other donors, is still learning what approaches work in LICUS contexts. Therefore, closely monitoring experiences to draw lessons is critical, and learning and sharing needs to become a more prominent feature of LICUS work. Second, given that progress is often slow in these countries, it is important to reassess continually whether the program is on course to achieve the desired outcomes. Third, a constantly changing and volatile LICUS environment, where the progress is often nonlinear, means that program adaptation is essential. Closely tracking performance will help determine when and what kind of adaptation is necessary.

Overall LICUS Approach

This section presents the limited available aggregate data relating to the effectiveness of the overall LICUS approach. The data sources are IEG's Stakeholder Survey, Bank ratings for active projects, QAG ratings for realism, IEG ratings for closed projects, and IEG CASCR Reviews. Trends in the KKZ governance indicator are also noted.

The results of the Stakeholder Survey show that the majority of in-country, Bank, and donor respondents said that the Bank's overall program has made a positive, though small, contribution to development in LICUS, and that without Bank support there would have been less development in the country (figures 2.6–2.10).

Given that familiarity with the LICUS approach was low among in-country respondents and other donor respondents, but also among Bank respondents working on LICUS (appendix Z), the LICUS approach cannot be assumed to have also made a small positive contribution to development in LICUS.

The percentage of projects rated satisfactory on the Bank's Development Objective (DO) ratings for the active LICUS portfolio increased from 89 percent in fiscal 2000–02 to 91 percent in fiscal 2003–05, and the difference in the percentage of projects rated satisfactory between the non-LICUS LIC and the LICUS portfolios declined from 5 percentage points during fiscal 2000–02 to 2 percentage points during fiscal 2003–05 (appendix P).

However, on average, 27 percent of the projects in the fiscal 2003–05 active LICUS portfolio were at risk of not meeting their development objectives. This is a marginal improvement from 28 percent in fiscal 2000–02. Year-on-year, the percentage of projects in the active LICUS portfolio at risk of not meeting their development objectives rose by one percentage point, from 32 percent in fiscal 2002 to 33 percent in 2003, but then declined to 27 percent in 2004 and 23 percent in 2005. The realism rating[26] for the LICUS is especially low, at 57 percent for fiscal 2003–05, compared with 80 percent for non-LICUS LICs (appendix P).

The realism of the Bank's DO rating is an issue. An in-depth assessment of a sample of projects conducted by QAG for the 2005 Annual Report on Portfolio Performance (ARPP) found 22 percent

Monitoring and evaluation have yet to be sufficiently incorporated into country strategies.

Monitoring and evaluation are essential to learning by doing.

Bank support has made a small positive contribution to development in LICUS.

On average, a fourth of the fiscal 2003–05 LICUS portfolio is at risk of not meeting objectives.

of the portfolio at risk of not meeting its development objectives, while assessments by the Regions rate only about 16 percent of projects as at risk. On quality-at-entry, the ARPP found that the Africa Region, especially in low CPIA countries, can improve quality further through simpler, more focused project design. The ARPP concluded that special attention is needed to improve candor and realism of project performance ratings during supervision and to address risky projects through more aggressive project restructuring and downsizing when needed.

There has been a narrowing gap in the percentage of projects rated satisfactory by IEG on outcome between LICUS and non-LICUS LICs.

Only one LICUS project approved since the start of the LICUS Initiative had closed and been evaluated by IEG by fiscal 2005. However, some of the projects that had closed during fiscal 2000–05 were active during the period since the beginning of LICUS Initiative, and their supervision may have benefited from the initiative.

IEG outcome ratings for closed projects in LICUS show an improving trend over time. The percentage of closed projects rated satisfactory on outcome in LICUS improved from 55 percent in fiscal 2000–02 to 68 percent (13 percentage points) in fiscal 2003–05. By comparison, the percentage of closed projects rated satisfactory on outcome in non-LICUS LICs improved from 74 percent to 76 percent (two percentage points), respectively, for the two time periods. Year-on-year, the percentage of closed LICUS projects rated satisfactory on outcome by IEG increased from 50 percent in fiscal 2002, prior to the LICUS Initiative, to 58 percent in fiscal 2003, 65 percent in fiscal 2004, and 82 percent in fiscal 2005. The corresponding numbers for projects in non-LICUS LICs ranged from 70 to 79 percent (appendix Q).

IEG ratings for LICUS CASs completed thus far have mostly been unsatisfactory.

While these results apply mainly to projects approved before the

LICUS Initiative, IEG's Bank performance ratings for closed projects in LICUS show an improvement from 65 percent satisfactory in fiscal 2000–02 to 72 percent satisfactory in fiscal 2003–05. The 2003–05 figures for Bank performance in LICUS are more-or-less similar to those for Bank performance in non-LICUS LICs (appendix Q).

IEG's CASCR Review ratings for country strategy outcomes have generally been in the unsatisfactory range, indicating that the objectives of the Bank's assistance programs in LICUS have been consistently underachieved. Of the four available CASCRs reviewed by IEG that covered at least part of the second period since the LICUS Initiative began, three were rated moderately unsatisfactory or unsatisfactory, and one was rated moderately satisfactory (only one of these CASCRs—rated moderately satisfactory—was for a CAS period fully within the initiative's tenure) (appendix R).

This underachievement of objectives was sometimes the product of overambitious Bank objectives (leading to a scaling down of objectives). But it was also partly a result of inadequate Bank effort or inappropriate input, as suggested by the mixed implementation experience documented in this review and in IEG's CASCR Reviews (thus requiring scaling up of effort).

IEG's CASCR Review for one country (of the four countries for which such reviews, covering at least part of the period since the LICUS Initiative began, are available) found that the Bank focused inadequately on project design and implementation issues. For example, the emphasis on the social sectors came at the expense of physical infrastructure, potentially constraining private sector growth; social sector projects did not appropriately reflect the division of responsibility in the country's federal system; and the approach to community development needed to be more cognizant of fiduciary and capacity issues and consistent across interventions. IEG's CASCR Review for another country found that Bank implementation was weak, with inadequate supervision and follow-up in many cases.

No IEG Country Assistance Evaluations have been done thus far for LICUS country programs

Perceptions of the Effectiveness of the LICUS Approach

Figure 2.6: The Majority of Stakeholder Respondents Said the Bank's Overall Program Made a Small Positive Contribution to Development of LICUS

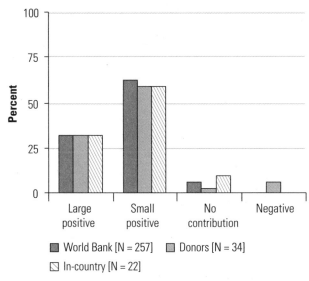

World Bank [N = 257]   Donors [N = 34]
In-country [N = 22]

Source: Appendix Z (Stakeholder Survey results).
Note: N indicates the number of valid responses.

Figure 2.7: The Majority of Stakeholder Respondents Said Development Would Have Been Smaller without Bank Support

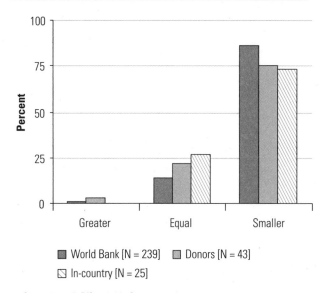

World Bank [N = 239]   Donors [N = 43]
In-country [N = 25]

Source: Appendix Z (Stakeholder Survey results).
Note: N indicates the number of valid responses.

Figure 2.8: The Majority of World Bank Respondents Said the Bank's Contribution to Development Was Greater Than That of Other Donors

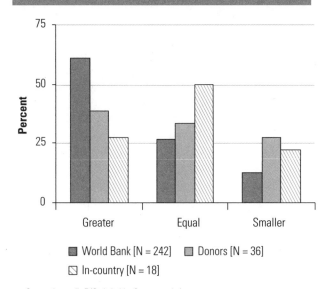

World Bank [N = 242]   Donors [N = 36]
In-country [N = 18]

Source: Appendix Z (Stakeholder Survey results).
Note: N indicates the number of valid responses.

Figure 2.9: The Majority of Stakeholder Respondents Said World Bank Lending and Grant Support to LICUS Has Achieved Its Intended Results to a Moderate or Slight Extent

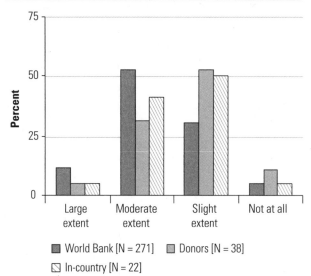

World Bank [N = 271]   Donors [N = 38]
In-country [N = 22]

Source: Appendix Z (Stakeholder Survey results).
Note: N indicates the number of valid responses.

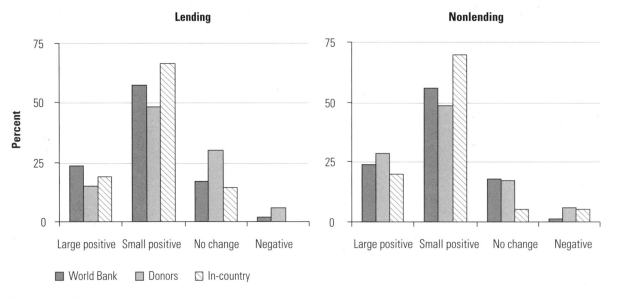

Figure 2.10: Comparing the Pre-LICUS and Post-LICUS Initiative Periods, the Majority of Stakeholder Respondents Said There Is Improvement in the Effectiveness of the Bank's Lending and Nonlending Support

Source: Appendix Z (Stakeholder Survey results).

Note: Number of valid responses ranges from 33 to 35 for other donors and 20 to 21 for in-country stakeholders and is 248 for the Bamk.

covering the period since the LICUS Initiative began (appendix R). The Bank needs to determine what it is likely to be able to achieve in the varying LICUS business model groups, set realistic objectives, and be held accountable for the achievement of those objectives.

IEG ratings for LICUS CASs completed thus far have generally been unsatisfactory.

While not fully attributable to the Bank, there is a deteriorating trend in KKZ's governance indicator for LICUS in the period since the LICUS Initiative began.[27] The deterioration is similar in LICUS and non-LICUS LICs, but for LICUS, the decline is from already low levels (chapter 1, figure 1.7).

Conclusion

The implementation experience across the core country-level LICUS principles has been mixed.

The first part of this chapter and table 2.3 show that the Bank's LICUS Initiative has been more effective with respect to some principles or specific aspects of them (staying engaged, supporting macroeconomic reforms, delivering physical infrastructure through alternative mechanisms, and coordinating with other donors at the international policy level) than others (supporting the transition from immediate post-conflict reconstruction to development, contributing to capacity development and governance, ensuring selectivity and prioritization in reforms, translating political understanding into country strategies, and donor coordination at the country level).

The second part of the chapter provides a patchwork of aggregate data. The Stakeholder Survey indicates a small positive contribution to development of the Bank's overall program in LICUS—a view that refers to Bank support generally, and not to the LICUS approach per se.

Table 2.3: Implementation Experience with the Core Country-Level LICUS Principles

LICUS principle	Implementation experience rating
Stay engaged	**Substantial**
Anchor strategies in stronger sociopolitical analysis	**Medium**
• Political understanding	• Medium-substantial
• Internalizing political understanding in strategy design and implementation	• Medium-low
Promote domestic demand and capacity for positive change	**Low**
Support simple and feasible entry-level reforms	**Medium-low**
• Macroeconomic reforms	• Substantial
• Delivery of physical infrastructure	• Substantial
• Transition from the immediate post-conflict reconstruction phase to the development phase	• Low
• Selectivity and prioritization	• Low
Explore innovative mechanisms for social service delivery.	**Medium**
Donor collaboration	**Medium**
• At international policy level	• Substantial
• At country level	• Medium-low
Measure and monitor results[a]	**Low**

Source: Fieldwork and thematic background analysis undertaken for this review.

a. Not specifically mentioned as a separate core principle by the Bank, but included by IEG because it is pivotal to the Bank's learning-by-doing LICUS agenda.

Chapter 3: Evaluation Highlights

- The Bank continues to rely almost exclusively on the CPIA to identify LICUS, although the CPIA does not sufficiently capture some key aspects of state fragility and conflict.
- The recently introduced LICUS business models are likely to permit a more tailored response to different groups of LICUS.
- But the operational guidance contained in the business models needs to be sharpened and the extent of operational usefulness of the business models tested through implementation.
- The Bank needs to review its aid-allocation criteria in light of its objectives for LICUS and ensure that LICUS are not under- or over-aided.

Operational Utility of the LICUS Identification, Classification, and Aid-Allocation System

T his chapter assesses the operational utility of three aspects of the LICUS approach: identification of LICUS, classification of LICUS into business models, and the aid-allocation system for LICUS. Operational utility is assessed against the objectives of the LICUS Initiative.

LICUS Identification

Distinguishing LICUS from other low-income countries

The Bank's 2002 LICUS Initiative was motivated by general aid effectiveness concerns within the Bank. The 2005 Fragile States Report focused the initiative on state-building and peace-building objectives.

Despite this focus, the criteria used to identify LICUS were not refined to capture these aspects sufficiently. The CPIA, on which the Bank relies almost exclusively to identify LICUS, has its advantages. Most important, because it is based on policy performance (not outcomes), the CPIA has the conceptual advantage of reflecting more recent policy situations, whereas outcomes may be the result of and capture past policy situations. However, there are also several shortcomings:

- First, the CPIA fails to capture sufficiently some key aspects of state fragility, such as accom-

modation of political dissent and of conflict, such as political instability and security or susceptibility to conflict.[1] The Bank has recognized that security-related variables are missing from the CPIA: "The CPIA . . . does not measure the reach of service provision and administrative control across geographical territory and it devotes greater weight to the economic, administrative, and service delivery functions of the state than to institutions dealing with security and rule of law" (World Bank 2005h, p. 7).

- Second, the CPIA gives equal weight to all its constituent elements, although some of them may have much more bearing on state building and peace building than others. It could be argued, for example, that improvements in the efficiency of resource mobilization or in the equity of public resource use should take precedence over some macroeconomic indi-

Despite the increased focus on state building and peace building, the criteria to identify LICUS have not been refined.

cators in the CPIA if state building is a key objective.

- Third, there is up to a 24-month lag between the period being measured by the CPIA rating and the time when the rating actually informs policy decisions. This makes it more difficult to identify—in a timely and effective way—policy improvements or deteriorations in LICUS that can guide resource allocation.
- Fourth, the confidentiality surrounding the CPIA (removed in June 2006), and consequent perceptions of the lack of transparency and objectivity, have not helped the dialogue among donors (who have had to devise proxies such as the CPIA-quintile-based definition of fragile states, since quintiles are publicly available, but not individual scores[2]) or among country clients (many of whom question their CPIA status relative to that of others).

A stronger approach to the identification of LICUS will require an analytical framework that more explicitly focuses on the objectives of the LICUS Initiative. Given the Bank's state-building and peace-building objectives and the shortcomings of the CPIA, the Bank will need to reexamine the appropriateness of the CPIA criterion to identify LICUS, and supplement it as needed.[3]

Donors and researchers have come up with different lists of difficult countries, using different definitions (Foreign Policy 2005; Van de Walle 2005). To the extent that the Bank's current list of LICUS misses some relevant countries, the effectiveness of the Bank's assistance is reduced. At the same time, to the extent that the Bank's current list includes some countries not fully relevant to its objectives, Bank resources that could be used to address those objectives are not.

The criteria used to identify LICUS need to derive from the objectives of the LICUS Initiative.

LICUS Classification

Differentiating within the LICUS group of countries

LICUS are a highly diverse group (see chapter 1), and it is useful for policy purposes to catego-rize them into smaller groupings, as the Bank has recently done using business models. The heterogeneity of LICUS was recognized by the 2002 LICUS Task Force, which identified six categories of LICUS: policy-poor but resource-rich; exceptionally weak government capacity; government/donor lack of consensus; limitations on engagement; countries emerging from conflict; and countries in early stages of a domestically generated reform process. The 2003 *Implementation Overview Report* (World Bank 2003a, pp. 3–4) also differentiated its guidance by type of LICUS—for example, countries in weak transition, countries with no progress or deterioration, post-conflict countries, and more stable and active countries.

This classification evolved into a more systematic, fourfold typology of business models in the 2005 Fragile States Report: deterioration, prolonged political crisis or impasse, post-conflict or political transition, and gradual improvement (appendix D). These business models are based on the extent of consensus between donors and government on development strategy and the pace and direction of change.

The first two types of LICUS (those experiencing deterioration and those facing prolonged political crisis or impasse) represent countries where there is little consensus between donors and government on development strategy. The other two (those that are post-conflict or in political transition and those experiencing gradual improvement) represent countries with such consensus. The pace and direction of change are then used to classify LICUS within each of these two groups for a total of four business models. These business models are likely to permit a more tailored response to different groups of LICUS but have yet to be fully developed.

Currently, for instance, the operational guidance on state capacity and accountability contained in each of the business models is broad and insufficiently customized to the institutional characteristics of countries that fall into various business models. For example, it states: "focus on transparency, dialogue and maintaining institutional capital to facilitate eventual turnaround" (deterioration business model); "focus on institutional analysis, dialogue and counterpart training" (prolonged crisis or impasse business model); "support for a broad state-building agenda, through institution building and, where appropriate, development policy operations with robust oversight mechanisms and sector programs" (post-conflict or political transition business model); and "development policy operations, where appropriate and restricted in scope, supported by sector and capacity-building projects and with strong oversight mechanisms" (gradual improvement business model).

Further refinement of the business models by more explicitly factoring in differences in capacity to perform core state functions (such as resource generation, resource allocation, basic social service and infrastructure provision, and political accommodation of dissent and security) is needed to enable the Bank to better reflect the institutional situations of different groups of LICUS in its response, and thereby to meet its state-building objective better. For example, the Bank's institutional response in political-transition LICUS, where state capacity to perform some or all core functions is lacking, will have to be different from that in political-transition LICUS with capable states.

The experience emerging from the implementation of the Bank's differentiated business models needs to be systematically monitored and will comprise the ultimate test of the operational relevance of the business models. Implementation data should be used to ascertain how much value the business models add over the CAS-driven country-by-country approach.

Aid-Allocation System for LICUS

Twenty-three of the 25 LICUS are IDA-only countries for which IDA financing has historically been allocated based on the Performance-Based Allocation (PBA) system. Implicit in the PBA system is the assumption that aid is more effective in environments with good policies, institutions, and governance, with the CPIA rating used to determine institutional quality across developing countries.[4] The policy

selectivity of the PBA system has increased over the years[5] and fewer IDA funds have been available for countries with weaker policies, institutions, and governance. This has raised the question of whether LICUS are receiving appropriate amounts of IDA funding.

Adjustments to the PBA have resulted in increased IDA financing, including some post-conflict LICUS and LICUS experiencing political transitions (box 3.1). Indeed, during fiscal 2003–05, post-conflict LICUS received a large share of the IDA financing to LICUS, averaging $8.1 per capita annually, compared with $1.5 per capita in non-post-conflict LICUS.

All seven post-conflict LICUS received higher per capita IDA financing, even when compared with the average for non-LICUS LICs (figure 3.1). Yet it remains far from clear whether the current levels of IDA ensure that LICUS are not under- or over-aided.

The aid-allocation issue has once again come to the fore with some research that questions the empirical evidence for the positive link between policies and aid effectiveness[6] (which underlies the PBA), and other research that argues that aid can be effective in promoting sustainable policy turnarounds in failing states by building and strengthening the preconditions for reform or by enhancing the chances that the reform will be sustained once it is set in place (Chauvet and Collier 2004). The latter research finds that potential returns from aid to LICUS can be extraordinarily high, even though the risks of failure are substantial (Chauvet and Collier 2005). For its part, the Bank has yet to address the aid-allocation issue for LICUS in a way that reflects its objectives for these countries and ensures that LICUS are not under- or over-aided.

The business models are likely to permit a more tailored response to different groups of LICUS.

Refining the business models by more explicitly factoring in differences in capacity would help the Bank to better address its state-building objective.

The extent of operational usefulness of the business models needs to be tested through implementation.

Figure 3.1: Highly Variable per Capita IDA and Trust Fund Financing across LICUS during Fiscal 2003–05

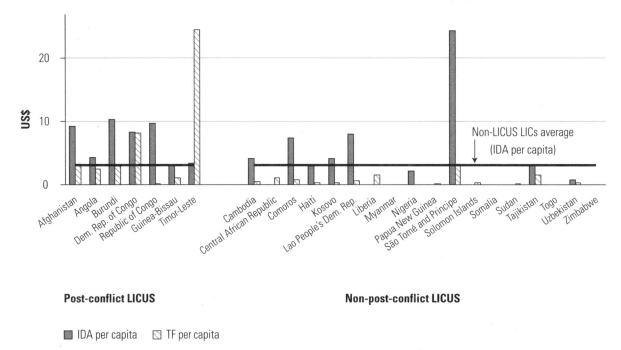

Post-conflict LICUS   Non-post-conflict LICUS

◼ IDA per capita   ◻ TF per capita

Source: Trust Funds and World Bank databases.

Box 3.1: Adjustments to IDA's Performance-Based Allocation System That Affect LICUS

- Agreement under IDA 12 authorizing special pre-arrears clearance allocations to aid-eligible countries coming out of active conflict and in the process of normalizing IDA relations.

- Agreement under IDA 13 to provide exceptional allocations to countries emerging from severe conflict in support of their recovery and in recognition of exceptional need.

- Agreement by the IDA deputies during the IDA 13 Mid-Term Review to stretch out the phasing of the special post-conflict allocations to fit the cycle of absorptive capacity of receiving countries, while maintaining the same total allocation.

- Agreement (since 1985) to provide exceptional access to IDA resources to small island economies, which have per capita incomes above the IDA eligibility cut-off but have no or very limited creditworthiness, which limits or precludes access to IBRD borrowing.

- Agreement under IDA 13 to provide additional allocations to

IDA countries in the aftermath of major natural disasters in cases where the existing allocation would not allow for a sufficient response.

- Agreement under IDA 13 (continued under IDA 14) to have a special provision for regional integration projects. Up to SDR 300 million of such projects yearly are envisioned under IDA 14.

- Agreement during IDA 14 that additional allocations may be provided on a one-time basis to countries in the process of reengaging with IDA after a prolonged period of inactivity on the basis of a strong transition plan with concerted donor support. The exception is to be used only after all other options have been exhausted and is not intended to last for more than two years, with a possible additional year, subject to strong performance.

- Agreement during IDA 14 also included exceptional IDA financing for natural disaster response and regional projects.

Sources: IDA 2002, 2004, 2005.

Early findings from the pilot implementation of the 12 Principles of International Engagement in Fragile States (OECD 2005d) show that there is a group of countries that receives low aid flows in relation to need and governance indicators, compared with other countries with similar governance indicators.[7] Overall, eight countries—Burundi, the Central African Republic, Chad, Guinea-Bissau, Niger, Sierra Leone, Tajikistan, and Togo—show the greatest imbalances and appear to attract relatively little donor attention.

Although trust funds have been an important supplement to IDA financing, these funds, for the most part, were concentrated in a few LICUS that already benefit from post-conflict IDA financing (for example, Afghanistan, the Democratic Republic of Congo) (figure 3.1). During fiscal 2003–05, average annual trust fund financing per capita in post-conflict LICUS was $5.6, compared with $0.2 in non-post-conflict LICUS.

In addition to the introduction of exceptional post-conflict IDA financing, the Bank has made several other adjustments to the PBA system. Some key questions that need to be addressed include the appropriate number and size of adjustments to the PBA; the basis for specific adjustments, including the robustness of the high-risk/high-reward argument; and the countries that should or should not receive exceptional treatment.

Conclusion

The Bank needs to conduct a technical review of the cumulative effect of the various adjustments to the PBA system on financing to LICUS, as well as develop criteria that enable it to determine assistance volumes that reflect its objectives for LICUS and ensure that these countries are not under- or over-aided.[8] While it does not necessarily follow that more should be provided to LICUS, the Bank needs to make a strategic assessment of the appropriate form and level of financial engagement in LICUS.

Earlier discussions have focused only on "more" or "less" aid but have not established "how much more" or "how much less." Whether and to what extent the Bank's aid-allocation criteria should be based on factors other than policy performance—such as levels of other donor assistance, assessment of potential risks and rewards, and regional and global spillovers—needs to be examined, keeping in mind that aid is limited and trade-offs will have to be made. While the aid allocation issue goes beyond the LICUS Initiative, it remains an issue of crucial importance for the achievement of the Bank's objectives in LICUS.

Beyond its own financing, the Bank needs to help address the gap in the international aid architecture in relation to the aggregate allocation for fragile states. Elements of a strategy to address this would include strengthened efforts at coordinated donor planning in which the Bank would have a role (and for which the OECD Watch List on Fragile States may be a starting point) (OECD 2005e).

Trust funds have played an important role in supplementing IDA financing, but have been highly variable across LICUS.

Chapter 4: Evaluation Highlights

- Substantial progress has been made in expanding analytical work and in developing guidance notes on specific topics.
- Progress on human resource reforms remains unsatisfactory, and LICUS do not yet consistently attract staff capable of effectively addressing the difficult LICUS situations.
- Learning by doing requires much more active and ongoing stock taking and knowledge sharing than currently takes place and needs to be a more prominent feature of LICUS work.
- The Bank needs to ensure a receptive institutional environment and management support for staff to feel at ease sharing negative experiences.
- Confidentiality and learning by doing are conflicting objectives.
- There is significant confusion between the roles of the LICUS and Conflict Prevention and Reconstruction Units.

The Bank's Internal Support for LICUS Work

T he 2002 LICUS Task Force Report identified four areas in the Bank's internal support for LICUS work that needed to be addressed to enhance effectiveness in LICUS: analytical work, staffing and incentives, operational policies and procedures, and management attention and operational guidance.

The report emphasized the need for an internal culture shift at the Bank to enable implementation of the LICUS approach (World Bank 2003a, p. 4). The Bank's 2005 Fragile States Report reinforced the need for such a shift, supporting all four change areas identified by the 2002 LICUS Task Force Report. This chapter assesses the Bank's progress in addressing the four areas of change.

Analytical Work

Stated Bank approach
The first area of change advocated in the 2002 LICUS Task Force Report called for increased analytical work and changing the overall balance between knowledge and finance to be more heavily weighted toward the former.

Implementation experience
Implementation progress on support for analytical work has been substantial and was discussed in chapter 2 under "Stay Engaged." The main conclusions are as follows:

- The Bank increased budgets for ESW and technical assistance to LICUS at the aggregate level during fiscal 2003–05 compared with fiscal 2000–02.

> *ESW budgets have increased at the aggregate level.*

- Resources for ESW and technical assistance have not increased in six LICUS.
- While the overall quality of analytical work in LICUS has improved, process aspects still need attention—the preparation of analytical work is insufficiently undertaken in coordination with governments and donors, and this has adversely affected its policy influence.

With respect to the overall balance between knowledge and finance, while this balance still favors finance, even in fiscal 2003–05, the change compared with fiscal 2000–02 is in the right direction for administrative budgets, but only marginally so for lending. This statement is based on definitions of "knowledge" and "finance" presented in the note to table 4.1.

Table 4.1: Overall Balance Between Knowledge and Finance for Administrative Budgets and Lending

	Knowledge (US$ million)			Finance (US$ million)			Knowledge: Finance	
	Fiscal 2000–02	Fiscal 2003–05	Percent change	Fiscal 2000–02	Fiscal 2003–05	Percent change	Fiscal 2000–02	Fiscal 2003–05
Lending	215	·397	84	2,265	3,740	65	0.09	0.11
Trust funds	774	403	−48	384	1,571	309	2.02	0.26
Administrative budget	23	48	109	80	113	41	0.29	0.42
Total	1,012	848	−16	2,729	5,424	99	0.37	0.16

Source: World Bank database.

Note: Lending for "knowledge" comprises lending for IDA, IBRD, and special financing projects that were either freestanding capacity development projects or where capacity development accounted for at least 80 percent of the project cost. Lending for "finance" comprises all other IDA, IBRD, and special financing projects. Trust funds for "knowledge" comprise trust funds for technical assistance, and trust funds for "finance" comprise all other trust funds. Administrative budgets for "knowledge" comprise the administrative budget for ESW and technical assistance, and administrative budgets for "finance" comprise the rest of the administrative budget.

Staffing and Incentives

Stated Bank approach

The 2002 LICUS Task Force Report pointed to the need to ensure high-quality staff in LICUS and noted the importance of providing the right incentives to encourage staff to work on LICUS.

Implementation experience

The forthcoming *Strengthening the Organizational Response to Fragile States* paper currently under way is welcome, even if late. Yet progress on staffing and incentive issues remains unsatisfactory three years into the LICUS Initiative.

Progress on staffing and incentives remains unsatisfactory three years into the LICUS Initiative.

The Bank made initial attempts to address the staffing problem in LICUS through three initiatives:

- The identification of elements of a strategy to address the staffing problem in LICUS (appendix S) with the intention that they would be further addressed in more detail by a human resources working group
- Introduction of an accelerated development program to provide a bridge between young professional and higher-level staff positions with a specific LICUS focus by giving staff direct exposure to LICUS contexts and issues while guaranteeing their re-entry into headquarters at a position consistent with their career trajectory prior to working on LICUS

- The development of field postings in LICUS as more attractive to staff by including a 5 percent premium on top of the existing hardship allowance for working in LICUS, more generous rest and relaxation allowance in some LICUS (such as Afghanistan), and allowing sector specialists based in neighboring countries to visit the LICUS country rather than live in it (as in the case of Tajikistan).

There has been little follow-up to these initial attempts. The proposed human resource working group was not formed until May 2005. While the accelerated development program has found some management support, there are concerns within human resources about the implications of establishing yet another separate program for staff when human resource reforms aim to simplify and streamline.

Furthermore, semistructured interviews found that the majority of staff had not heard of any specific changes in human resource policy with respect to working in LICUS, while several commented that small changes, such as the 5 percent premium or generous rest and relaxation policies, were insufficient to make a difference.

In the Stakeholder Survey, the majority of Bank respondents said that there has been no change when working in LICUS with respect to the following human resource matters—overall career prospects, overall financial compensation, realism in expectations by Bank management about what can be accomplished, level of support from Bank management, and efforts made by the Bank to ensure personal security and safety (figure 4.1).

While staffing numbers and quality are less of an issue in some high-profile post-conflict countries, finding specialist staff to work on other LICUS, especially in field offices, remains a problem. In 2005, about 70 percent of LICUS did not have a professional specialist in the field, compared with about 25 percent for non-LICUS LICs.[1] The Bank's recent move to state building and peace building as central objectives would also suggest the need to ensure adequate staff with public sector management skills and staff who are comfortable seeking and using (if not necessarily producing) political knowledge in decision making.

In the Stakeholder Survey only about half of Bank respondents said that their colleagues working in LICUS are to a large extent competent. While 63 percent of other donor respondents said that Bank staff who work in LICUS are competent to a large extent, only 33 percent of in-country respondents agreed (appendix Z).

Understanding of country circumstances is often best achieved through substantial field presence, though that alone is not enough. Internalizing analysis throughout all involved Bank units, and applying its lessons to all interventions, is equally important.

Staffing numbers and quality are not an issue in high-profile LICUS, but they are in other LICUS.

In Cambodia, for example, the Bank's field presence has significantly improved understanding of the political situation, but discussions with country team members and other stakeholders suggest that this knowledge may still be highly concentrated among a few managers and staff (mostly in the country office and Bangkok hub), with relatively limited dissemination to the broader country team.

The issue appears to have shifted from a partial understanding of the political realities of Cambodia to one of where this knowledge is located within the Bank's country team and how

Field presence alone is insufficient for adequately addressing country circumstances.

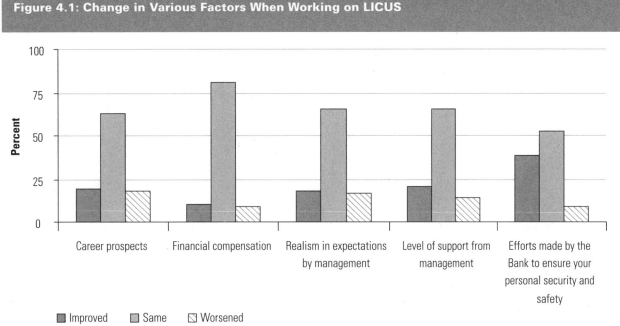

Figure 4.1: Change in Various Factors When Working on LICUS

Legend: ■ Improved ■ Same ▨ Worsened

Source: Appendix Z (Stakeholder Survey results).

Note: Number of valid responses ranges from 213 to 238. The question in the survey did not differentiate between staff who had worked on a LICUS country and those who had worked on a non-LICUS country in their previous assignment.

it is used to guide decision making in strategy and program implementation. The concentration of in-depth country knowledge among a few staff implies that only some Bank activities and interventions benefit. In general, greater knowledge transfer is needed between donor country offices and headquarters-based country and sector staff.

Effective donor coordination depends, in part, on the personalities of field staff.

Effective donor coordination by the Bank requires having the right kind of staff involved in the country. In semistructured interviews, several donors emphasized that coordination is unusually susceptible to the strengths and the foibles of the individuals involved. More appropriate training for staff posted to difficult field assignments and improved incentives within the Bank that encourage staff to collaborate with other donors might ameliorate these idiosyncratic risks.[2]

Staff evaluations focus on the delivery of outputs or products, while change in LICUS is often process oriented and incremental.

Bank staff expressed concern about the performance criteria for staff working on LICUS, and in particular how the Bank is interpreting "success" in these countries. The fact that LICUS are, by definition, often "off-track" or making only modest headway against zero or first-generation reforms leaves staff wondering how best to present their contribution to Bank outputs.

In semistructured interviews, Bank staff noted that change is often highly incremental and process oriented in LICUS. They stated that it is sometimes difficult to ascribe to specific interventions. In contrast, staff evaluations are centered on the delivery of tangible outputs or products.

To ensure the desired staff behavior, the Bank needs to communicate to staff how success will be measured and what constitutes a reasonable level of risk-taking.

Such a strong emphasis on the delivery of outputs, as opposed to the processes necessary to bring about effective delivery in difficult environments, tends to inflate expectations of staff impact. In a LICUS country this is problematic because of the very strong likelihood that programs will not work out as planned. Several staff noted the importance of working on both a non-LICUS and a LICUS country so that they could rely on a stream of outputs delivered in the former to boost their overall performance assessment.

Clarity among Bank staff about how success is measured and interpreted is especially important with respect to the Bank's relatively harder-to-measure state-building and peace-building agendas. To avoid creating unrealistic expectations and discouraging staff from working toward these huge agendas, it will be critical to establish realistic interim benchmarks for state-building and peace-building outcomes for which Bank staff will be accountable. How will the Bank measure success in these areas and for what actions and results will staff be rewarded?

Similarly, staff needs clear signals about how much risk it is reasonable to take in LICUS. Given that these are high-risk countries, will there be fewer penalties for failure? How will success be judged in staff evaluations and career development—how much will the achievement of small, incremental steps be rewarded? The answers to these important issues will influence staff behavior.

Operational Policies and Procedures

Stated Bank approach

The third area of change identified by the 2002 LICUS Task Force Report was for the Bank to clarify further, disseminate, and revise its operational policies and procedures for LICUS work to enable a faster and more effective response in LICUS.

Implementation experience

Progress on adapting relevant Bank operational policies and procedures to the special circumstances of LICUS has been slow and small. No specific operational policies in the Bank govern LICUS work, and existing operational policies do not provide adequate guidance for working in the full range of LICUS environments. The LICUS concept has been superimposed onto the Bank's existing set of Operational Policies and Bank Procedures (OPs/BPs).

Appendix T summarizes the main OPs and BPs identified by the LICUS Unit as particularly relevant for LICUS.

Bank respondents point to a host of difficulties in working with existing OPs/BPs in LICUS. One of the main difficulties with these OPs/BPs is the assumption that there is sufficient capacity in the recipient government/administration to engage in the Bank's investment lending procedures.

For example, although OP/BP 8.50[3] allows staff to speed up the project preparation process in emergency situations, it requires staff to refer back to standard Bank OPs for the remaining phases of the project, including project implementation. The expectation is that a normal way of doing business is possible, largely premised on the idea of a single event or disaster that still leaves government institutions intact.

In many LICUS, and particularly in those emerging from conflict, such an assumption is rarely tenable and can lead to undue delays (box 4.1). The result is that emergency operations designed under OP/BP 8.50 are prepared quickly but can take several months to become effective.

Some recent revisions to OPs are relevant and effective overall, but others have been slow in coming. The Bank has undertaken or is undertaking important revisions to some OPs/BPs, such as OP/BP 6.0[4] and OP/BP 8.50. The Bank has revised OP/BP 6.0 on Bank financing to allow for Bank financing of recurrent costs, local expenditures, and local taxes and duties, providing much-needed flexibility given weak state capacity and the low tax/gross domestic product (GDP) ratio in most LICUS. Bank staff working on Tajikistan noted a major change in flexibility as a result of revisions to OP/BP 6.0. Work continues on revisions to OP/BP 8.50, which have been under way since late 2003.

The proposed revisions to OP 8.50 will ensure that emergency procedures are not applied to the more unstable and unpredictable LICUS environments, where speed may not be appropriate and a more deliberate approach would, in fact, be

more appropriate. Pending finalization, it is not clear if the conceptual problems in applying OP/BP 8.50 to LICUS conditions will be adequately addressed (box 4.2).

Procurement procedures are considered too cumbersome in most LICUS. The Bank's official stance on procurement is that nothing in the policy framework governing procurement prevents the Bank from working effectively in LICUS, as long as the Bank's activities are transparent, legitimate, and accountable. On paper, this would appear to be largely true. There are provisions for projects executed by the Bank and by third parties in the event that recipient execution is not possible. There are provisions for local competitive bidding, national competitive bidding, and single sourcing of goods and services if there is no alternative or if alternatives would be too high risk.

However, staff noted difficulties in finding the right procurement solution in specific LICUS and noted that procurement staff were not

The LICUS concept has been superimposed onto the Bank's existing policies with no specific policy governing LICUS work.

Some recent changes in operational policies have increased flexibility, but other changes have been pending for a long time.

Procurement procedures are seen by Bank staff as too cumbersome in most LICUS.

Box 4.1: OP/BP 8.50: A Major Source of Delays in Liberia

Bank staff on the Liberia country team noted major difficulties in drawing on OP/BP 8.50 to prepare project proposals under the newly created Liberia Trust Fund. The presence of a transitional government in Liberia made it very difficult to engage through a framework largely designed with more capable, IDA-eligible countries in mind.

The result was protracted dealings among different Bank departments, causing serious delays. The high internal transaction costs appeared to contradict the principle of "emergency" and of the need for speed and flexibility in a LICUS context.

Source: Interview with the Bank's Liberia Country Team, 2005.

Box 4.2: Conceptual Problems in Applying OP/BP 8.50 to LICUS Environments

OP 8.50 on emergency recovery assistance, currently also applicable to post-conflict reconstruction, focuses mainly on events of short duration, such as earthquakes, floods, or hurricanes, that do not affect institutions and that require a rapid response to rebuild physical infrastructure. Civil conflicts, in contrast, are of a protracted duration and destroy the social fabric of a country. Their causes typically go back in time and result in situations that require long-term development efforts. Furthermore, unlike natural disasters, civil conflicts require major efforts in dealing with institutional frameworks and macroeconomic conditions.

Source: IEG 1998.

always aware of the flexibility provided for in the current procurement guidelines. Several operational staff noted high levels of risk aversion among procurement staff with respect to LICUS. The perception among staff is that project designs or grant proposals are expected to conform with generic low-income country or IDA standards rather than being adapted to the different risk-reward contexts of LICUS.

Because corruption is a real danger in LICUS, procurement should be closely watched.

Box 4.3 provides examples of procurement problems faced in LICUS. In the Stake-

Box 4.3: Examples of Procurement Problems in LICUS

In Tajikistan, the threshold for international competitive bidding is considered too low, given the weak interest from foreign bidders.

In Liberia, Bank execution for procurement is used widely because of the risk environment, but Bank execution does not allow for certain types of purchases, especially of equipment. Using a third party for execution (such as the UN Office of Project Services) allows the Bank to get around this, but at a cost that, in a budget-constrained program, diverts scarce resources from other uses.

Bank staff note a lack of lesson sharing across countries and regions on procurement issues, resulting in a great deal of "reinventing the wheel," particularly in arrangements with other development partners such as multidonor trust funds.

Source: Bank staff interviews.

holder Survey, more than 60 percent of Bank respondents said that the Bank's procurement procedures are not adapted or are only adapted to a slight extent to the low-capacity or higher-risk environment of LICUS (appendix Z).

Procurement problems have typically led to significant delays in Bank operations in LICUS. In the Central African Republic, it took more than six months to deliver to the government three 4 × 4 vehicles badly needed to cut down on blatant smuggling abuses, while millions of dollars in forgone customs receipts were lost each month. Similarly, in countries where the UN is a major executing agent, staff point to a huge amount of time spent clarifying whose procurement and financial management procedures apply, leading to a loss of crucial time in responding to changing circumstances in the country.

The Bank has begun to discuss the need for staff training on procurement options in LICUS. That would involve both procurement staff and program team members. It would also consider the possibility of carving out a core group of LICUS (those with limited Bank country presence) in which the UN is encouraged to take over procurement altogether on behalf of the Bank.

Discussions on both of these topics are at an early stage, and no timetable has been set. The merits of these arrangements will need to be assessed. The key is to find procurement solutions that do not hamper the Bank's operational work in LICUS, while at the same time ensuring that the Bank's fiduciary standards are not compromised.

Compared with some other portfolios in the Bank, quality-at-entry of safeguard compliance in LICUS projects has been relatively better (88 percent moderately satisfactory or better), though it is still short of the zero tolerance policy.

Safeguard compliance during implementation is much weaker (37 percent moderately satisfactory or better) than compliance at entry and is similar to some other portfolios. Safeguard compliance during implementation warrants attention by the Bank and the borrower and could be challenging, given the weak capacity environment in LICUS (appendix U).

Other Bank operational procedures are also in need of adaptation. In the Stakeholder Survey, half of Bank respondents said that the Bank's project preparation is adapted to the low-capacity or higher-risk environment of LICUS to a large or moderate extent. The other half said that it is only so to a slight degree or to no extent. Bank respondents were also roughly equally divided on the extent to which the Bank's project supervision is adapted to the environment of LICUS. With regard to both the Bank's financial management procedures and the Bank's legal framework, about 60 percent of Bank respondents said they are not at all adapted or only slightly adapted to the LICUS environment (appendix Z).

Management Attention and Operational Guidance

Stated Bank approach

The fourth area of change identified by the 2002 LICUS Task Force Report was the need for a more balanced approach to LICUS country programs, underpinned by enhanced institutional support and management attention. The report also identified the need for further clarifying and disseminating good practices for LICUS.

Implementation experience

Progress on ensuring that LICUS managers have access to the Bank's senior management has been substantial, but this has yet to be translated into adequate management attention that yields clear improvements in human resource policies and incentives to undertake LICUS work. The introduction of quarterly LICUS meetings with Regional vice presidents and country directors, chaired by the managing director, has helped spotlight specific countries and helped staff navigate technical and procedural hurdles when they are brought to light.

Staff also noted greater attention to LICUS issues at the Regional vice presidential level and from OPCS. In Zimbabwe, the country team felt that the LICUS Unit had ensured high-level senior management attention to a difficult situation.

The attention of individual country directors is more limited, especially if they are also covering a larger, more "successful," or higher-profile country. Countries that are LICUS but of low international interest tend to lose out, both to better performers and to front-burner LICUS. In the Stakeholder Survey, about 40 percent of Bank respondents said the Bank's lending and nonlending support to LICUS has only slightly or not at all attracted adequate management attention or involvement (appendix Z).

IEG's fieldwork for this review noted appreciation from field staff for the role played by the LICUS Unit. In particular, they appreciated its advocacy and strategic role. Several Bank staff referred to the importance of the unit in promoting the LICUS agenda with external partners. However, a number of other staff were unclear about what exactly the LICUS Unit did.

The majority of Bank respondents in the Stakeholder Survey said the Bank's LICUS Unit has been effective to a large or moderate extent, with regard to providing access to trust funds as well as substantive support for country strategy development and implementation. However, the majority also said that the Bank's LICUS Unit has been only slightly or not at all effective in providing substantive support for projects, providing substantive support for research or analytical work, unlocking procedural or policy difficulties at headquarters, and facilitating donor collaboration and harmonization (figure 4.2 and appendix Z).[5] Sector staff (that is, sector directors, sector managers, sector economists, and sector specialists) were statistically significantly more likely to report greater effectiveness of the LICUS

> *The key is to find procurement solutions that do not hamper the Bank's operational work in LICUS, while at the same time ensuring that the Bank's fiduciary standards are not compromised.*

> *Country directors are less likely to pay attention to LICUS if they are also covering a larger, more "successful," or higher-profile country.*

> *Operational staff appreciate the role played by the LICUS Unit, but the extent of knowledge about its role varies.*

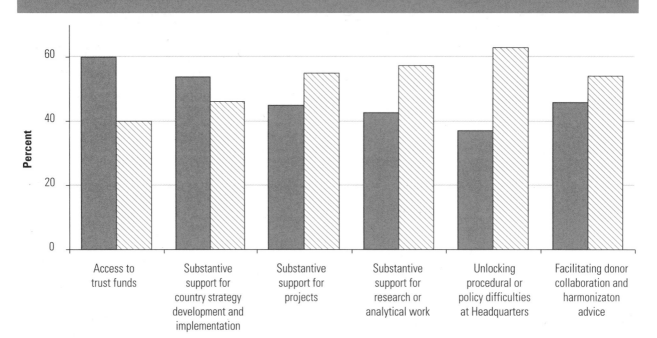

Figure 4.2: Bank Respondents' Views on Effectiveness of LICUS Unit

Legend: ■ To a large or moderate extent   ▨ To a slight extent or not at all

Source: Appendix Z (Stakeholder Survey results).

Note: Number of valid responses ranges from 162 to 169. Seventy-five percent of Bank headquarters staff, staff with less than two years of experience, or staff not working full time on LICUS did not respond to these questions.

Unit for all categories, compared with other staff.

Staff capacity within the LICUS Unit is a potential concern, especially with regard to the provision of substantive support. With a very small staff,[6] the amount of support that the LICUS Unit can provide is inevitably constrained. While the unit's staff work hard to respond and to be consistent across Regions and country teams—and this is appreciated by field-level staff—gaps and inconsistencies arise because of the sheer breadth and complexity of the agenda.

Unit staff themselves note particular difficulties in keeping up with the regular review of country strategies and other operational support to the Regions, fielding staff at short notice to support multi-

Guidance notes have been prepared on specific topics, but the topics are not widely known among staff.

donor processes, and ensuring coherence between external policy debates and ongoing country work.

Guidance notes on specific topics have been prepared for staff working on LICUS, although only recently. Few interviewees mentioned any of these guidance notes directly. Based on country experience, the LICUS Unit has distilled guidance on a number of important issues (appendix V) and has fed it into both operational advice to country teams and broader external policy debates.

However, country-level staff, in semi-structured interviews for this review, said that the lack of country knowledge sometimes constrains technical input from the unit. They also noted that advice from the unit has tended to be in response to specific problems rather than being comprehensive, strategic, and systematic.

In some key areas, the Bank's operational approach is clearly lacking—for example, on state building and peace building. What actions and reforms will effectively contribute to which aspects of state building? As noted in chapter 3, the Bank's record on capacity development has generally been weak. Unless the Bank provides fresh guidance on effective approaches to state building and strengthening accountability in LICUS—where governance and institutional challenges are greatest—the Bank's state-building efforts are likely to meet with little success.

Other areas where the Bank needs to further develop its operational approach include prioritizing and sequencing reforms; at the same time, the Bank should avoid partial solutions. The Bank needs to deliver services quickly without harming long-term government capacity development; address trade-offs between fostering political reconciliation with development of effective and legitimate local institutions and translate political understanding into country strategy; prevent conflict; and address linkages between politics, security, and development. The Bank has recently taken an important initial step with respect to providing staff guidance on the political, security, and development nexus from the Bank's perspective by developing a framework (World Bank 2005e).

The balance of the Bank's recent operational guidance on LICUS is tilted more toward what instruments should be used than on outlining actual operational approaches with respect to what needs to be done differently and how. LICUS country teams would also benefit from more narrative-based guidance, of the kind presented in chapter 2 of this review, and through short, problem-oriented notes rather than more formal guidance notes, which are often too condensed and devoid of sufficient country context.

While the Bank's approach in post-conflict LICUS has been articulated more clearly, a number of shortcomings in the approach need to be addressed. The approach needs to be developed further—for example, to guide the transition and development phases that follow the immediate post-conflict reconstruction phase.

The Bank also still needs to develop a more effective approach for the political crisis or impasse and deteriorating governance business models. In Papua New Guinea, the Bank has stayed engaged, but it is not clear what the engagement is achieving. The Bank's country team expressed concern about where the country is heading and how the Bank can contribute. The implicit objective seems to be simply to "stay engaged" while continuing to think about possible courses of action.

The Bank's operational approach is lacking in some key areas.

Australia too—one of Papua New Guinea's major donors—seems unsure of the best way forward, seemingly reverting back to the previously tried and failed government capacity-development approaches of the 1980s. Lack of donor coordination and widespread confusion concerning the best course of action to promote a sustained and effective development agenda has left the Bank somewhat inactive and ineffective in Papua New Guinea; that has also left it struggling to define a coherent operational approach, given that everything seems by and large to have failed in the past.

The Bank has recognized that, as with other international partners, it is still learning what works in fragile contexts (World Bank 2005e, p. vii). In cases where the Bank is not ready to produce a guidance note, it will be critical to ensure more active and ongoing learning. This underlines the need for the strong monitoring and evaluation of experiences.

The Bank needs to invest more in actively monitoring and evaluating LICUS experiences.

The Bank is not likely to be able to rely on client monitoring and evaluation systems in these countries. It therefore needs to invest adequately in monitoring and evaluating the performance of its LICUS support and to distill emerging experience continually. The implementation narratives presented in chapter 2 of this review illustrate how this may be done.

Sharing experiences of what is working and what is not in different LICUS situations can foster learning. Though the Bank has done some sharing of lessons through its LICUS Learning Group Seminar Series, much more attention is needed to intensify the systematic sharing and dissemination of emerging LICUS experiences—both those of the Bank and those of other donors. Creating a more receptive institutional environment and ensuring management support for sharing negative experiences will be key. So far, the Bank seems willing mainly to share positive examples, as in its recent LICUS reports (World Bank 2005e, 2005h).

Familiarity with the LICUS approach is low among in-country respondents and other donor respondents, but also among Bank respondents working on LICUS. In the Stakeholder Survey almost a quarter of Bank respondents said that they are familiar with the Bank's LICUS approach only to a slight extent or not at all (appendix Z).

Widespread lack of awareness of the Bank's LICUS approach raises questions about the utility of the approach in informing country strategies.

In Lao PDR, the 2005 CAS does not mention the country as a LICUS country, and neither the government nor other donors were aware that the concept existed or that their country was part of this group. Several Bank staff working in Lao PDR were also unaware that the country fell in this category; they were aware that Myanmar did (despite the fact that all these countries come under the same Bank country management unit). The rather widespread lack of awareness of the Bank's LICUS classification and approach inside and outside the Bank does raise questions about the extent of its influence so far.

The confidentiality of the LICUS list and criteria (removed in June 2006 through the Bank's disclosure of the country-level CPIA ratings) has not helped foster active learning and sharing of experiences around the LICUS approach. Some countries (Nigeria, Tajikistan, Zimbabwe) have vehemently opposed their classification into the LICUS category—and insufficient transparency in assigning CPIA ratings has not helped the dialogue.

Confidentiality hinders learning and sharing.

Going forward, openness during country strategy design discussions about which business model(s) pertain to specific LICUS will be critical to ensure constructive debates about effective solutions among donors and country clients, as well as to ensure ongoing refinement of the business models themselves. The resistance of some governments to being classified as LICUS or fragile states, and possible future resistance to being classified into one or more business model(s), underlines the need for more effective communication of the Bank's objectives and approach in this area. Finding more neutral or objective terms to describe both the overall category of LICUS and the different business model groups could also help. But confidentiality can only hinder learning and consensus building.

There is confusion about the role of the LICUS Unit relative to the Conflict Prevention and Reconstruction (CPR) Unit. While Bank staff commented on the high quality of staff in both units, they also expressed significant confusion over their roles. Both units deal with re-engagement issues in post-conflict countries, and both provide technical advice and support to country transition processes. The confusion arises when country teams are looking for specific guidance on procedural and policy matters.

Several staff noted the advantage of going to the LICUS Unit because of its strategic location in OPCS, which can help attract senior management attention more easily. Others who have been working in post-conflict countries for some time noted the technical knowledge of the CPR Unit and its larger staff complement. That knowledge enables the unit to provide more operational support.

Of concern to staff are the practical questions of which unit to turn to for specific types of advice and what kinds of support could be expected from each unit. In semistructured interviews conducted for this review, Bank staff in Afghanistan and Haiti said they were unclear about the relative roles of the LICUS and the CPR Units, and there was a general feeling that there is considerable duplication.

Staff expressed confusion about why the LICUS and CPR Units were undertaking seemingly parallel work on Poverty Reduction Strategy Papers (PRSPs). They were also confused about the distinctions among Post-Conflict Multilateral Needs Assessments, JAMs, and Transitional Results Matrices.

Bank staff also noted that there is confusion among external partners and field-level counterparts over which of the two units to engage. This confusion is aggravated at times by inadequate collaboration and communication between the two units.

In the Stakeholder Survey, about two-thirds of Bank respondents saw some problem with the current organizational arrangement: 37 percent said that there is some duplication between the support of the Bank's LICUS Unit and that of the CPR Unit; 15 percent said that there is a lot of duplication, and 12 percent that there is even a conflict or contradiction (appendix Z). One Bank staff member remarked that the CPR Unit and the LICUS Unit are the "most conflictual units around."

Given that conflict and state fragility influence each other, the Bank needs to consider whether it would be more effective to combine the two units into one. The Bank aims to address the overlap between these units through an ongoing study of the Bank's Regional and sector mappings. Issues to consider in determining the right organizational arrangement are the following:

- Ensuring that there is no duplication or fragmentation of support to country teams and that they have easy access to expert technical advice with no conflicting messages
- Ensuring an efficient use of the Bank's administrative budget and managerial resources
- Determining the need for a continued central strategic role with respect to both the internal and external agenda for LICUS/fragile states and related donor processes
- Assessing the need for continued operational support from central teams.

The 2002 LICUS Task Force Report noted a potentially important role for the World Bank Institute (WBI) because of the importance of knowledge sharing and capacity development for a turnaround in LICUS. The WBI has been important in some LICUS, but not in others. Appendix W provides an overview of WBI activities in LICUS.

The significant duplication and overlap between the CPR and LICUS Units needs to be resolved.

While working on such countries often requires an opportunistic approach and is likely to be better when led by country teams, the limited availability of core WBI resources for the vast majority of LICUS has constrained both the scale and scope of WBI's work. A notable exception is Sudan, where WBI has been a driving force from the very early days of reengagement.

In the Stakeholder Survey, more than two-thirds of Bank respondents said that the technical input from WBI was slightly or not at all sufficient or timely. Sixty percent said it was slightly or not at all of good quality (figure 4.3).

The Development Economics Vice Presidency (DEC) is involved in some highly relevant LICUS research—for example, on political economy, terrorism, drugs, and conflict (appendix X). DEC was one of the leading voices in the early aid effectiveness debates, yet this has not been kept up more recently.

Furthermore, DEC's LICUS work has primarily focused on conflict and has given relatively little attention to other forms of state fragility. The key question of how to break the low-performance trap still needs further examination. In the Stakeholder Survey, more than 70 percent of Bank respondents said that the technical input from DEC was slightly or not at all sufficient or timely, and 54 percent said it was slightly or not at all of good quality (figure 4.4).[7]

Conclusion

There has been substantial progress in increasing analytical work in a number of LICUS and in ensuring that LICUS managers have access to the Bank's senior management. However, progress has been slow and slight in adapting OPs/BPs to the high-risk, low-capacity circumstances of LICUS. It has also been slow in ensuring sufficient management attention, which yields clear improvements in staffing numbers, staffing quality, and incentives.

There is confusion about the role of the LICUS Unit relative to the CPR Unit, with two-thirds of Bank respondents in the Stakeholder Survey noting some problem with the current organizational arrangement. Finally, the Bank has yet to benefit fully from the contributions DEC and WBI could potentially make to LICUS work.

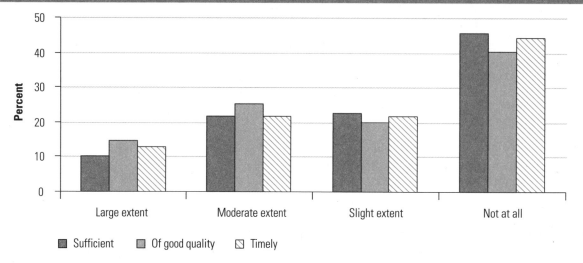

Figure 4.3: World Bank Institute's Technical Input

Source: Appendix Z (Stakeholder Survey results).

Note: Number of valid responses ranges from 158 to 169.

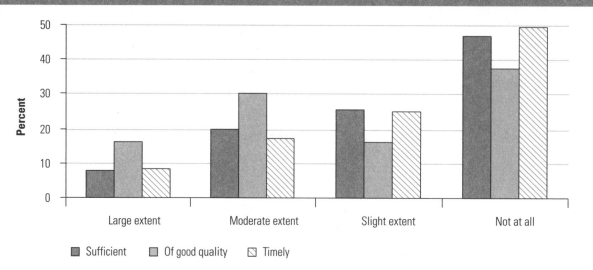

Figure 4.4: Development Economics Vice Presidency's Technical Input

Source: Appendix Z (Stakeholder Survey results).

Note: Number of valid responses ranges from 123 to 132.

Conclusions, Lessons, and Recommendations

This chapter summarizes the conclusions of this review, distills lessons of experience relevant both for the Bank and other donors, and then presents the recommendations.

Conclusions

Early successes

There have been several notable early successes with regard to the LICUS principles. The Bank's operational readiness to support LICUS has improved since the LICUS Initiative began and the Bank has engaged with a number of these countries from the early days of peace or political transition. The Bank has also contributed to macroeconomic stability and to the delivery of significant amounts of physical infrastructure, especially in post-conflict LICUS.

Substantial progress has been made in donor coordination at the international policy level, exemplified by the recent agreement to the 12 OECD-DAC principles of international engagement by a wide spectrum of donors, including the Bank. The Bank has often played a leading role as co-chair of international donor events and coauthor of jointly undertaken policy papers. The Bank's recently introduced business models, which differentiate between different types of LICUS, are likely to permit a more tailored response to these countries.

The Bank's internal support for LICUS work has also progressed in several areas, notably the following: (i) expanding analytical work by de-linking administrative budgets for ESW and technical assistance from lending volumes; (ii) using ISNs, which allow for the design of strategies that cover a shorter period to accommodate the volatile LICUS conditions; (iii) developing guidance notes on specific topics; (iv) providing access to LICUS managers to the Bank's senior management; and (v) introducing the LICUS Trust Fund to finance countries in non-accrual (for which the Bank previously lacked an instrument). Results from the Stakeholder Survey indicate a small positive contribution to development of the Bank's overall program in LICUS—a view that refers to Bank support generally, and not to the LICUS approach per se.

Challenges

The Bank's initial engagement with a number of LICUS has not been adequately followed up by a focused and well-sequenced reform agenda. Furthermore, the Bank has not yet sufficiently internalized political understanding in strategy design and implementation. The Bank also needs to strengthen the quality of its country-level coordination with other donors, especially with respect to implementation follow-through.

In addition, the Bank has made one of its traditional areas of weakness (capacity development and governance) a central part of its focus by adopting the more complex state-building objective. This new emphasis requires that the Bank identify more effectively its comparative advantage; improve performance, including through the development of innovative approaches; and identify partners that can complement its work to ensure the achievement of intended outcomes. Finally, the choice of the term "state-building" may itself be inappropriate, given its political and ideological connotations.

The Bank needs to develop its operational approaches in LICUS, especially for the deterioration and prolonged crisis or impasse business models. Further refinement of the business models by more explicitly factoring in differences in the capacity to perform core state functions (for example, resource generation, resource allocation, basic social service and infrastructure provision, and political accommodation of dissent and security) is also needed. That will enable the Bank to achieve a better fit between its operational approaches and the varying institutional environments of different LICUS.

The Bank's work on post-conflict countries predates the LICUS approach, and the corresponding business model for post-conflict LICUS is articulated more clearly than the other business models. However, it has shortcomings and needs to be further developed to guide the transition and development phases that follow the immediate post-conflict reconstruction phase.

Furthermore, while the Bank has given more attention to conflict prevention, there is limited knowledge about the effectiveness of those efforts. The Bank's role and comparative advantage in this area have yet to be clearly established, especially as conflict prevention requires the Bank to give greater attention to the *root causes* of conflict.

The policy selectivity of the PBA system has increased over the years, and fewer IDA funds have been available for countries with weaker policies, institutions, and governance. This has raised the question of whether LICUS are receiving appropriate amounts of IDA funding. Adjustments to the PBA have resulted in increased IDA financing, including to some post-conflict LICUS and LICUS experiencing political transitions. Yet it remains far from clear whether the current levels of IDA ensure that LICUS are not under- or over-aided.

The aid-allocation issue has once again come to the fore with some research questioning the empirical evidence for the positive link between policies and aid effectiveness (which underlies the PBA). Other research argues that aid can be effective in promoting failing states' sustainable policy turnarounds by building and strengthening the preconditions for reform or by enhancing the chances that the reform will be sustained once it is set in place. The latter research finds that potential returns from aid to LICUS can be extraordinarily high, even though the risks of failure are substantial. For its part, the Bank has yet to address the aid-allocation issue for LICUS in a way that reflects its objectives for these countries and ensures that LICUS are not under- or over-aided.

The Bank's internal support for LICUS work has progressed little on critical human resource reforms relating to staffing numbers, staffing quality, and incentives to undertake LICUS work. In IEG's Stakeholder Survey, the majority of Bank respondents said that there has been no change when working in LICUS with respect to the following human resource matters: overall career prospects, overall financial compensation, realism in expectations by Bank management about what can be accomplished, level of support from Bank management, and efforts made by the Bank to ensure personal security and safety.

The Bank, as other donors, is still learning what approaches work in LICUS contexts. Therefore, closely monitoring experiences in LICUS to draw lessons is critical, and learning and sharing needs to become a more prominent feature of LICUS work. Although the Bank has developed guidance notes that distill lessons of experience in specific areas (such as development policy loans), there is need for much more active and ongoing stock-taking and sharing of experiences among those working on LICUS.

The implementation narratives presented in chapter 2 of this review illustrate the kind of stock-taking that could prove useful for LICUS. A new series of informal field-oriented discussion notes that strive for timely lesson learning would also be useful. To achieve an open exchange of negative experiences, a more receptive institutional environment that ensures management support for the sharing of negative experiences will be key. So far, the Bank seems much more willing to share positive examples, as in its recent LICUS reports (World Bank 2005e, 2005h). The LICUS Unit's learning-by-doing objective would be much better served by giving adequate attention to both positive and negative experiences.

There is significant duplication of and confusion over the roles and responsibilities of the LICUS Unit and the CPR Unit, which need to be resolved. Of concern to staff were the practical questions of which unit to turn to for specific types of advice and what kinds of support to expect from each unit. In IEG's Stakeholder Survey, about two-thirds of Bank respondents saw some problem with the current organizational arrangement: 37 percent said that there is some duplication between the support of the Bank's LICUS Unit and that of the CPR Unit; 15 percent said that there is a lot of duplication, and 12 percent that there is even a conflict or contradiction.

Lessons of Experience for the Bank and Other Donors

Several lessons emerge from this review's assessment of the Bank's experience in implementing the core principles of the LICUS approach. Many of the issues covered under these lessons were noted as areas in need of improvement in the 2002 LICUS Task Force Report, such as the need to anchor strategies in stronger sociopolitical analysis or support highly focused reform agendas. They were also emphasized in the Bank's 2005 LICUS reports. The lessons derive from the Bank's own implementation experience but may also be useful in guiding other donor assistance in LICUS.

LICUS engagement

Staying engaged is only a means to an end and needs to be quickly followed by a clear and relevant reform agenda in LICUS. In the absence of a clear and relevant reform agenda, early successes of engagement may be short lived and contribute little to the achievement of country strategy objectives. The examples of the Central African Republic and Haiti show that various obstacles may make the follow-up to a successful initial LICUS engagement difficult.

For example, as political successes were insufficiently backed up on the economic side in the Central African Republic, the government is now faced with a potentially disastrous budget crisis. In Haiti, the donor community seems to have given inadequate attention to ensuring a minimum level of security. In both cases, good initial results of the LICUS Initiative are now at risk of being diminished.

In certain instances, strategic disengagement—with the exception of in-house analytical work—may be needed, at least for periods of time, especially when involvement with the Bank is seen as inappropriately giving legitimacy to the LICUS government or when such involvement dampens internal pressure for reform, and thus potentially hinders the emergence of conditions needed to bring about serious and sustainable political reform.

In the deterioration and prolonged crisis or impasse business models, where there is often little consensus between donors and government on development strategy, engagement needs to include policy dialogue aimed at creating an opening for reform, while simultaneously working on a reform agenda should a window of opportunity appear.

In the post-conflict or political transition and gradual improvement business models, engagement will need to have more technical content and a stronger focus on implementing the reform agenda, given the existence of greater reform consensus between donors and government. The Bank's guidance for prolonged conflict or political impasse countries states, "Relatively noncontroversial development issues may provide an entry point for constructive dialogue between the parties to a conflict." For deteriorating governance countries, the Bank's guidance states that the Bank should provide "input on specific economic issues which are important for mediation efforts and may serve as a way to restart dialogue" (World Bank 2005e).

Country ownership and absorptive capacity constraints apply as much to knowledge products as to financial products. The involvement of country counterparts in the Bank's analytical work remains limited to administrative aspects, with much less country-client participation in selecting topics and undertaking analysis. This thereby reduces national buy-in. Yet the involvement of country counterparts is key to ensuring client ownership and improving impact of analytical work.

In Tajikistan, the lack of government involvement in the selection and preparation of the Bank's analytical work limited the government's interest in the results, which subsequently hindered effective implementation. In Angola, senior government officials saw some Bank-led analytical work (for instance, the recent Country Economic Memorandum) as an imposition of Bank views on internal affairs, leading to limited ownership and capacity development. Without country ownership, the chance of analytical work influencing government policy is small.

LICUS governments' absorptive capacity constraints in using analytical work may also limit possible knowledge transfer. The Angolan government, for instance, endorsed the Bank's ISN but expressed concern regarding the amount of foreseen analytical and advisory activities. This has raised doubt about whether the government would fully use analytical products. The absorptive capacity of the government is severely limited, and analytical and advisory activities undertaken mostly by the Bank risk straining relations with the government, regardless of their technical quality.

In Cambodia, plans for analytical and advisory services in the 2005 CAS—totaling 30 tasks to be completed over fiscal 2005–07—appear overly ambitious, considering the country's limited institutional capacity.

Political understanding and its use in country strategy

Commissioning and consuming—not necessarily producing—good political analysis is critical for LICUS donors. The objective of a country team should be to commission or consume (not necessarily produce) analysis that is directly relevant to and usable in the development of a strategy. In LICUS situations, especially in environments where speed is of the essence, donors need to ensure that existing political analysis is mined before commissioning a new analysis.

For example, in Lao PDR, the Bank effectively tapped existing political analysis and invited a political scientist who had published extensively on the country to make a presentation to the country team on politics and reform in the country. This allowed for the preparation of an independent summary of relevant political analysis (tailored to the needs of the donor community in general and the Bank in particular) and its dissemination to a relevant group of Bank staff and other donors. It avoided the higher costs of preparing a "Bank" analysis, as well as potential tension with the government because it allowed the Bank to avoid getting bogged down in some of the sensitivities surrounding the analysis. For the Bank, the acquisition of existing knowledge as well as its dissemination proved more important and effective in Lao PDR than knowledge creation.

The main focus of donor efforts needs to be on helping staff internalize political analysis in strategy design and implementation. Though the Bank has conducted or had access to good political analysis in some LICUS, it has inadequately reflected such analysis in its strategy. For example, the interim strategy in Papua New Guinea contains a good discussion of the political system and recognizes problems such as clan loyalties, political patronage, corruption, and lack of capacity. Yet the strategy treats these problems as technical in nature and does not adequately use them to underpin the overall approach.

Specific types of political analysis that can help strategy design are as follows:

- Political risk analysis, which can help make the decision whether the Bank should engage in a certain country and, if so, how to engage
- Structural analysis, which can help identify major characteristics of the political situation that will affect the Bank's work, no matter what specific strategy is chosen
- Analysis of day-to-day politics, which can help assess the distribution of power among different political forces in the capital and in the Regions, or even localities—which needs to go beyond the political gossip about who is up and who is down in the capital
- Analysis of the history of reform in the country as well as neighboring countries, which can help avoid past reform failures, such as failed privatization attempts that may have created a strong backlash in the past.

Focused reform agenda

In complex LICUS environments, where virtually every sector requires reform, appropriate sequencing of reforms and sufficient time to implement them are crucial for achieving results without overwhelming limited LICUS capacity. Donors must strive for collective donor selectivity, yet this is far from being achieved, as the examples of Afghanistan's donor-endorsed reform agenda and Haiti's ICF (presented below) indicate. However, even if collective donor selectivity is not immediately achieved, the Bank itself needs to ensure focus and selectivity in its own assistance program, based on its core competences. Such Bank selectivity has been increasing in recent years but remains a challenge, as the example of São Tomé and Principe suggests.

In Afghanistan, the reforms covered by donors are wide ranging, show lack of sufficient priority, and have led to 120 pieces of pending legislation. These reforms, dealing with virtually every economic and social aspect of the country, need to be carefully prioritized and sequenced. Donors have yet to do this.

In Haiti, the ICF was meant to guide international assistance and cooperation through September 2006 and covers practically all basic state functions, ranging from security, to national dialogue, to economic governance, to

economic recovery, to basic services. Individually, all these areas seem important, but together they add up to a formidable agenda.

With respect to the Bank's own assistance program, São Tomé and Principe is an example where the Bank was far too ambitious in relation to the resources allocated to the country, with the result that many of the CAS objectives were not achieved or were only partially achieved.

Beyond selectivity in CASs, it is critical to ensure that actual reform agendas in the field are focused and well prioritized. The lack of selectivity and prioritization in the reform agendas raises questions of effectiveness, especially given the limited capacity in LICUS. While it is difficult to be selective in a country where many things need fixing urgently, the appropriate sequencing of reforms is key to ensuring that limited LICUS capacity is not overtaxed and that partial solutions are avoided.

Well-sequenced reforms spanning a sufficient number of years, along with donor commitment to see them through, will be essential. In Timor-Leste, donors may have pulled out too quickly, without sufficiently dealing with the country's pressing capacity needs. In Haiti, development assistance has fluctuated greatly, with the country having gone through several feast-or-famine cycles in its relations with the donor community. This could have been avoided if various donors had better timed and sequenced their aid.

Capacity development in post-conflict LICUS

Capacity development and governance programs need to start early, even in post-conflict LICUS. Immediately following the cessation of conflict, the international donor community tends to focus its assistance on physical reconstruction. Because capacity to use aid effectively in post-conflict LICUS is low and governance is often poor, the focus from the beginning also needs to be on the development of capacity and improvement of governance, not merely on reconstruction of physical infrastructure. This may require the creation or strengthening of public institutions, civil service reform, and use of local expertise. If foreign experts are brought in to provide technical assistance, this must not compromise the long-term development of local capacity.

Donor coordination

Donor coordination cannot succeed without a common vision and purpose among donors—when donor objectives cannot be fully harmonized, it is important that they at least be complementary. The Bank's approach has not fully recognized the differing motivations of donors for engaging with LICUS. Although the broad concept of fragility is widely understood and accepted, the countries identified by donors as fragile vary. Motivations for supporting fragile states range from security, to aid effectiveness, to equitable development, to poverty reduction, to state building, to conflict prevention.

In both Afghanistan and Tajikistan, IEG's fieldwork found that major donors did not subscribe to a single clear objective. Without a common overall objective, policy coherence is unlikely.

The Bank's donor coordination efforts and modalities are insufficiently informed by the objectives of the different players in a country. That said, donor coordination is a form of collective action, requiring that other donors similarly improve their outreach to the Bank and subordinate bilateral agendas to agreed multilateral objectives.

Coordination needs to begin within each donor agency. Coordination is not only important among multilateral and bilateral donor agencies, but it is also a vital issue within each donor agency. Projects in different sectors of the same country often work in parallel and fail to tap synergies, as was the case, for example, with the Bank's Community Empowerment and Agricultural projects in Timor-Leste.

A side effect of the Bank's decentralization to country offices has been the concentration of country knowledge among local staff and its inadequate dissemination across the country team, especially to those based in Washington. Addressing the problems of coordination across the various departments of donor agencies (such as among Bank departments dealing with public sector management, conflict prevention and reconstruction, LICUS, capacity development, and research departments) is particularly important in LICUS, where problems are complex and widespread and often require multisectoral solutions.

Results measurement and monitoring

Monitoring and evaluation are at least as important in LICUS as they are in any other country. Monitoring and evaluation are crucial in LICUS for several reasons. First, the Bank, like other donors, is still learning what approaches work in LICUS contexts. Therefore, closely monitoring experiences to draw lessons is critical, and learning and sharing needs to become a more prominent feature of LICUS work.

Second, given that progress is often slow in these countries, it is important to reassess continually whether the program is on course to achieve the desired outcomes. Third, a constantly changing and volatile LICUS environment, where progress is often nonlinear, means that program adaptation is essential—closely tracking performance will help determine when and what kind of adaptation is necessary. Effective learning by doing to improve the Bank's future effectiveness in LICUS can only happen with strong monitoring and evaluation.

The Bank has stated that state building and peace building should be the goals by which to measure the LICUS Initiative's success. However, it has yet to identify performance indicators by which this can be done, or yardsticks against which performance may be measured. Where change is often more process oriented—especially in the deterioration and prolonged crisis or impasse business models—outputs and outcomes that may be expected in the other business models may not be appropriate yardsticks of success. Objectives should be appropriate to particular LICUS contexts, which would in turn determine yardsticks and ensure that the bar of success is set at an appropriate height.

Improving internal organizational support for LICUS work

Field presence alone is insufficient for effective country strategy implementation. It needs to be complemented by adequate communication between field and headquarters donor agency staff, as well as an adequate number of field staff with the appropriate authority and skills. Understanding of country circumstances is often best achieved through substantial field presence, though that alone is not enough. Internalizing analysis of the country conditions throughout all involved donor agency departments, and applying its lessons to all interventions, is equally important.

In Cambodia, for example, the Bank's field presence has significantly improved understanding of the political situation. Discussions with country team members and other stakeholders, however, suggest that this knowledge may still be highly concentrated among a few managers and staff (mostly in the country office and Bangkok hub), with relatively limited dissemination to the broader country team.

The issue appears to have shifted from a partial understanding of the political realities of Cambodia to one of where this knowledge is located within the Bank's country team and how it is used to guide decision making in strategy and program implementation. The concentration of in-depth country knowledge among a few staff implies that only some Bank activities and interventions benefit. In general, greater knowledge transfer is needed between donor country offices and their headquarters-based country and sector staff.

Despite the cost, field offices need to be adequately staffed if they are to engage effectively with clients. In Angola, the initially small group of field staff faced a multiplicity of tasks, from strategic dialogue with government and donors to logistics such as moving the office to new premises. The situation was made more difficult by the lack of operational-level staff in the field office who could, in consultation with ministry staff, prepare the ground before high-level meetings between the ministers and the Bank. Moving issues to the top too quickly—

because of the lack of lower levels—led to unnecessary tensions. Donor decisions regarding the number of staff in each LICUS should reflect the extent and nature of intended engagement, considering respective donor's objectives in those countries.

Apart from the absolute numbers, field office staff also need to have sufficient authority to ensure that not every decision has to be approved by headquarters. Effective field presence requires having the right kind of staff involved in the country.

In semistructured interviews, several donors emphasized that coordination is unusually susceptible to the strengths and the foibles of the individuals involved. More appropriate training for staff posted to difficult field assignments and improved incentives within the Bank that encourage staff to collaborate with other donors might ameliorate these idiosyncratic risks.

In the deterioration business model, where there might be a breakdown of dialogue with the government, donor agency staff will need strong diplomatic and persuasion skills to ensure that the door remains open for a dialogue with the government, while simultaneously mobilizing nongovernmental groups, including civil society.

In the prolonged crisis or impasse business model, where problems are chronic or there is political stalemate, the necessary staff skills will include immense patience as well as creativity, with constant innovation relating to ways of breaking the persisting logjam. In the post-conflict or political transition business model, the necessary staff skills will include specific technical knowledge of how to develop sound economic systems, institutions, and key infrastructure.

Staff should also possess the ability to act quickly and decisively in these environments, before the optimism following peace dissipates. Staff needs to help guard against these countries' falling back into conflict. As these situations often attract massive international aid, donor staff needs strong coordination and sequencing skills to organize both the development partners and their activities.

In the gradual improvement business model, the primary skill needed is the ability to provide customized technical assistance and work hand in hand with a client that is already reforming.

Sharing experiences—both positive and negative—is essential for learning, but doing so effectively requires a receptive institutional environment and management support. Sharing experiences of what is working and what is not in different LICUS situations can foster learning. Learning is especially important in LICUS work, because the donor community is continuing to grapple with the question of how best to assist these challenging countries. While the Bank has shared some lessons through its LICUS Learning Group Seminar Series, much more attention is needed to intensify the systematic stock-taking and dissemination of emerging LICUS experiences—those of both the Bank and other donors, and both positive and negative.

Creating a more receptive institutional environment and ensuring management support for the sharing of negative experiences will be key. So far, the Bank seems mainly willing to share positive examples.

Effective communication is essential to ensure country acceptance of donor approaches for LICUS and to temper unrealistic country expectations about what can be achieved, especially immediately after the cessation of conflict. Better communication of donors' objectives and approaches for LICUS will be needed to ensure country buy-in and to prevent disillusionment among stakeholders about what can be achieved in a specific period of time.

In the Bank's deterioration and prolonged crisis or impasse business models, where the economic and social situation is for the most part worsening or stagnant, the communication strategy would need to disseminate actively the benefits of reform both to the government and to civil society.

In the Bank's post-conflict or political transition business model, to prevent disillusionment from unrealistic expectations, the communication strategy should target the entire population and be explicit about what donors will do, when, and how, and what results should be expected. The communication strategy in the gradual improvement business model will need to be more informational, presenting relevant cross-country and cross-sectoral experiences.

Immediately following the cessation of conflict, international donors, including the Bank, have often committed large amounts of aid coupled with overly ambitious agendas. This has frequently created high expectations among the population and led to subsequent disillusionment when expectations have remained unfulfilled and day-to-day living has seen few tangible improvements. Avoiding overambitious agendas and providing better communication to lower expectations to realistic levels are critical; the Bank needs to invest in this effort.

Better operational guidance is needed for tailoring donor approaches to the special conditions of LICUS. The LICUS Initiative has raised awareness of the need to act differently in LICUS, but the Bank and other donors have yet to identify precisely *how* to do this. The extent to which donor approaches to LICUS need to, and can, efficiently address the causes—not just symptoms—of countries becoming or remaining characterized as LICUS also need greater attention. Solutions that view causes as givens may miss all-important contextual factors. Donor operational guidance must ensure that areas outside the comparative advantage of particular donors be left to others, while their own work both adequately factors in the work done by others and complements it.

The Bank's deterioration and prolonged crisis or impasse business models, and the transition and development phases that follow the immediate reconstruction phase in the post-conflict or political transition business model, pose some of the biggest challenges for the donor community. These are areas in which there has been relatively little innovative thinking.

Issues for which operational guidance is particularly needed include ways to prioritize and sequence reforms, while avoiding partial solutions; ways to deliver services quickly, without harming long-term government capacity development; ways to foster political reconciliation, while also contributing to effective and legitimate governance; ways to internalize political understanding within country strategy design and implementation; and ways to address linkages between politics, security, and development effectively.

The balance of the Bank's recent guidance on LICUS is tilted more toward what instruments should be used than on an outline of actual operational approaches for what needs to be done differently, and how. LICUS country teams would also benefit from more narrative-based guidance, of the kind presented in chapter 2 of this review, and through short, problem-oriented notes rather than only more formal guidance notes, which are often too condensed and devoid of sufficient country context.

Recommendations

- *Clarify the scope and content of the Bank's state-building agenda, and strengthen the design and delivery of capacity development and governance support in LICUS.*

    Given its weak record on capacity development and governance, as well as its focus on the more ambitious and complex state-building objective in LICUS, the Bank needs to clarify its areas of comparative advantage in relation to other donors. The Bank needs to adopt innovative approaches that ensure better capacity and governance outcomes. Innovative approaches need to be developed for achieving a better fit between the Bank's interventions and the capacity of LICUS to perform core state functions; ensuring implementation of focused and well-sequenced interventions in LICUS environments, where virtually every aspect of capacity and governance may need significant improvement; and effectively monitoring capacity and governance outcomes.

- *Develop aid-allocation criteria for LICUS that ensure that these countries are not under- or over-aided.*

    The Bank needs to conduct a technical review of the cumulative effect of the various adjustments to the performance-based allocation system on aid volumes to LICUS. Aid-allocation criteria that reflect the Bank's objectives in LICUS and ensure that these countries are not under- or over-aided need to be developed. Whether and to what extent the criteria should be based on factors other than policy performance (such as levels of other donor assistance, assessment of potential risks and rewards, and regional and global spillovers) needs to be examined, keeping in mind that aid is limited and trade-offs will have to be made.

- *Strengthen internal Bank support for LICUS work over the next three years.*

    Two aspects of internal Bank support need attention. First, staffing numbers, skills, and incentives for working on LICUS need to be prioritized. Ensuring adequate incentives to attract qualified staff—both at headquarters and in field offices—will require giving clear signals of what is deemed to be success in LICUS, what outcomes staff will be held accountable for, how much risk it is reasonable to take, how failure will be judged, and how overall performance evaluation ratings and staff career development will take these into account.

    As in Olympic diving, where the scoring system factors in both the technical perfection and the difficulty of the dive, staff performance in LICUS should be similarly judged by assigning due weight to the extent of challenges presented by varying LICUS environments. Signaling the importance of LICUS work throughout the management hierarchy will also be required.

    Apart from incentives, the Bank needs to ensure that staff working on LICUS have relevant skills, are capable of seeking and using political knowledge, and are willing and able to work in interdisciplinary teams. Current plans to address these issues in the forthcoming *Strengthening the Organizational Response to Fragile States* paper are welcome, even if late.

    More systematic thinking is needed on staffing decisions for LICUS within the context of the Bank's overall staffing, recognizing that assigning more and better-qualified staff to work on LICUS would likely mean trade-offs for other Bank country teams. Trade-offs to benefit LICUS may or may not be justified, depending on the Bank's objectives for LICUS, as well as other Bank clients' need for assistance.

Second, the organizational structure for LICUS and conflict work needs to be streamlined. The Bank needs to ensure an efficient organizational arrangement that removes duplication and fragmentation of support between the LICUS and CPR Units.

- **Reassess the value added by the LICUS approach after three years.**

  The value of the LICUS category and approach, including the operational usefulness of the business models, needs to be independently evaluated after three years, when sufficient experience on the outcomes of the approach will be available. At that time, it should be possible to address the more fundamental question of whether and to what extent Bank assistance can effectively support sustainable state building. Continued Bank support for the LICUS category and approach should be based on the findings of that reassessment.

APPENDIXES

APPENDIX A: DEFINITIONS AND DATA SOURCES

Term	Definition and data sources
AAA	Analytical and advisory activities (AAA) is an umbrella term for several product lines. Examples of AAA include economic and sector work, technical assistance, donor and aid coordination, research services, the *World Development Report*, and impact evaluation. *Source:* http://intranet.worldbank.org/WBSITE/INTRANET/UNITS/INTOPCS/INTDELIV ERYMGMT/ 0,,contentMDK:20267395-menuPK:764245~pagePK:64137152~piPK:64136883~the SitePK:388672,00.html#1
Administrative budget	Administrative budget refers to the allocations made to each vice presidential unit and then to country units based on country benchmarks for resource allocation, seen as a function of the supervision needs, lending requirements, and AAA requirements. Lending requirements were dropped from the formula in fiscal 2004 (thus disconnecting the administrative budget from lending). The elements of AAA requirements in the setting of country benchmarks are related to population size, poverty, and countries that are relatively new members of the Bank. *Source:* http://intranet.worldbank.org/WBSITE/INTRANET/UNITS/INTRMAy0,,content MDK:20336533-menuPK:422043~pagePK:64088751~piPK:64087868~theSitePK:330235- ROLE:(ALS),00.html
Analytical work	Analytical work is synonymous with AAA. See AAA above.
Africa Catalytic Growth Fund	The Africa Catalytic Growth Fund (ACGF) was launched in March 2006 to provide rapid, targeted support to countries with credible programs to accelerate growth, poverty reduction, and attainment of the Millennium Development Goals (MDGs). The group of countries that ACGF aims to serve is almost entirely separate from the group served by the LICUS Trust Fund grants. In some cases, the "transforming countries" could be countries where the LICUS Trust Fund has already prepared the groundwork, but that are now ready to graduate, shifting from post-conflict or LICUS status to a more substantial scale of funding based on clearer evidence of government reforms. *Source:* ACGF Board Report-Africa Catalytic Growth Fund http://siteresources.world bank.org/INTAFRCATGROFUND/Resources/board_report.pdf
Conflict-affected countries	Conflict-affected countries are countries that have recently experienced, are experiencing, or are widely regarded as at risk of experiencing violent conflict. These countries are identified by the Regional vice presidencies. The conflict-affected LICUS are: Afghanistan, Angola, Burundi, Cambodia, Central African Republic, Comoros, Democratic Republic of Congo, Republic of Congo, Guinea-Bissau, Haiti, Kosovo, Liberia, Myanmar, Nigeria, Solomon Islands, Somalia, Sudan, Tajikistan, and Timor-Leste. *Source:* World Bank data.

Term	Definition and data sources
CPIA	The Country Policy and Institutional Assessment (CPIA) assesses the quality of a country's present policy and institutional framework, particularly how conducive that framework is to fostering poverty reduction, sustainable growth, and the effective use of development assistance. The CPIA consists (as of 2004) of a set of 16 criteria representing the policy and institutional dimensions of an effective poverty reduction and growth strategy, which are divided into four clusters: economic management, structural policies, policies for social inclusion/equity, and public sector management and institutions. For each criterion, countries are rated on a scale of 1 (low) to 6 (high). A rating of 1 corresponds to very weak performance, and a 6 rating to very strong performance. Intermediate scores of 1.5, 2.5, 3.5, 4.5, and 5.5 may also be given. *Source:* OPCS, "Country Policy and Institutional Assessments: 2004 Assessment Questionnaire."
ESW	Economic and sector work (ESW) supports World Bank country operations by adapting research to specific projects or circumstances. *Source:* http://intranet.worldbank.org/WBSITE/INTRANET/UNITS/INTOPCS/INTDELIV ERYMGMT/0,,contentMDK:20267395-menuPK:764245-pagePK:64137152-piPK:64136883-the SitePK:388672,00.html#1
HDI	The Human Development Index (HDI) is a composite index that measures average achievement in three basic dimensions of human development—a long and healthy life (measured by life expectancy at birth), knowledge (measured by adult literacy rate and gross enrollment ratio), and a decent standard of living (measured by GDP per capita). *Source:* http://hdr.undp.org/reports/global/2005/pdf/HDR05_HDI.pdf
HIPC	The Heavily Indebted Poor Countries (HIPC) Initiative was launched in 1996 and modified in 1999 to create a framework for all creditors, including multilateral creditors, to provide debt relief to the world's poorest and most heavily indebted countries, and thereby reduce the constraint on economic growth and poverty reduction imposed by the debt build-up in these countries. The HIPC decision point is the date at which a heavily indebted poor country with a record of good performance under adjustment programs supported by the International Monetary Fund (IMF) and the World Bank commits to undertake additional reforms and to develop and implement a poverty reduction strategy. The HIPC completion point is the date at which the country successfully completes the key structural reforms agreed at the decision point, including the development and implementation of its poverty reduction strategy. The country then receives the bulk of debt relief under the HIPC Initiative without any further policy conditions. The HIPC Initiative currently identifies 40 countries, including 12 LICUS, as potentially eligible to receive debt relief. The 12 LICUS are: Burundi, Central African Republic, Comoros, Democratic Republic of Congo, Republic of Congo, Guinea-Bissau, Haiti, Liberia, São Tomé and Principe, Somalia, Sudan, and Togo. None of the 12 LICUS is at HIPC completion point. *Sources:* http.7/intranet.worldbank.oig/WBSITE/INTRANET/UNITS/INTPREMNET/INTDEBT DEPT/0,,content; World Bank and IMF 2006a.

Term	Definition and data sources
IDA PC	IDA Post-Conflict Exceptional Financing (IDAPC) is based on Post-Conflict Progress Indicators (PCPIs).
ISN	Interim Strategy Note (ISN) is the umbrella term for Transitional Support Strategies (TSSs) and Country Re-engagement Notes (CRNs). When country circumstances are not conducive to a normal Country Assistance Strategy (CAS) approach, the Bank may prepare an ISN. An ISN may also be used for countries affected by or emerging from conflict or in countries in which the Bank has not recently been engaged. The ISN may be put in place for a period of up to 24 months and may be renewed for additional periods with the endorsement of the executive directors. An ISN normally includes a discussion of the country context, including the legal context, the history of the Bank's involvement in the country, and the roles of regional and international partners. It establishes immediate priority assistance objectives along with a proposed program of assistance to meet these objectives. An ISN also includes an assessment of risks, strategies for entry and exit, and contingency responses to a reversal of progress, especially renewed conflict. Finally, it describes benchmarks and performance monitoring indicators for assessing progress, and a schedule for periodic consultations with the Board. The term "Watching Brief "refers to a phase in World Bank engagement in conflict-affected countries. A country is determined to be in the Watching Brief phase when conflict is ongoing and prevents the Bank from continued assistance or other business. The Watching Brief was introduced in 1996 as a way of maintaining constructive engagement with countries where the Bank might otherwise have been absent.
KKZ	Kaufmann, Kraay, Mastruzzi (KKZ) indicators reflect the statistical compilation of responses on the quality of governance given by a large number of enterprise, citizen, and expert survey respondents in industrial and developing countries, as reported by a number of survey institutes, think tanks, nongovernmental organizations, and international organizations (drawn from 37 separate data sources constructed by 31 different organizations, including the CPIA). The KKZ scale ranges from −2.5 to +2.5. *Source:* http://www.worldbank.org/wbi/governance/data.html
Lending	Lending refers to commitments for projects financed by (i) IDA (credits, exceptional IDA post-conflict grants, guarantees, and other grants); (ii) IBRD; or (iii) Special Financing. Other grants under IDA include: debt vulnerability, poorest countries, natural disasters, and HIV/AIDS.
LIC	Sixty-two countries were classified as low-income countries (LICs) by the 2005 *World Development Indicators*. The list includes the 25 LICUS, 35 non-LICUS LICs, and Chad and Sierra Leone. *Source:* World Bank 2005j.

Term	Definition and data sources
LICUS	The Bank classifies a country as LICUS if it is a low-income country (falling within the threshold of IDA eligibility) scoring = 3.0 on both the overall and governance CPIA averages, plus low-income countries without CPIA data (including Afghanistan, Liberia, Myanmar, Somalia, Timor-Leste, and the territory of Kosovo). The fiscal 2005 LICUS list of countries (created using the fiscal 2004 Gross National Income [GNI] threshold of $865 or less per capita and 2003 CPIA ratings) includes 25 countries: Afghanistan, Angola, Burundi, Cambodia, Central African Republic, Comoros, Democratic Republic of Congo, Republic of Congo, Guinea-Bissau, Haiti, Kosovo, Lao People's Democratic Republic, Liberia, Myanmar, Nigeria, Papua New Guinea, São Tomé and Principe, Solomon Islands, Somalia, Sudan, Tajikistan, Timor-Leste, Togo, Uzbekistan, and Zimbabwe. *Source:* LICUS Unit, World Bank.
LICUS Trust Fund	The Bank created the LICUS Trust Fund on January 15, 2004. The fund targets the most marginalized LICUS in non-accrual that cannot use IDA funds for basic reforms or capacity building. Under exceptional circumstances, it also permits a Bank contribution to an agreed multidonor strategy in an active IDA LICUS, where existing IDA funds are inappropriate for this purpose and executive directors have endorsed such a cofinancing program in the country strategy document. LICUS classified as post-conflict by the Resource Mobilization Department (FRM) and that are eligible for IDA post-conflict financing are not eligible for support under the trust fund. Activities eligible for financing under the LICUS Trust Fund include capacity building to support governance reform and strengthening social service delivery, including the fight against HIV/AIDS. To date, beneficiaries of the LICUS Trust Fund have been Central African Republic, Comoros, Haiti, Liberia, Somalia, Sudan, Togo, and Zimbabwe. A total of $23.8 million has been committed through 37 LICUS Trust Funds in 8 non-accrual LICUS since the establishment of the trust fund. *Source:* http://imagebank.worldbank.org/servlet/WDSContentServer/IW3P/IB/2004/10/07/ 000090341_ 20041007095849/Rendered/PDF/275350GLB0rev.pdf
Non-accrual status	Loans to, or guaranteed by, a sovereign are placed in non-accrual status when the oldest payment arrears are six months overdue—that is, when the second consecutive payment is missed on the loans with the oldest arrears. In order to be eligible for new loans, the sovereign concerned must clear all payment arrears in full. Once all arrears are cleared, all loans to, or guaranteed by, the sovereign are generally restored to accrual status. *Source:* http://intranet.worldbank.org/WBSITE/INTRANET/UNITS/SRM/0,,contentMDK: 20669963-menuPK:1748372-pagePK:67677-piPK:64094917~theSitePK:134920,00.html
Non-LICUS LICs	Non-LICUS LICs are low-income countries, excluding those that were classified as "core" or "severe" LICUS in fiscal 2003–05. This excludes from LICs the 25 LICUS (mentioned above), Chad, and Sierra Leone. Chad and Sierra Leone were excluded because they were not classified as LICUS in fiscal 2005, although Chad was classified as LICUS in fiscal 2003 and Sierra Leone was classified as LICUS in fiscal 2003 and 2004. The non-LICUS LICs thus include: Bangladesh, Benin, Bhutan, Burkina Faso, Cameroon, Côte d'Ivoire, Eritrea, Ethiopia, The Gambia, Ghana, Guinea, India, Kenya, Democratic People's Republic of Korea, Kyrgyz Republic, Lesotho, Madagascar, Malawi, Mali, Mauritania, Moldova, Mongolia, Mozambique, Nepal, Nicaragua, Niger, Pakistan, Rwanda, Senegal, Tanzania, Uganda, Vietnam, Republic of Yemen, and Zambia. *Sources:* World Bank 2005j and LICUS Unit, World Bank.

Term	Definition and data sources
ODA	Official development assistance (ODA) comprises grants or loans to developing countries and territories on the OECD Development Assistance Committee list of aid recipients that are undertaken by the official sector with promotion of economic development and welfare as the main objective and at concessional financial terms (if a loan, having a grant element of at least 25 percent). Technical cooperation is included. Grants, loans, and credits for military purposes are excluded. Also excluded is aid to more advanced developing and transition countries, as determined by DAC. *Source:* http://sima.worldbank.org/gmis/mdg/UNDG%20documeiTLfinal.pdf
Post-conflict countries	Post-conflict countries are a subset of conflict-affected countries. They are identified based on Post-Conflict Progress Indicators (PCPI) for purposes of determining exceptional IDA grants. Eligible countries receive up to 4 years of full post-conflict allocations. In years 5, 6, and 7, allocations are reduced by 25 percent, 50 percent, and 75 percent, respectively, of the excess above the CPIA norm. By year 8, they return to CPIA-based allocations. The LICUS that became eligible for these exceptional loans are: Guinea-Bissau (fiscal 2001), Democratic Republic of Congo (fiscal 2002), Republic of Congo (fiscal 2002), Afghanistan (fiscal 2003), Angola (fiscal 2003), Burundi (fiscal 2003), and Timor-Leste (fiscal 2003). *Source:* LICUS Unit, OPCS, Financial Resource Mobilization (FRM), World Bank.
PCF	The Post-Conflict Fund (PCF) was established in 1997 and became a trust fund in 1999, eligible to receive contributions from donors. The PCF supports research, planning, piloting, and analysis of ground-breaking activities through funding to governments and partner organizations in the forefront of this work, including nongovernmental organizations, United Nations agencies, transitional authorities, governmental institutions, and civil society groups. The main focus has widened from that of mainly rebuilding infrastructure to promoting economic recovery, creating effective and accountable institutions, assisting vulnerable groups, working to improve health and education services, supporting community-driven reconstruction processes, and demobilizing and returning ex-combatants and displaced people to their communities. As of July 2005, PCF beneficiaries were Afghanistan, Burundi, Cambodia, Comoros, Democratic Republic of Congo, Republic of Congo, Haiti, Kosovo, Nigeria, Somalia, Sudan, Tajikistan, and Timor-Leste. *Source:* http:/Aveb.worldbank.orgMBSITBEXTERNAL/TOPICS/EXTSOCIALDEVELOPMENT/EXTCPR/0,,menuPK:407746-pagePK:1'49018-piPK:149093-theSitePK:407740,00.html; http://siteresources.worldbank.org/INTCPR/21'4578-1115615449417/20698452PCFAnnualReport05.pdf
PCPI	The Post-Conflict Performance Indicators (PCPI) ratings framework is designed to measure change in countries that are eligible for exceptional post-conflict allocations from IDA. The scale of the PCPI is 1–6 (low to high). A rating of 1 is equal to a situation of ongoing or re-ignited conflict, and therefore no positive change; a rating of 6 indicates very strong performance, which roughly equals a rating of 4 on the CPIA scale, and would be very unusual for any country under the PCPI framework. *Source:* http://siteresources.worldbank.org/INTCPRi1090479-1115613025365/20482305/Post-Conflict+Performance+Indicators,+2004-05.pdf

Term	Definition and data sources
Special Financing	Country-specific trust funds.
TA	Technical assistance (TA) supports external clients to implement reforms or strengthen institutions. For example, a Bank ESW report may recommend that a government establish a unified body to regulate the power and water sectors, while a follow-on Bank technical assistance activity assists the government in developing a draft act for the establishment of such a multisectoral regulator. *Source:* http://intranet.worldbank.org/WBSITE/INTRANET/UNITS/INTOPCS/INTDELIV ERYMGMT/ 0,,contentMDK:20267395~menuPK:764245~pagePK:64137152~piPK:64136883~the SitePK:388672,00.html#1
TRM	The Transitional Results Matrix (TRM), also referred to as a Transitional Calendar or Results-Focused Transitional Framework (RFTF), is a planning, coordination, and management tool developed by the UNDG and the World Bank that national stakeholders and donors can use to prioritize actions necessary to achieve a successful transition in fragile states. The TRM helps launch a poverty-reduction strategy (PRS) approach in these environments, either as an early framework to lay the groundwork for a PRS or, later, as a way to operationalize a PRS in low-capacity countries. TRMs are organized by clusters and sectors that are key to the recovery process and include the following: (i) strategic objective or goal, (ii) baseline (or current situation), (iii) time intervals for actions and priority outputs, (iv) targets and monitoring indicators, and (iv) agencies/units responsible for implementation of each action. *Source:* World Bank and UNDP 2005.
Trust funds	Financial and administrative arrangements between the World Bank and external donors under which donors entrust funds to the Bank to finance specific development-related activities. Formal legal agreements with donors designate the Bank as trustee and define the terms and conditions for use of the funds. Donors include many Bank member countries, the private sector, foundations, and nongovernmental organizations, including the World Bank Group. The top 10 trust fund programs in LICUS are HIPC, Afghanistan Reconstruction Trust Fund (ARTF), Single-Purpose Trust Funds (SPTF), Trust Fund for East Timor–Bank Executed (ETBK), Japan Social Development Fund (JSDF), Trust Fund for East Timor–ADB Executed (ET-ADB), Global Environment Facility–IBRD as Implementing Agency (GEFIA), Debt Service Trust Fund (DS), LICUS, and Institutional Development Fund (IDF). *Source:* http://intranet.worldbank.oip/WBSITE/INTRANET/UNITS/INTCFP/0,,contentlVIDK: 20153435-menuPK:323877~pagePK:64060698~piPK:64060705~theSitePK:299971,00.html

APPENDIX B: LICUS, FISCAL 2003–06

Country	Conflict status	Fiscal 2003	Fiscal 2004	Fiscal 2005	Fiscal 2006	Core/ severe LICUS in all 4 years
		C = Core; S = Severe; M = Marginal				Y = Yes
Africa						
Angola	Post-conflict and conflict-affected	C	S	S	C	Y
Burundi	Post-conflict and conflict-affected	C	C	C	C	Y
Cameroon	Non-conflict-affected	M	M	—	—	—
Central African Republic[a]	Conflict-affected	M	S	S	S	—
Chad	Non-conflict-affected	C	M	M	M	—
Comoros	Conflict-affected	M	C	C	S	—
Congo, Democratic Republic of	Post-conflict and conflict-affected	C	C	C	C	Y
Congo, Republic of	Post-conflict and conflict-affected	M	C	C	C	—
Côte d'Ivoire[a]	Conflict-affected	—	—	M	C	—
Equatorial Guinea	Non-conflict-affected	—	S	—	—	—
Eritrea	Conflict-affected	—	—	M	C	—
Gambia, The	Non-conflict-affected	—	M	M	M	—
Guinea	Non-conflict-affected	—	M	M	C	—
Guinea-Bissau	Post-conflict and conflict-affected	C	S	C	C	Y
Liberia[a]	Conflict-affected	C	S	S	S	Y
Niger	Non-conflict-affected	—	M	M	—	—
Nigeria	Conflict-affected	M	C	C	C	—
São Tomé and Principe	Non-conflict-affected	—	C	C	M	—
Sierra-Leone	Conflict-affected	C	C	M	M	—
Somalia[a]	Conflict-affected	C	S	S	S	Y
Sudan[a]	Conflict-affected	C	S	S	C	Y
Togo[a]	Non-conflict-affected	M	S	C	C	—
Zimbabwe[a]	Non-conflict-affected	C	S	S	S	Y
East Asia and Pacific						
Cambodia	Conflict-affected	M	M	C	C	—
Lao People's Democratic Republic	Non-conflict-affected	C	C	C	C	Y
Papua New Guinea	Non-conflict-affected	M	C	C	M	—
Solomon Islands	Conflict-affected	—	S	S	C	—
Timor-Leste	Post-conflict and conflict-affected	—	C	C	C	—
Tonga	Non-conflict-affected	—	—	—	M	—
Vanuatu	Non-conflict-affected	—	—	—	C	—

(Continues on the following page.)

Country	Conflict status	Fiscal 2003	Fiscal 2004	Fiscal 2005	Fiscal 2006	Core/ severe LICUS in all 4 years Y = Yes
		C = Core; S = Severe; M = Marginal				
Europe and Central Asia						
Kosovo	Conflict-affected	—	C	C	C	—
Kyrgyz Republic	Non-conflict-affected	M	—	—	—	—
Tajikistan	Conflict-affected	C	C	C	M	—
Uzbekistan	Non-conflict-affected	C	S	C	M	—
Latin America and the Caribbean						
Haiti	Conflict-affected	C	S	S	C	Y
Middle East and North Africa						
Djibouti	Non-conflict-affected	C	—	—	M	—
West Bank and Gaza	Conflict-affected	—	—	—	C	—
Yemen	Non-conflict-affected	M	—	—	—	—
South Asia						
Afghanistan	Post-conflict and conflict-affected	C	S	S	S	Y
Myanmar[a]	Conflict-affected	C	S	S	S	Y
Total (core and severe only)[b]		17	26	25	26	12

Sources: For LICUS list of countries—OPCS, World Bank. For list of countries in non-accrual—World Bank 2005g.

Note: S indicates LICUS classified as "severe" (an overall and governance CPIA of 2.5 or less); C indicates LICUS classified as "core" (an overall and governance CPIA of 2.6–3.0); and M indicates LICUS classified as "marginal" (an overall and governance CPIA of 3.2). The criteria for identifying LICUS have undergone modification over time.

a. Countries in non-accrual.

b. Marginal LICUS score on the edge of what is considered LICUS and are identified by the Bank only for monitoring purposes (hence, the total includes only "core" and "severe" LICUS, not "marginal" LICUS).

APPENDIX C: PROGRESS ON MILLENNIUM DEVELOPMENT GOALS

Most LICUS are unlikely to achieve the Millennium Development Goal (MDG) targets by 2015. Six LICUS—Burundi, the Democratic Republic of Congo, Liberia, Nigeria, Papua New Guinea, and Sudan—are unlikely to meet four or more of the six (for which the data is available) MDG targets. Another seven LICUS—the Republic of Congo, Haiti, Myanmar, Tajikistan, Togo, Uzbekistan, and Zimbabwe—are unlikely to meet three of the six targets. Countries that are doing relatively better are Angola, Cambodia, and Lao People's Democratic Republic. These countries will be able to achieve three of the six MDG targets if they continue to progress according to the past trend. While this analysis is simplistic, it does shed light on the challenge the World Bank and other donors face in helping the LICUS to achieve the MDGs.

Goal	Target	Indicator	Likely	Possible	Improving, but unlikely	Unlikely
Goal 1: Eradicate extreme poverty and hunger	Reduce by half the proportion of people who suffer from hunger	Population below minimum level of dietary energy consumption (%)	Angola, Cambodia, Central African Republic, Republic of Congo, Haiti, Lao People's Democratic Republic	Myanmar	Comoros, Solomon Islands,[a] Zimbabwe, LIC	Burundi, Democratic Republic of Congo, Liberia, Nigeria, Sudan, Tajikistan, Togo, Uzbekistan
Goal 2: Achieve universal primary education	Ensure that all boys and girls complete a full course of primary schooling	Primary completion rate, total (% of relevant age group)	Cambodia, Lao People's Democratic Republic, Liberia,[b] São Tomé and Principe, Solomon Islands, Tajikistan, Togo	Comoros, Uzbekistan[c]	Republic of Congo, Myanmar, Papua New Guinea, Sudan, Nigeria,[b] LIC	Burundi, Democratic Republic of Congo, Guinea-Bissau, Zimbabwe
Goal 3: Promote gender equality and empower women	Eliminate gender disparity in primary and secondary education, preferably by 2005, and at all levels by 2015	Ratio of girls to boys in primary and secondary education (%)	Angola, Myanmar, Sudan, Uzbekistan, LIC	Cambodia, Comoros, Lao People's Democratic Republic, Papua New Guinea, Togo, Zimbabwe[c]	Nigeria	Burundi, Republic of Congo, Liberia, Tajikistan

(Continues on the following page.)

Goal	Target	Indicator	Likely	Possible	Improving, but unlikely	Unlikely
Goal 4: Reduce child mortality	Reduce by two-thirds the mortality rate among children under five	Under-5 mortality rate (per 1,000)	Lao People's Democratic Republic	Comoros, Solomon Islands	Guinea-Bissau, Haiti, Myanmar, Nigeria, Papua New Guinea, Sudan, Tajikistan, Timor-Leste, Togo, Uzbekistan, LIC	Angola, Burundi, Cambodia, Central African Republic, Democratic Republic of Congo, Republic of Congo, Liberia, São Tomé and Principe, Somalia, Zimbabwe
Goal 5: Improve maternal health	Reduce by three-quarters the maternal mortality rate	Maternal mortality ratio				
Goal 6: Combat HIV/AIDS, malaria, and other diseases	Halt and begin to reverse the spread of HIV/AIDS	Prevalence of HIV, total (percent of population aged 15–49)	Burundi, Cambodia, Republic of Congo, Nigeria, Zimbabwe, Togo	Lao People's Democratic Republic,[d] Democratic Republic of Congo,[d] Central African Republic,[d] Uzbekistan,[d] LIC [d]		Angola, Haiti, Liberia, Sudan, Myanmar, Papua New Guinea
Goal 7: Ensure environmental sustainability	Reduce by half the proportion of people without sustainable access to safe drinking water	Access to an improved water source (percent of population)	Angola, Burundi, Central African Republic, Comoros, Myanmar, Zimbabwe, LIC	Nigeria	Democratic Republic of Congo, Haiti, Liberia, Sudan	Papua New Guinea, Togo, Uzbekistan

Source: World Bank 2005j.

Note: LIC refers to low-income countries with a Gross National Income (GNI) per capita of $825 or less in 2004.

(i) The calculations are based on past trends between two points, the earliest taken from the period 1990–94 and the other from 1997 to 2003. Then it was determined how long it would take a country to achieve the MDG based on the growth rate between the two points (in a few cases extrapolations are based on data from 2000 and 2003, for example, Haiti Target 1). Countries that would achieve the MDG based on the past trend on or before 2015 were considered "likely"; countries that were close to the target by 2015, or close to the target in 2003, regardless of past trends, were considered "possible"; countries that are moving in the right direction, but are unlikely to achieve the target by 2015, were considered "improving, but unlikely"; and countries that have made no progress or are moving in the reverse direction were considered "unlikely."

(ii) No data available on Afghanistan and Kosovo; LICs include all countries with a Gross National Income (GNI) per capita of $825 or less in 2004.

a. Because data were lacking on the indicator, an alternative indicator—prevalence of underweight in children (under five years of age) was used.

b. Because data were lacking on the indicator, an alternative indicator—net primary enrollment ratio (% of relevant age group)—was used.

c. "Possible" if declining trend controlled.

d. Stagnant growth rates for prevalence of HIV, total (% of population aged 15–49).

Deterioration

- Interim Strategy Note, focusing on stemming decline in governance and social services, and contributing in economic and development areas to multidonor conflict-prevention efforts. Limited new financing; focus on portfolio restructuring.
- Increased use of CDD, private sector, NGO, and ring-fenced mechanisms (including service delivery and local economic development in areas of insecurity).
- State capacity and accountability: focus on transparency, dialogue, and maintaining institutional capital to facilitate eventual turnaround.
- Contribute to community-level conflict prevention and to multidonor efforts for peace-building or governance reform at a national level.

Post-Conflict or Political Transition

- Interim Strategy Note, focusing on rebuilding state capacity and accountability and delivering rapid, visible development results in support of peace building.
- Exceptional IDA allocation.
- Joint needs assessment/recovery planning that links political, security, economic, and social recovery.
- State capacity and accountability: support for a broad state-building agenda through institution building and, where appropriate, development policy operations with robust oversight mechanisms and sector programs (including transitional projects that work through CDD or NGO mechanisms). Leadership and civil society support.

- Public administration, service delivery, and economic development to address areas with crime, insecurity, or conflict.

Prolonged Crisis or Impasse

- Interim strategy note, focusing on maintaining operational readiness for reengagement and providing economic inputs to early peace or reconciliation dialogue.
- Small grant-based finance, aiming at local economic development and protection of human capital, generally through nongovernmental recipients (including service delivery and local economic development in areas of insecurity).
- Capacity and accountability: focus on institutional analysis, dialogue, and counterpart training.
- Use of socioeconomic issues for restoration of dialogue/identification of entry points for change.

Gradual Improvement

- Country Assistance Strategy, focusing on building state capacity and accountability, achieving selective development results, and boosting support for reform currents, supported by moderate IDA allocation.
- Activities to boost domestic reform currents, including leadership support, communications initiatives, training, and capacity building.
- State capacity and accountability: development policy operations (where appropriate and restricted in volume), supported by sector and capacity-building projects and with strong oversight mechanisms. Asymmetric reforms.
- Public administration, service delivery, and economic development to address areas with crime, insecurity, or conflict.

Source: World Bank 2005e.

APPENDIX E: SUMMARY OF OECD-DAC PRINCIPLES FOR INTERNATIONAL ENGAGEMENT IN FRAGILE STATES

- ***Take context as the starting point.*** Conduct political analysis above and beyond quantitative indicators of governance, institutional strength, or conflict.
- ***Move from reaction to prevention.*** Share and respond to risk analysis, address the root causes of state fragility, and strengthen the capacity of regional organizations.
- ***Focus on state building as the long-term vision.*** Strengthen the capacity of state structures to perform core functions. Help ensure the legitimacy and accountability of those structures and their ability to provide an enabling environment for strong economic performance.
- ***Align with local priorities.*** Acknowledge and accept priorities where governments demonstrate the political will to foster their countries' development; where donor and government consensus is lacking, seek wider consultations and partial or shadow alignment.
- ***Recognize the political-security-development nexus.*** Support national reformers in developing unified planning frameworks for political, security, humanitarian, economic, and development activities at the country level.
- ***Promote coherence between donor agencies.*** Involve those responsible for security, political, and economic affairs as well as those responsible for development aid and humanitarian assistance.
- ***Agree on practical coordination mechanisms between international actors.*** Include upstream analysis, joint assessments, shared strategies, coordination of political engagement, joint offices, multidonor trust funds, and common reporting frameworks.
- ***Do no harm.*** Avoid activities that undermine national institution building, such as bypassing budget processes or setting high salaries for local staff.
- ***Mix and sequence instruments.*** Use both state recurrent financing and nongovernmental delivery to fit different contexts.
- ***Act fast . . .*** and with flexibility at short notice when opportunities occur . . .
- ***. . . but stay engaged long enough to give success a chance.*** Capacity development in core institutions will take at least 10 years.
- ***Avoid pockets of exclusion.*** Address "aid orphans" and coordinate with donors to prevent excessive aid volatility.

Sources: OECD 2005c, http://www.oecd.org/dataoecd/59/55/34700989.pdf.

APPENDIX F: FOUR BANK THEMES BASED ON THE OECD-DAC PRINCIPLES

- **Building state capacity and accountability.** A long-term focus on state capacity and accountability is critical if these countries are ever to find a durable exit from crisis.
- **Peace, security, and development linkages.** Political, security, and development linkages are particularly important in fragile states.
- **Donor coordination for results.** Particularly close partnerships between international actors are needed, because low counterpart capacity and difficult political environments mean that fragmented international dialogue or donor programs are unlikely to deliver results.
- **Institutional flexibility and responsiveness.** Donor organizational responses must be calibrated to the specific needs of the countries, acting faster and more flexibly, staying engaged for the long term, and coordinating to address problems of aid orphans and donor-driven aid volatility.

Source: World Bank 2005e.

APPENDIX G: FISCAL 2003–05 COUNTRY STRATEGY DOCUMENTS FOR FISCAL 2005 LICUS

Fiscal year	Date	Country	Strategy document
2003	Jul-02	Kosovo	Transitional Support Strategy
	Feb-03	Afghanistan	Transitional Support Strategy
	Feb-03	Tajikistan	Country Assistance Strategy
	Mar-03	Angola	Transitional Support Strategy
	Apr-03	Somalia	Country Reengagement Note
	Jun-03	Sudan	Country Reengagement Note
	Jan-03	Haiti	Country Reengagement Note
2004	Aug-03	Republic of Congo	Transitional Support Strategy
	Jan-04	Democratic Republic of Congo	Transitional Support Strategy
	Mar-04	Liberia	Country Reengagement Note
	Apr-04	Kosovo	Transitional Support Strategy
2005	Jul-04	Central African Republic	Country Reengagement Note
	Nov-04	Togo	Country Reengagement Note
	Dec-04	Haiti	Transitional Support Strategy
	Jan-05	Angola	Interim Strategy Note
	Mar-05	Lao People's Democratic Republic	Country Assistance Strategy
	Mar-05	Papua New Guinea	Strategy Note
	Mar-05	Zimbabwe	Interim Strategy Note
	Apr-05	Burundi	Transitional Support Strategy
	Apr-05	Cambodia	Country Assistance Strategy
	May-05	São Tomé and Principe	Country Assistance Strategy
	May-05	Solomon Islands (Pacific Islands)	Country engagement
	Jun-05	Nigeria	Country Assistance Strategy
	Jun-05	Timor-Leste	Country Assistance Strategy
Total number of strategies, fiscal 2003–05: 24			

Source: World Bank database.

Background work was carried out on the implications of the Enhanced HIPC Initiative for LICUS as part of this review.[1] The main findings are presented below.

- *LICUS have lagged behind in establishing a record to qualify for HIPC debt relief, but a large number of these countries could potentially benefit from debt relief if they fulfill requirements for eligibility before the sunset clause expires at end 2006.*

Of the 25 LICUS, none has reached the completion point, five are between the decision and completion points[2] (Burundi, Democratic Republic of Congo, Guinea-Bissau, Republic of Congo, and São Tomé and Principe), and seven are potentially eligible for the HIPC Initiative (Central African Republic, Comoros, Haiti, Liberia, Somalia, Sudan, and Togo).[3] Three of these potentially eligible LICUS (Central African Republic, Haiti, and Togo) satisfy the policy performance criterion for eligibility under the Enhanced HIPC Initiative. The Central African Republic and Haiti are moving toward qualification for decision point under HIPC, because they have Emergency Post-Conflict Assistance arrangements and are preparing their PRSP and I-PRSP, respectively. Togo has expressed its willingness to seek support for its programs as soon as the security condition stabilizes and has recently prepared an I-PRSP (Interim Poverty Reduction Strategy Paper), although the paper has not yet been submitted to the Boards of the Bretton Woods Institutions. The other four potentially eligible LICUS (Comoros, Liberia, Somalia, and Sudan) have not had an IMF- or IDA-supported program since 1995, which they would need before end-2006 in order to be eligible for relief under the enhanced HIPC.

- *It may be more difficult for LICUS to establish a macroeconomic record than it is for other countries. This is not to imply that entry requirements should be relaxed, but rather that a concerted effort should be made to help LICUS meet HIPC requirements.*

The weak capacity and volatility in LICUS will make it more difficult for them to establish a policy record before HIPC sunset in 2006, suggesting that the Bank needs to pay more attention to supporting policy measures necessary for LICUS to meet HIPC decision point and completion point requirements. This is particularly important in light of the Multilateral Debt Relief Initiative for 100 percent debt cancellation for completion point HIPC countries, which will be implemented in July 2006 (World Bank 2006e). A 2003 IEG evaluation of the HIPC Initiative found that in the case of the "millennium rush" countries that qualified in late 2000, the relaxation of eligibility requirements raises the risk of not achieving HIPC objectives, given that the majority of these countries experienced policy slippages after reaching their decision points and are ceteris paribus less likely to achieve good development results (IEG 2003a). Similarly, Collier (2005) argues that "debt relief is an aid modality that, unless carefully managed, comes closest to turning aid into oil."[4]

- *Changes under IDA 14 linking grant financing with debt distress are a welcome development, particularly for LICUS, but long-term debt sustainability depends on sustained improvements in policy.*

During the IDA 14 discussions it was agreed that debt sustainability will be the basis for the allocation of grants to IDA-only countries in IDA 14, so that the share of grants in total IDA financing will emerge from a country-by-country analysis of the risk of debt distress (IDA 2005, p. 25). The Joint Bank-Fund debt sustainability framework, which links the risk of debt distress to the quality of policies and institutions in low-income countries,[5] was endorsed as the analytical underpinning for the link between debt sustainability and grant eligibility (IDA 2005, p. 25). This move is particularly important for debt sustainability in LICUS, since under the new framework, LICUS qualify for 100 percent grant financing. In addition, an exception to the debt-distress grant eligibility criterion was made for Kosovo and Timor-Leste, which are thus made eligible for grants.

Both the extension of the HIPC sunset clause and the grant allocation mechanism are important steps in helping LICUS relieve their debt burden. However, as suggested by a recent IEG Evaluation Update on HIPC (IEG 2006b), debt reduction alone is not a sufficient instrument to affect the multiple drivers of debt sustainability.[6] Sustained improvements in export diversification, fiscal management, and public debt management are also needed (IEG 2006b). Moreover, as suggested by Collier (2005), debt relief faces a potentially severe time consistency problem—that is, once debts are cancelled, there is no incentive for the government to abide by any continuing conditions. Sustained improvements in policies in LICUS will be crucial for debt sustainability.

BREAKDOWN BY COUNTRY: LENDING AND ADMINISTRATIVE
BUDGET—TOTAL AND FOR ANALYTICAL WORK

Table I.1: Total Dollar (US$) Amounts: Lending and Administrative Budget (total and for analytical work)

Country	Lending (million US$)		Administrative budget ('000 US$)		Analytical work ('000 US$)	
	Fiscal 2000–02	Fiscal 2003–05	Fiscal 2000–02	Fiscal 2003–05	Fiscal 2000–02	Fiscal 2003–05
Afghanistan	100	793	4,190	19,992	1,094	7,693
Angola	33	176	2,886	5,791	537	1,987
Burundi	131	223	2,942	4,270	385	860
Democratic Republic of Congo	500	1,332	4,621	11,422	956	2,990
Guinea-Bissau	51	14	2,193	2,658	197	494
Republic of Congo	90	110	1,934	4,407	582	922
Timor-Leste	112	15	6,146	5,915	2,401	1,934
Post-conflict		**2,664**		**54,455**		**16,879**
Cambodia	135	167	9,624	13,937	1,700	4,073
Central African Republic	45	0	1,328	1,878	98	758
Comoros	17	13	2,143	1,759	137	211
Haiti	0	75	1,788	3,623	202	1,661
Kosovo	63	30	7,240	5,921	2,302	1,946
Lao People's Democratic Republic	87	136	7,525	17,598	638	2,065
Liberia	0	0	386	2,069	169	1,239
Myanmar	0	0	320	322	320	272
Nigeria	682	881	19,432	22,755	7,229	5,352
Papua New Guinea	190	0	5,098	5,426	1,144	2,183
São Tomé and Principe	10	12	1,538	2,107	457	448
Solomon Islands	4	0	823	639	37	290
Somalia	0	0	37	1,084	25	831
Sudan	0	0	908	5,354	778	3,900
Tajikistan	122	59	6,060	11,605	748	3,578
Togo	0	0	2,656	1,729	443	1,017
Uzbekistan	105	100	6,341	7,530	1,518	2,118
Zimbabwe	5	0	5,506	1,332	1,245	855
Non-post-conflict		**1,473**		**106,668**		**32,899**
LICUS	**2,480**	**4,137**	**103,665**	**161,123**	**25,342**	**49,778**
Non-LICUS LICs	**18,557**	**20,400**	**379,941**	**449,637**	**69,088**	**109,947**
Non-LICUS LICs (excluding India)	**12,011**	**14,569**	**318,967**	**380,754**	**56,040**	**89,723**

Source: World Bank database.

Table I.2: Per Capita Annual Amounts: Lending and Administrative Budget (total and for analytical work)

Country	Lending (US$)		Administrative budget (US$)		Analytical work (US$)	
	Fiscal 2000–02	Fiscal 2003–05	Fiscal 2000–02	Fiscal 2003–05	Fiscal 2000–02	Fiscal 2003–05
Afghanistan	1.2	9.2	0.051	0.232	0.013	0.089
Angola	0.9	4.3	0.075	0.143	0.014	0.049
Burundi	6.3	10.3	0.141	0.198	0.018	0.040
Democratic Republic of Congo	3.3	8.4	0.031	0.072	0.006	0.019
Guinea-Bissau	12.1	3.1	0.520	0.595	0.047	0.111
Republic of Congo	8.4	9.8	0.181	0.391	0.055	0.082
Timor-Leste	46.6	5.7	2.560	2.248	1.000	0.735
Post-conflict		**8.2**		**0.167**		**0.052**
Cambodia	3.5	4.2	0.248	0.347	0.044	0.101
Central African Republic	4.0	0.0	0.118	0.161	0.009	0.065
Comoros	10.1	7.2	1.249	0.977	0.080	0.117
Haiti	0.0	3.0	0.073	0.143	0.008	0.066
Kosovo	8.7	4.2	1.006	0.822	0.320	0.270
Lao People's Democratic Republic	5.3	8.0	0.464	1.036	0.039	0.122
Liberia	0.0	0.0	0.040	0.204	0.018	0.122
Myanmar	0.0	0.0	0.002	0.002	0.002	0.002
Nigeria	1.7	2.2	0.050	0.056	0.019	0.013
Papua New Guinea	12.0	0.0	0.323	0.329	0.073	0.132
São Tomé and Principe	22.1	25.4	3.393	4.462	1.008	0.949
Solomon Islands	3.1	0.0	0.636	0.466	0.029	0.212
Somalia	0.0	0.0	0.001	0.038	0.001	0.029
Sudan	0.0	0.0	0.009	0.053	0.008	0.039
Tajikistan	6.5	3.1	0.324	0.614	0.040	0.194
Togo	0.0	0.0	0.190	0.119	0.032	0.070
Uzbekistan	1.4	1.3	0.085	0.098	0.020	0.028
Zimbabwe	0.1	0.0	0.143	0.034	0.032	0.022
Non-post-conflict		**1.5**		**0.110**		**0.034**
LICUS	**2.0**	**3.2**	**0.084**	**0.124**	**0.020**	**0.038**
Non-LICUS LICs	**3.4**	**3.6**	**0.070**	**0.080**	**0.013**	**0.020**
Non-LICUS LICs (excluding India)	**5.2**	**6.0**	**0.138**	**0.158**	**0.024**	**0.037**

Source: World Bank database.

APPENDIX J: POLITICAL ANALYSIS RELEVANT FOR STRATEGY DEVELOPMENT IN LICUS

The objective of a country team should be to commission or consume (not necessarily produce) analysis that is directly relevant to and usable in the development of a strategy. Many types and layers of political analysis are useful for this purpose. Some illustrations are outlined below.

Political risk analysis underlies the decision of whether the Bank should engage in a certain country and, if so, how it should engage. This analysis can provide an overall evaluation of the level of stability and instability in the country and suggest the different scenarios that might unfold. Political risk analysis needs to be repeated regularly in LICUS.

Structural analysis seeks to identify major characteristics of the political situation that will affect the work of the Bank, no matter what the specific strategy chosen. For example, structural analysis focuses on the existence of major ethnic or religious conflicts in the country and the distribution of various groups over the national territory that may transform a policy that would work well in a homogeneous environment into one that discriminates against a particular group. This analysis can be carried out at the national, regional, or local level, or for particular sectors. Structural analysis focuses on the weakness of a particular state, leading to the development of strategies that avoid undermining it further.

Analysis of day-to-day politics needs to go beyond the political gossip about who is up and who is down in the capital, but also needs to look at the distribution of power among different political forces in the capital and in the regions, or even localities. Such analysis is crucial in deciding, for example, whether a more centralized or decentralized approach to reform in a particular sector is desirable. Depending on the situation, decentralization may lead to policies that are more responsive to local needs or, for example, put even more power in the hands of warlords.

Analysis of the history of reform in the country, and often in neighboring ones, is critical for designing an effective strategy. Botched privatization attempts that created a strong backlash in the recent past, for example, would suggest that further privatization should not be part of the Bank strategy immediately, but a compromise solution might be sought instead—for example, commercialization rather than privatization of utilities.

Source: Background work undertaken by Marina Ottaway for this review, 2005.

APPENDIX K: CAPACITY DEVELOPMENT PROJECTS IN LICUS

Over fiscal 2000–05, 206 projects were approved in the 25 LICUS—148 IDA, 10 IBRD, 38 Special Financing, and 10 project-related Global Environment Facility (GEF) grants. Of these 206 projects, 30 were free-standing capacity development, institutional strengthening, or technical assistance projects, or were projects in which such *components* added up to 80 percent of the total project cost (see table below).

Similarly, over fiscal 2000–05, a large number of grants were approved under different trust fund programs; for example, 29 grants were approved under LICUS Trust Funds and 56 under Institutional Development Funds (IDFs). The Post-Conflict Fund (PCF) is not a trust fund program, but since 1999 it has been eligible to receive contributions from donors. PCF supports

countries emerging from conflict—many of which are LICUS—through research, planning, piloting, and analysis of ground-breaking activities.

Given the large number of trust funds, the analysis was restricted to the LICUS Trust Fund, PCF, and IDF. Eighteen grants under the LICUS Trust Fund and 30 grants under PCF were free-standing capacity development, institutional strengthening, or technical assistance grants, or were grants in which such *components* added up to 80 percent of the total cost (see table below). The list of LICUS Trust Fund capacity-development grants was provided by the Bank's LICUS Unit and the list of PCF capacity-development grants was provided by the Bank's Social Development Department. All IDF grants were deemed to be capacity-development grants.

Country	Project/program title	Instrument
Afghanistan	Emergency Public Administration Project	IDA
	Programmatic Support for Institution Building	IDA
	Second Emergency Public Administration Project	IDA
	Public Administration Capacity Building Project	IDA
	Enhancing Knowledge and Partnerships	PCF
	Reconstruction Strategy for Afghanistan with Afghan and Other Stakeholder Participation	PCF
	Afghanistan Priority Sectors Support Program, and Launch Package for Community Empowerment Program	PCF
	Launch Package for Community Empowerment Program	PCF
	Afghan Female Teacher in-Service Training in Peshwar (Pakistan)	PCF
	Teacher Training Programs for Afghan Refugees	PCF
	Balochistan Refugee Teacher Training Project	PCF
Angola	Economic Management Technical Assistance	IDA
Burundi	Planning for Burundi's Future: Building Leadership Capacity	PCF
	Ex-Combatants Assistance (BEAP)	PCF
	(PREVCONB) Program for Prevention of Conflict in Burundi	PCF

(Continues on the following page.)

Country	Project/program title	Instrument
Cambodia	Land Management and Administration Project	IDA
	Rural Investment and Local Governance	IDA
	Economic and Private Sector Capacity Building Project	IDA
	Cambodian Center for Conflict Resolution—Capacity Development Program	PCF
Central African Republic	Policy Support Project	IDA
	Public Financial Management and Education Sector	LTF
	Public Financial Management and Governance	LTF
	Strategic Leadership Seminar for Central African Republic	LTF
Comoros	Support to the Comorian Transition Process	LTF
	Support to the Comorian Transition Process	LTF
	Support to the Comorian Transition Process - Leadership Seminars	LTF
	Anjouan Professional Integration of Militia	PCF
	Transitional Support to Comoros Economic Management	PCF
	Reintegration of Young Militias in Anjouan	PCF
Democratic Republic of Congo	Pilot Post-Conflict Rapid Assessment of Living Conditions and Infrastructure	PCF
	Demobilization & Rehabilitation Program: Preparatory Phase, Social Reintegration Program - Pilot Activities	PCF
Guinea Bissau	Private Sector Rehabilitation and Development	IDA
Haiti	Economic Governance Reform Operation	IDA
	Governance Technical Assistance Grant	IDA
	Support for Economic Governance Reform	LTF
	Building Institutional Capacity & Strengthening Provision of School Feeding Program	LTF
	Haiti Disaster Risk Management Pilot	LTF
Kosovo	Economic Policy/Public Expenditure Management	IDA
	Energy Sector Technical Assistance 2	IDA
	Business Environment Technical Assistance	IDA
	Energy Sector Technical Assistance 3	IDA
	Kosovo Youth Development Grant	PCF
	Energy Sector Technical Assistance	SF
	Private Sector Development Technical Assistance	SF
Lao People's Democratic Republic	Financial Management Capacity Building Credit	IDA
Liberia	Liberia: Community Empowerment Project	LTF
	Liberia: Support for Economic Management & Development Strategy	LTF
	Public Financial Management	LTF
	Reactivation of the Forestry Sector and Forest Management	LTF
	Support to Donor Coordination (RIMCO)	LTF
	Regional Support for Reconstruction of the Liberian Legal System	LTF
Nigeria	Local Empowerment and Environmental Management Project	GEF
	Economic Management Capacity Building	IDA
	State Governance and Capacity Building TAL (fiscal 2005)	IDA
	Economic Reform and Governance Project	IDA
Papua New Guinea	Governance Promotion Adjustment Loan	IBRD

Country	Project/program title	Instrument
Republic of Congo	Transparency and Governance Capacity Building	IDA
	Emergency Support for Integration of Ex-Combatants and Unemployed Youth into Agricultural Sector (FAO)	PCF
São Tomé and Principe	Public Resource Management	IDA
	Public Resource Management Technical Assistance	IDA
	Capacity Building and Technical Assistance	IDA
Somalia	Capacity Building for Somali Planners	LTF
	Livestock Project: Puntland Pastoralists Program	LTF
Sudan	Capacity Building for Development in Post-Conflict Sudan	LTF
	Expanded Watching Brief - Part 1	PCF
	Expanded Watching Brief - Part 2	PCF
	Nuba Mountains Project	PCF
Tajikistan	Empowering Women: Socioeconomic Development in Post-Conflict - 1st Phase	PCF
	Women's Empowerment and Socio-economic Development - 2nd Phase	PCF
Timor-Leste	Transition Support Program	SF
	Administrative Services Capacity Building Project	PCF
	Post-Conflict Reconstruction and Reintegration Program - Part 1	PCF
	Post-Conflict Reconstruction and Reintegration Program - Part 2	PCF
	Post-Conflict Reconstruction and Reintegration Program - Part 3	PCF
	Support to Poor Widows: Widows, War and Welfare	PCF
	Capacity Building Assistance & Development Project	PCF
	Leadership Capacity Building for Economic Development (LED)	PCF
	Economic Institutions for Capacity Building	SF

APPENDIX L: ACCOUNTABILITY IN THE MANAGEMENT OF NATURAL RESOURCES IN LICUS

Background work on accountability in the management of natural resources in LICUS was done as part of this review. The main findings are presented below.

The Bank has emphasized issues of governance in natural resource management in country strategies in recent years.

Of the 25 LICUS, 7—Angola, the Central African Republic, the Democratic Republic of Congo, the Republic of Congo, Nigeria, Papua New Guinea, and Togo—were identified as "extractive industries–dependent countries" in the IEG 2005 evaluation *Extractive Industries and Sustainable Development* (IEG 2003b). The LICUS Task Force report pointed out high levels of opportunistic behavior in LICUS, especially in natural resource extraction activities, and recommended that measures to improve governance and intensify scrutiny over the uses of natural resource rents be among the high priorities. A review of the Bank's strategies in the seven resource-rich (extractive industries–dependent) LICUS listed above suggests that issues of governance in natural resource management have indeed been emphasized in recent years. In most cases, this takes the form of analytical work on governance in the natural resource sectors[1] or general financial management and fiduciary studies.[2]

Natural resource management is also included in progress indicators and triggers.

In Angola, financial support beyond the Transitional Support Strategy was contingent on (i) publication of all government tax revenues and (ii) completion of the Oil Diagnostic Study, and movement to the Central Bank of all oil revenues (except those earmarked to service oil-backed debt) and their inclusion in the Central Bank's annual audit. In the Republic of Congo, publication of the annual audit of accounts of the national oil company was among the post-conflict performance indicators (PCPI).

Implementation arrangements, however, are inadequate.

In the Central African Republic, necessary actions for the forestry and mining sectors are outlined in the Bank's country strategy, but it is unclear how they will be implemented, or what happens if they are not implemented. In Papua New Guinea, similarly, the Bank's Interim Strategy (2005) mentions that better management of revenues from the extractive industries sector is a priority, and that the Bank will support the International Finance Corporation's (IFC's) investment in the mining sector through advisory work (World Bank 2005l, p. 27). At the same time, the Interim Strategy Note lacks details on its engagement, benchmarks, milestones, or other monitoring indicators against which progress could be effectively measured.

Furthermore, emphasis on governance in natural resource management is not LICUS-specific; instead, it is part of the overall trend within the Bank to base strategies more strongly on governance considerations. The IEG evaluation of extractive industries suggests, with regard to the evolution of Bank's policy and role in extractive industries, that "in the latter part of the 1990s, there was an increased focus on reform and deregulation programs in an effort to further good governance as a central element in the improvement of country economic performance" (IEG 2003b, p. 61). Given the particularly weak governance environment in LICUS, and the abundant evidence of the negative impact of natural resource windfalls, additional attention and more focused approaches may be required. Even in the Chad-Cameroon Oil Pipeline Project, where the Bank applied some of the strongest safeguards, including a revenue management law designed to ensure that earnings from oil are directed toward poverty reduction, an oversight commit-tee with members from civil society and Parliament, and a Future Generations Fund in the amount of 10 percent of oil revenues, these provisions proved to be insufficient. The independent oversight committee proved to be understaffed and did not have sufficient information from the government and Exxon Mobil.

APPENDIX M: DEVELOPMENT POLICY LENDING

The LICUS Initiative suggested that while development policy lending (DPL) is not always appropriate in all fragile-state contexts, it could be under two business models—the *post-conflict or political transition* and *gradual improvement* business models. When successful, DPL can potentially deliver larger, country-wide benefits by stabilizing government during a transition, alleviating liquidity pressures in a cash-strapped environment, supporting institution building, and fostering harmonized donor support for a focused set of policy and institutional actions. According to the OPCS Note on Development Policy Operations in Fragile States (World Bank 2005f), where revenue collections are weak, the stability of state institutions and improvements in service delivery will require budgetary support, as well as a rapid donor response, in order to maintain momentum.

DPL was introduced in 2004 and its use in LICUS has so far been minimal—two approved DPL operations (in Lao PDR) and nine more in the pipeline for fiscal 2005–06. Adjustment lending, which DPL replaces, has also been limited, with only nine operations approved during fiscal 2002–05. This limited experience reveals better outcomes associated with post-conflict transitions (Democratic Republic of Congo, Kosovo, Timor-Leste); government commitment was an important success factor. At the same time, the Financial Management Adjustment Credit in Lao PDR faced weak compliance and government resistance to reforms, which produced *unsatisfactory* outcomes. In design, programmatic single-tranche operations have also performed better than multiple-tranche loans by avoiding second-tranche release delays caused by difficulties in fulfilling release conditions (the Financial Management Adjust-ment Credit experienced a one-year delay).

A review of adjustment operations approved during fiscal 2002–04 and evaluated by IEG[1] suggests a direct relationship between outcomes and institutional quality (table M.1). While unsatisfactory outcomes are few,[2] they tend to be identified with countries that have lower CPIA ratings.

While the experience of adjustment operations approved during fiscal 2002–05 is similar to that of investment projects, there is a notable difference in borrower performance (tables M.2 and M.3). The stronger link with CPIA in adjustment operations can be explained in part by their heavier reliance on budgetary and financial management procedures of partner countries and agreement on overall development objectives.

Similarly, a review of recent adjustment and investment lending in LICUS[3] suggests that investment lending has fared somewhat better in overall outcome attainability and institutional development impact. While 44 percent of adjustment operations (4 out of 9) resulted in unsatisfactory results,[4] similar outcomes are found in only 18 percent (4 out of 22) of investment projects.

Table M.1: Mean CPIA, by IEG Outcome Ratings

Outcome mean	Mean	Standard deviation	Obs.
Highly satisfactory	3.93	0.41	4
Satisfactory	3.71	0.43	41
Marginally satisfactory	3.67	0.41	30
Marginally unsatisfactory	3.55	0.07	2
Unsatisfactory	3.25	0.30	6
Total	3.67	0.43	83

Source: IEG and World Bank databases.

Table M.2: Performance and CPIA in Adjustment Lending (fiscal 2002–05)

Overall borrower performance	Mean CPIA	Standard deviation	Obs.
Highly satisfactory	4.00	0.26	3
Satisfactory	3.69	0.44	71
Unsatisfactory	3.43	0.17	9
Total	3.67	0.43	83

Source: IEG and World Bank database.

Table M.3: Performance and CPIA in Investment Lending (fiscal 2002–05)

Overall borrower performance	Mean CPIA	Standard deviation	Obs.
Satisfactory	3.78	0.35	9
Unsatisfactory	3.76	0.66	7
Total	3.77	0.49	16

Source: IEG and World Bank database.

Recent experience suggests that while there may be a *prima facie* argument for providing budget support in post-conflict countries, their higher dependence on institutional quality and good borrower performance will require a more cautious approach when considering DPL in LICUS, as compared with non-LICUS, as well as careful design and additional monitoring. As suggested by Koeberle and Stavreski (2005), "budget support is most appropriate for countries with a good track record, strong ownership of the reform program, a reasonably sound policy and institutional framework, and commitment and sufficient capacity to allocate resources effectively and in accordance with development priorities." Indeed, most of the Poverty Reduction Support Credits (PRSCs) to date have gone to countries in the top two quintiles of the CPIA distribution. Therefore, careful consideration of the appropriateness of DPL in countries with no obvious political or post-conflict turnaround and weaker government ownership and reform consensus will be particularly important.

This does not necessarily imply, however, resorting to free-standing investment projects. Approaches such as SWAps may also be considered as they too address the limitations of fragmented project approaches and provide benefits similar to budget support operations, while allowing for additional safeguards through the use of various financing modalities (budget support, pooled and project financing) within a common program, as well as common policy dialogue and joint monitoring against one set of targets and indicators.[5] At the same time, SWAps may not be an approach of choice, given their long-term view, when the goal is alleviating short-term cash needs, for instance. The choice of assistance modalities will be a complex one, particularly in fragile environments. The pros and cons of different options should be weighed (box M.1) in light of country conditions.

Box M.1. Projects versus Budget Support: Pros and Cons

Projects can facilitate implementation and monitoring, both in terms of the Bank's ability to ensure quick project implementation and to collect the necessary data to report on project progress.

Common criticisms of the project approach include: (i) fragmented environment that is not conducive to the formulation of a unified long-term reform program by the government; (ii) parallel implementation mechanisms that fail to facilitate, or even undermine, longer-term institutional development; (iii) increased transaction costs associated with duplication of effort necessary to meet different procedural requirements and multiple donor missions; and (iv) mis-alignment of donor funds with the government's budget cycle and the often off-budget aid flow that limits the predictability of aid flows.

Benefits associated with budget support and SWAps include: (i) increased predictability of funds; (ii) greater efficiency of budgetary programming and spending; (iii) capacity development; (iv) greater ownership on part of the government; and (v) being in line with current Bank strategy, as embodied in the Comprehensive Development Framework.

In very poor governance environments, the Bank may find it difficult to monitor and control the use of resources provided through budget support and SWAps.

APPENDIX N: THE CHALLENGES OF ENGAGING CIVIL SOCIETY ORGANIZATIONS IN LICUS

From its Angola, Guinea-Bissau, and Togo case studies, the World Bank report on engaging civil society organizations (World Bank 2005d) concluded that:

- In Angola, extensive donor presence during the conflict led to a significant yet uncoordinated rise of civil society organizations (CSOs) dominated by high-capacity international NGOs.
- In Guinea-Bissau, several NGOs support the CSOs that were created by the citizens to counteract a weak state and other problems, but do so project by project, lacking the resources and capacity to build institutions and ensure sustainability.
- In Togo, neither government nor civil society is able to provide minimal social services because of a repressive state and drastic donor cutbacks, enabling fraudulent NGOs to take advantage of poor communities.

The study found that financing CSOs project by project was especially problematic in the rapidly changing environments of conflict-affected and fragile states, because it gave the organizations limited opportunity to develop capacity, specialization, strategic planning, and long-term investments in beneficiary communities. Competition for scarce resources made CSOs donor-driven, with accountability focused upward to donors rather than downward to citizens. The report's main recommendation was for donors to shift from the project-by-project approach of supporting CSOs to a more sustained engagement, with less ad hoc project funding and one-time training events and more systematic cooperation and commitment, including partnering and funding the long-term institutional development of CSOs.

To understand the challenges of working with civil society organizations in LICUS better, the Participation and Civic Engagement Group and CPR Unit are piloting a Civil Society Assessment Tool. On May 25, 2006, the Bank and Inter Action hosted a joint workshop on CSOs in fragile states. The results from the workshop are expected to provide input to the OECD-DAC work on service delivery in fragile states.

Sources: World Bank 2004c, 2005d.

APPENDIX O: THE WORLD BANK'S ECONOMIC AND SECTOR WORK IN LICUS

There has been an increase in the number of economic and sector work (ESW) products in fiscal 2003–05 compared with fiscal 2000–02 for both LICUS and non-LICUS LICs. While the increase in the number of ESW products was 60 percent in non-LICUS LICs, it was 166 percent in LICUS (table O.1).

The 2002 LICUS Task Force Report noted that a minimum set of good practice ESW should be feasible, even in countries where there is no or little government interest. This "minimum set" of ESW includes core diagnostic ESW such as Development Policy Reviews (DPRs), Poverty Assessments (PAs), Integrative Fiduciary Assessments (IFAs), and Institutional and Governance Reviews (IGRs).[1] Country Financial Accountability Assessments (CFAAs) and Country Procurement Assessment Reports (CPARs) can be integrated into the IGR where a separate exercise may be difficult.

Yet there are some LICUS without a single core diagnostic ESW product (minimum or otherwise) over fiscal 2003–05: Afghanistan, the Central African Republic, Comoros, Haiti, Liberia, Myanmar, the Solomon Islands, and Zimbabwe. Overall, countries with 3 or more core diagnostic reports have increased from 2 to 10 (5 times) among LICUS, compared with an increase from 8 to 20 (2.5 times) among non-LICUS LICs (table O.2).

While the administrative budget for ESW in LICUS has more than doubled since the LICUS Initiative, one-fourth or more of LICUS do not have any ESW being conducted in Sector Boards such as Education; Environment; Health, Nutrition, and Population; Social Development; Social Protection; Transport; Urban Development; and Water Supply and Sanitation (table O.3). This lack of ESW in important Sector Boards in several LICUS raises some questions about the effectiveness of future Bank assistance.

Table O.1: ESW Products

Product	LICUS (25)		Non-LICUS (34)	
	Fiscal 2000–02	Fiscal 2003–05	Fiscal 2000–02	Fiscal 2003–05
Core diagnostic reports	17	43	67	112
Other diagnostic reports	3	29	17	105
Advisory reports	22	52	126	158
Not assigned	23	49	141	188
Total	65	173	351	563

Source: World Bank database.

Table O.2: Core Diagnostic ESW Reports by Country

Country	Fiscal 2000–02	Fiscal 2003–05
Post-conflict LICUS		13
Afghanistan		
Angola		CFAA, CPAR, IFA
Burundi		CFAA, CPAR
Democratic Republic of Congo		CFAA, CPAR, PER
Guinea-Bissau		PER
Republic of Congo		PER
Timor-Leste	CFAA, CEM	CPAR, PA, PER
Non-post-conflict LICUS		30 (29)
Cambodia	PA	CFAA, CPAR, PER
Central African Republic		
Comoros		
Haiti	CPAR	
Kosovo	PA	CEM, CFAA, PER, PA
Lao People's Democratic Republic	CFAA, CPAR, PER	CEM
Liberia		
Myanmar	CEM	
Nigeria	CFAA, CPAR, PER, IGR[a]	CFAA, CPAR, PA
Papua New Guinea	PA	CPAR, PA, PER
São Tomé and Principe		CEM,PA
Solomon Islands		
Somalia		CEM
Sudan		CEM (2)
Tajikistan	PA, CEM	CFAA, CPAR, PA, PER
Togo		CPAR, DPR, PA
Uzbekistan	CPAR	CEM, CFAA, PA, PER
Zimbabwe		
LICUS (25)	16	43 (42)
Non-LICUS LICs (34)	66 (56)	111(99)

Source: World Bank database.

Note: CEM = Country Economic Memorandum, CFAA = Country Financial Accountability Assessment, CPAR = Country Procurement Assessment Report, DPR = Development Policy Review, IFA = Integrative Fiduciary Assessment, IGR = Institutional and Governance Review, PA = Poverty Assessment, PER = Public Expenditure Review. The IGR has also been included in the list of LICUS core diagnostic reports because the 2002 LICUS Task Force report identified it as an essential piece of ESW for LICUS.

Table O.3: Number of Countries Covered by a Sector Board's ESW Product, Fiscal 2003–05

Sector Board	LICUS	Non-LICUS
Economic policy	15	29
Education	6	18
Energy and mining	8	12
Environment	3	11
Financial management	8	25
Financial sector	6	23
Gender and development	4	12
Global information/communications technology	0	2
Health, nutrition, and population	5	20
Operational services	2	3
Poverty reduction	9	23
Private sector development	11	24
Procurement	10	21
Project finance and guarantees	0	1
Public sector governance	10	20
Rural sector	10	16
Social development	3	10
Social protection	6	10
Transport	1	9
Urban development	1	9
Water supply and sanitation	0	11

Source: World Bank database.

APPENDIX P: PERFORMANCE OF ACTIVE PROJECTS

Projects in 25 LICUS Evaluated by QAG

Quality Assessment Group (QAG) assessments show a decline in quality at entry for projects in LICUS assessed in fiscal 2000–03. Quality of supervision, however, shows a marked improvement from a low of 61 percent before fiscal 2000 to 85 percent for fiscal 2000–03 (table P.1).[1] The percentage of projects in LICUS rated satisfactory for quality at entry and quality of supervision for fiscal 2000–03 are comparable to the percentage of projects rated satisfactory in non-LICUS LICs. However, projects in non-LICUS LICs show an improvement in both ratings over time, while projects in LICUS show a decline in quality at entry.

Composition of the LICUS Portfolio

Over fiscal 2000–05, the Bank had 104–137 active projects per year in the 25 LICUS. Over the same period, the Bank had 465–510 active projects per year in the non-LICUS LICs. Table P.2 illustrates the percentage of projects rated as problems on development objectives and implementation progress and the percentage of projects and commitments "at risk" for the active portfolio for each year during fiscal 2000–05 and the average for two time periods: fiscal 2000–02 and 2003–05.

Table P.1: QAG Ratings for Active Projects

	Time period	Quality at entry		Quality of supervision	
		Number of projects	Percent satisfactory	Number of projects	Percent satisfactory
LICUS	Fiscal 1997–99	12	92	36	61
	Fiscal 2000–03	30	84	13	85
Non-LICUS LICs	Fiscal 1997–99	89	79	212	70
	Fiscal 2000–03	76	84	90	84

Source: World Bank database.

Table P.2: Project Performance of the Active Portfolio

	Fiscal year						Average	
							Fiscal 2000–02	Fiscal 2003–05
	2000	2001	2002	2003	2004	2005		
Post-conflict LICUS								
Number of projects				39	50	57		49
Net commitments				1,569	2,942	2,840		2,450
Development objective (% problem)				10	0	7		5
Implementation progress (% problem)				13	0	7		6
At risk (%)				41	20	21		26
Realism (%)				44	0	42		32
Non-post-conflict LICUS								
Number of projects				84	74	80		79
Net commitments				2,200	2,369	2,829		2,466
Development objective (% problem)				11	12	10		11
Implementation progress (% problem)				20	22	15		19
At risk (%)				30	31	24		28
Realism (%)				68	78	68		72
LICUS								
Number of projects	105	105	117	123	124	137	109	128
Net commitments	2,510	2,220	3,098	3,790	5,340	5,471	2,609	4,867
Development objective (% problem)	14	12	7	11	7	9	11	9
Implementation progress (% problem)	13	12	10	18	13	12	12	14
At risk (%)	27	26	32	33	27	23	28	27
Realism (%)	71	63	32	59	55	58	53	57
Non-LICUS LICs								
Number of projects	517	521	500	497	488	481	513	489
Net commitments	32,873	34,762	34,130	34,267	33,697	33,529	33,922	33,831
Development objective (% problem)	6	5	5	7	7	8	6	7
Implementation progress (% problem)	10	9	11	9	11	13	10	11
At risk (%)	15	12	18	14	16	19	15	16
Realism (%)	78	87	67	81	85	76	76	80

Source: World Bank database.

APPENDIX Q: PERFORMANCE OF CLOSED PROJECTS AND LESSONS IN LICUS

This appendix first presents the trends in project performance in the 25 countries categorized as LICUS by the Bank in fiscal 2005 based on ICR Reviews conducted by IEG for 129 projects that *closed* over fiscal 2000–05. All ICR Reviews in IEG's ICR Review and Tracking Database for projects in each of the 25 LICUS that were evaluated by July 2005 were also assessed for implementation experience (107 total). The most frequently noted significant outcomes, shortcomings, and lessons from these projects are presented in tables Q.2–Q.4.

Composition of the 2005 Closed LICUS Projects Evaluated by IEG

IEG evaluated 1,672 closed projects from fiscal 2000 to June of fiscal 2006. This evaluated cohort includes 129 projects approved in the 25 LICUS and 529 projects approved in non-LICUS LICs (the approval years are given in figure Q.1). In nominal net commitment terms, the LICUS cohort covers $3.3 billion and the non-LICUS LIC cohort covers $31.6 billion. Table Q.1 illustrates the IEG ratings for the exiting LICUS and non-LICUS cohorts.

Figure Q.1: Approval Years of Evaluated Projects

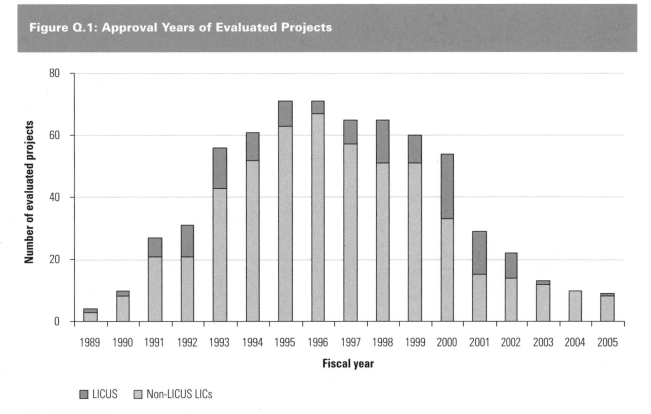

Source: World Bank database.

Only two projects that were approved after the LICUS Initiative had been evaluated by IEG as of June 2006. Both were rated satisfactory on outcome. Project performance of the LICUS cohort (approved prior to the initiative, but exited after it began) has shown an improving trend, from 58 percent for projects exiting in fiscal 2003 to 82 percent for projects exiting in fiscal 2005. In contrast, the percentage of projects rated satisfactory on outcome for the non-LICUS LICs increased from 70 percent in fiscal 2003 to 77 percent in 2005 (figure Q.2, table Q.l).

QAG has argued in its fiscal 2004 ARPP that the improving trend in outcome ratings in LICUS over fiscal 2002–04 is due to improved Bank performance. Ratings for Bank performance were found to be significantly correlated (positively) to outcome ratings.

The net disconnect has been higher for the LICUS cohort than for non-LICUS LICs for all years over fiscal 2000–05, except for 2003 (table Q.l). The net disconnect has, however, declined over time for both the LICUS and non-LICUS LICs and was about 6 percent for LICUS and 4 percent for non-LICUS LICs for projects exiting in fiscal 2005.

Figure Q.2. Percentage of Projects Rated Satisfactory on Outcome by IEG

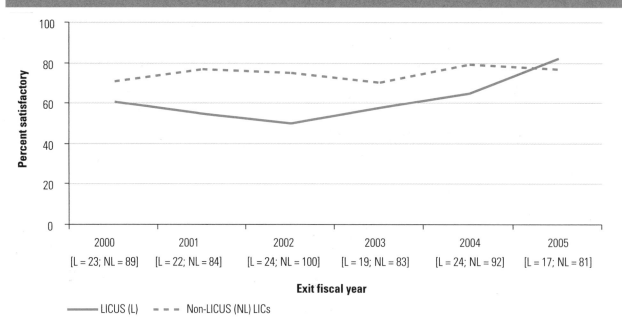

Source: World Bank database.

Table Q.1: Performance of Projects That Exited and Were Evaluated by IEG Between Fiscal 2000 and 2005 for LICUS and Non-LICUS LICs

	Exit fiscal year							
	2000	2001	2002	2003	2004	2005	2000–02	2003–05
LICUS cohort								
Number of projects	23	22	24	19	24	17	69	60
Net commitments	751	669	468	695	266	420	1,888	1,381
Outcome (% satisfactory)	61	55	50	58	65	82	55	68
Sustainability (% likely)	41	38	32	44	43	67	37	50
Institutional development impact (% substantial)	35	18	14	32	22	59	22	36
Bank overall performance (% satisfactory)	83	59	54	79	63	76	65	72
Borrower overall performance (% satisfactory)	61	50	33	53	67	76	48	65
Net disconnect (%)	17	27	23	11	9	6	22	8
Non-LICUS LICs								
Number of projects	89	84	100	83	92	81	273	256
Net commitments	4,774	4,412	6,496	4,927	5,625	5,347	15,682	15,899
Outcome (% satisfactory)	71	77	75	70	79	77	74	76
Sustainability (% likely)	63	72	75	70	77	80	70	76
Institutional development impact (% substantial)	42	49	40	46	53	63	43	54
Bank overall performance (% satisfactory)	73	74	75	72	75	78	74	75
Borrower overall performance (% satisfactory)	64	77	74	70	75	72	72	72
Net disconnect (%)	11	17	20	20	8	4	16	11

Source: World Bank database.

Note: (i) Exit fiscal year denotes the year in which the project leaves the World Bank's active portfolio, normally at the end of disbursements—percents exclude projects not rated. (ii) The data for fiscal 2005 exits represent a partial lending sample and reflect all IEG project evaluations through June 2006. The processing of the remainder of the fiscal 2005 exits is on-going and is expected to be completed by the end of fiscal 2006.

Table Q.2: Outcomes of Closed Projects in LICUS

	Outcome	Examples
1	Increased amounts of physical infrastructure constructed or rehabilitated (schools, health facilities, roads, power grids, water and drainage works)	The Lao PDR Southern Province Rural Electrification Project connected 51,805 provincial households (exceeding the target of 50,000) through grid extension, and the GEF-supported off-grid component provided electricity to 6,097 households (32% greater than the target of 4,600), mainly through solar home systems and microhydropower. It thereby achieved an electrification ratio in the project provinces of 42%, exceeding significantly the appraisal target of 20%.
		Angola's Social Action Project supported the construction of significant amounts of physical infrastructure: 232 schools; 66 health clinics; 338 water and sanitation facilities; 38 productive and 9 economic subprojects. The output was simple but efficient and cheaper than that funded by other organizations.
2	Improved quality of and access to social services	While Uzbekistan's First Health Project experienced difficulties with some of its components, its objective of improving the quality and cost effectiveness of primary health care services was substantially achieved through the construction, consolidation, and rehabilitation of rural medical centers (SVPs); the upgrading of services (clinical, primary and preventive care, child health services, reproductive health, emergency care, and the provision of drugs, medical supplies, logistical support); and health promotion, including communications equipment, technical assistance, and training. Rehabilitation and equipment of SVPs improved the availability of key primary health care services, with the population's appreciation of these services (proxy for quality) evident in the dramatic increases in use of services offered (prenatal services, vaccination rates) as well as in the results of a survey.
		Despite data inconsistencies and difficulty in attributing outcomes solely to this project, Timor-Leste's Health Sector Rehabilitation and Development Project laid the groundwork for strengthening the quality and quantity of basic primary health care at the district level. The project's objective to provide high-priority primary care via contracted NGOs, improve the supply and logistics of essential drugs, rehabilitate and equip health centers, and strengthen administrative/technical capacity at district and central levels was substantially achieved. Outpatient utilization rates were very encouraging (0.75 visits per capita in 2000 versus 2.13 visits in 2004; target was 2.5 visits), indicating a growing appreciation and trust of government health services by the population as well as the greater availability of health centers.
3	Increased community participation	The Comoros Pilot Agricultural Services Project was restructured at midterm, adding the third and new objective of reinforcing the capacity of local communities and producer groups. While neither of the two original objectives was fully achieved, results from demand-driven productive investments showed significantly increased revenue-generating capacity of small farmers and financing productive investments increased producers' incomes by at least 25 percent. Sixty-one producers' organizations were established as legal entities, and members received training and are fully functioning; 60 private extension agents were trained and 58 subprojects were approved and financed (116 percent of the target), involving about 1,000 farmers in various crop and livestock production initiatives. The actual cost of the project was $2.1 million, making this a cost-efficient learning exercise.
		By financing activities to carry out participatory rural appraisals (PRAs), the objective of Cambodia's Northeast Village Development Project—to introduce a decentralized, participatory poverty-

Outcome	Examples
	focused rural development planning system, starting at the village level with the formation of Village Development Committees (VDCs)—was substantially achieved. The targeting process was satisfactory, VDCs were elected in 120 targeted villages, village-level PRAs were completed, and village action plans were formulated according to the priorities of the villagers. Training was provided to each community and their VDCs, and operation and maintenance committees were organized in participating villages. The objective to gain experience in managing such programs needed by the Cambodian government was also substantially achieved. Technical guidelines on subproject implementation and operations and maintenance were developed, tested, and revised during project implementation, and lessons learned were disseminated through national and provincial-level workshops.
4 Advances in institutional development	Cambodia's Disease Control and Health Development Project resulted in enormous strides in planning, budgeting, and elaboration of specific implementation strategies in all three national disease programs. Health management agreements were set up in all 11 provinces and have become the basis for a realignment of the health system, with national centers responsible for technical direction and strategy and provinces for managing implementation. Substantial capacity building in management and technical areas and effective leadership elevated the National AIDS Office from "a collection of small and scattered donor-supported pilot schemes to a cohesive national program" (ICR) within the Ministry of Health that could spearhead the national response with complete national ownership. Substantial investment in monitoring and evaluation through surveys, surveillances, and outreach programs provided a foundation for and commitment to evidence-based decision making.
	Tajikistan's Institution Building Technical Assistance Project helped the government develop a legal basis for privatization. The project conducted training in privatization procedures and had substantial progress in privatizing small-scale enterprises (95 percent privatized) as well as medium- and large-scale firms (95 percent corporatized and 30 percent privatized). A plan for privatization of the cotton processing and marketing organization was prepared, technical assistance was provided for privatization of 22 cotton ginneries, and MOA was provided with the required legal framework to initiate the farm restructuring program, including land access rights, transfer of these rights, and implementation of farm restructuring. The project also saw: a new banking law implemented, more efficient payment clearing, training in implementing new prudential regulations, a new accounting system, and on-site supervision of banks. Significant progress was made in privatization, the legal basis for private property, and the skills of officials working in these areas. The banking sector was strengthened as a result of a new banking law, better bank supervision, and a payment-clearing system that reduced clearing time from four days to one. Twenty-two state-owned cotton ginneries were prepared for privatization, and a large number of enterprises were privatized.
5 Increased economic stabilization and improved financial management	Guinea-Bissau's Economic Management Credit supported the introduction of prior authorization of expenditure commitments by the Ministry of Economy and Finance and partial integration of recurrent and capital budgets; financed audits of public expenditure procedures identifying

(Continues on the following page.)

Table Q.2: Outcomes of Closed Projects in LICUS (continued)

Outcome	Examples
	actions to strengthen budgetary management; trained staff in West African Economic and Monetary Union (WAEMU) procedures; and enacted a comprehensive tax reform consistent with WAEMU countries. The country's economic management improved by taking several steps: increasing the budgetary revenue/GDP ratio by about 5 percentage points to 15.4 percent of GDP during the same period; improving the current primary balance/GDP ratio by almost 4 percent to 5.5 percent of GDP from 1993 to 1997; liquidating or placing under tender 17 public enterprises and transferring 7 to private management; facilitating accession to the WAEMU; improving technical skills of civil servants in key ministries; and improving the informational and financial management of the civil service. The Democratic Republic of Congo's Economic Recovery Credit aimed to support economic stabilization and structural reforms to lay the basis for recovery within the I-PRSP strategy. The 2003 budget was adopted with improved estimates for public and capital expenditures, the budgeting process was streamlined, communications on fiscal data between the Treasury and the Central Bank were improved, and expenditure tracking systems were created to trace spending to ultimate beneficiaries, particularly to assess poverty reduction expenditures. The independence of the Central Bank was confirmed by a new charter; an audit of the operations of the Central Bank was completed; new legislation was prepared for financial institutions; audits and strategies were completed to determine the liquidation, privatization, or restructuring of several public and private banks; and a financial sector strategy was adopted. With assistance from other donors, the project permitted the DRC to reestablish relations with the international donor community and regain its creditworthiness, due to the clearance of arrears to the Bank and the IMF.

Source: ICR Reviews from the ICR Review and Tracking Database.

Table Q.3: Shortcomings of Closed Projects in LICUS

	Shortcoming	Examples
1	Weak or irrelevant monitoring and evaluation	In Timor-Leste's Community and Local Governance Project, there was inadequate tracking of project outputs, with certain basic output indicators identified by the project—such as number of O/M committees formed—remaining unmonitored. While the project emphasized gender considerations in its design, it failed to prepare gender-disaggregated information concerning the project's beneficiaries. Another aim of the project was to reduce poverty, with a subcomponent set to specifically measure poverty impact, yet no such measurement was undertaken. One of the four revised project objectives in Togo's Lome Urban Development Project sought to alleviate urban poverty. The project design assumed that the beneficiaries would primarily be the urban poor, yet it failed to include indicators to monitor and measure the impact on the poor, resulting in insufficient analysis of whether and to what extent the objective had been achieved.
2	Insufficient understanding of the political environment: project too complex/ambitious for local circumstances and extent of political resistance	In the Comoros Emergency Economic Recovery Credit, although the Bank had identified the risk that the reconciliation process could stall or be reversed, the measure to guard against this risk was only modest. By only requiring stakeholders to express their commitments to the reconciliation process ex ante, the Bank seemed to have seriously underestimated the extent of mistrust and political disagreements between the varying levels of government. This lack of understanding on the Bank's end further spurred on political instability, resulting in limited achievements of the credit's objectives. The Bank overestimated the borrower's ability to carry out Nigeria's Primary Education Project in deteriorating economic and social circumstances. The large-scale cascade model—whereby tertiary institutions would train trainers, who would train education officers, who would train teachers—that was created for teacher training on textbook use and student assessment was too complex and proved impossible to implement in the context of the Nigerian situation. Certain regional initiatives linked to the project could not be carried out because of the highly centralized nature of Nigeria's military government, and extensive governance problems undermined project implementation.
3	Unclear/inappropriate project design, procedures, or poverty targeting at appraisal	The design of São Tomé and Principe's Health and Education Project was flawed. Baseline indicators and quantifiable objectives were not established, and the planned interventions were not clearly linked to stated objectives. The health infrastructure investments, which represented more than half of total project costs (the exact percent is not given in the ICR), were highly inefficient. Constructed drainage canals collapsed during the project's first five years, resulting in their total replacement and project extension. Drainage was, however, not even the correct intervention—as the vector involved prefers small accumulations of clean water—and the number of reported cases of malaria increased approximately 40 percent from 1995 to 2000. Despite the project's heavy emphasis on infrastructure, infrastructure specialists were not included on Bank supervisory teams until September 2000. Tajikistan's Post-Conflict Reconstruction Project had an ambiguous project objective, which was treated differently in different project-related documents. The legal agreement cited the objective as addressing specific post-conflict reconstruction needs in order to restore assets and productivity. According to the MOP and Bank ICR, the objective was to implement the Peace Agreement. And in the borrower ICR, the objective was stated as providing assistance and creating favorable conditions for economic growth in the project area.

(Continues on the following page.)

Table Q.3: Shortcomings of Closed Projects in LICUS (continued)

	Shortcoming	Examples
4	Procurement problems caused by weak ownership, insufficient training on Bank procedures, political interference, and delays in government formation	The borrower did not comply with IDA procurement guidelines in Haiti's Road Maintenance and Rehabilitation Project, which resulted in the formal declaration of 19 contracts as misprocured and the suspension of disbursements from the Credit.
		In Angola's Lobito Benguela Urban Environmental Rehabilitation Project, key project management and procurement decisions were regularly deferred for months because of inadequate communication between the project's management, implementing entities, and IDA.
5	Overestimation of government and local support, capacity, and commitment to project implementation	Papua New Guinea's Emergency El Nino Drought Response Project overestimated the country's institutional capability as well as the commitment to adopt participatory principles. The Bank worked on the false assumption that participating provinces would have the recurrent financial resources to support the project activities. The project's components demanded provincial and district authorities to adopt a more participatory approach to subproject selection and management, yet the two provinces involved demonstrated little eagerness or institutional capacity to do this.
		Unexpected on the Bank side, despite the clearly distinct roles of the federal and state governments, Nigeria's federal government was unwilling to involve local communities in the design of the Small Towns Water Project and failed to devolve ownership to local government and communities. The federal government's unwillingness to pass on completed facilities inhibited the creation of local agreements to operate and manage them. In opposition to the design's intentions, the project further deepened the gulf between the local and federal governments, increasing the mistrust of the former.
6	Delays in implementation and audits	Project implementation for Nigeria's Water Rehabilitation Project was slow from the start. The first civil works contract was not awarded until approximately 30 months after the date of project effectiveness. This was caused by persistent delays in the design and preparation of bidding documents.
		While planned in the project design, Kosovo's Emergency Farm Reconstruction Project did not become effective in time for the first cropping season after the 1999 conflict. The project experienced delays in establishing effective institutional arrangements for implementing the project between the three principal parties (IDA, UNMIK, and FAO).
7	Difficulty in recruiting counterpart staff and heavy dependence on expatriates because of lack of incentives for locals, causing high attrition rates and little institutional memory	The impact of training on MOH capacity and service quality remained limited in Guinea-Bissau's Social Sector Project, as most of those trained under the project left government service because of the war and low pay relative to donors, NGOs, and other countries. Some staff quit after training when they did not receive expected promotions. Lao PDR's District Upland Development and Conservation Project experienced difficulties in its education initiative because of Department of Education tardiness in providing adequate incentives to non-formal education workers in the villages.
		Little capacity was built in the district and provincial agriculture offices, and there was low commitment because of the lack of incentives to cooperate. As a result, the project had problems recruiting provincial and district officers for relocation to the isolated villages and applying existing expertise where it was most needed.

Source: ICR Reviews from the ICR Review and Tracking Database.

Table Q.4: Lessons from Closed Projects in LICUS

1. Projects must be especially flexible in an evolving context of fragile and changing circumstances, with continuous reappraisal to see whether they are still practicable and subsequent restructuring to respond appropriately to new conditions. Conducting rigorous social and economic evaluations can help make important midcourse changes in project design and implementation.

2. In countries with uncertain economic performance and fragile institutions, the Bank should be particularly vigilant in creating objectives realistically calibrated and focused, taking into account the stability of the political system, degree of administrative capacity, and extent to which the government owns the project's objectives. While this may mean the Bank expends more resources over a longer period to achieve the end result, a series of limited successes is better than attempting to attain all desirable goals at once, with all the attendant risks. This is particularly the case when the appraisal team is faced with impending elections with uncertain results.

3. Roles and responsibilities should be clearly articulated when different units are in charge of administration and execution to minimize conflict and disagreements over the use of funds and execution of contracts.

4. Especially in risky circumstances, projects should contain minimal conditions of effectiveness, and conditions that establish satisfactory accounting and financial management systems should be formulated as conditions of Board presentation.

5. Before project effectiveness, the Bank should make an intensive effort to identify clear benchmarks and indicators that are easily measurable by the implementation agencies to make it easy to assess whether implementation is working well; monitoring indicators should reflect incremental stages of achievement and be adapted as necessary during project implementation.

6. The Bank's sustained support is critical to achieving overall development impact and can contribute to developing a strong working relationship with local authorities while attracting other donors to the area.

7. Before agreeing to hire project directors, who may have networks of connections and obligations that conflict with their project-related obligations and may be hard to remove, the Bank should ascertain that these directors can be replaced in their role easily and quickly (even if they retain their position in the public sector).

8. Extensive training of local staff in the Bank's procurement policies and financial management procedures should be planned in the project's design and conducted before start-up to build project implementation capacity and ensure timely disbursement in low-capacity environments. Procurement irregularities can be eliminated if procurement audits are done after the first year of project implementation.

9. Rather than one large project spanning multiple sectors in a country with limited implementation capacity, multiple small loans can be useful instruments to introduce significant reforms on a minor scale in difficult countries and enable learning before scaling up good-practice outcomes.

10. Human Resources should not limit its focus to training; issues such as incentives, career development, public/private partnership, and decentralization also need to be addressed.

Source: ICR Reviews from the ICR Review and Tracking Database.

APPENDIX R: COUNTRY ASSISTANCE EVALUATIONS AND CAS COMPLETION REPORT REVIEWS

Five Country Assistance Evaluations (CAEs) are available for the 25 LICUS. They assess the pre-LICUS Initiative period (1986–2002) and rate all but one country program as moderately unsatisfactory or unsatisfactory (see table R.1). The main reasons are for the unsatisfactory ratings are as follows:

- **Poor assessment of political and governance constraints.** In Haiti, the Bank's objectives were consistent with major economic problems, but relevance was limited by the failure to give highest priority to resolving the political and governance problems that undermined economic development. The poor assessment of political constraints has resulted in excessive optimism on the Bank's part, for example, in Papua New Guinea. In Zimbabwe during 1998–2000, when there were clear signs that the Bank's strategy was not working, the Bank continued to appraise and approve new projects, as well as negotiate the third Structural Adjustment Credit, with poor results.

- **Inadequate assessment of priorities/ timing.** In Zimbabwe, the Public Expenditure Reviews at the end of 1995 came too late to inform the design of the Structural Adjustment Credits, and although many analytical products were completed during the 1990s, there was no substantive analytical work on poverty. In Papua New Guinea, the Bank's attention was inconsistent, with a period of intense activity followed by inactivity. In Cambodia, projects in the areas of agricultural and rural development were not immediately supported despite their importance.

Country Assistance Strategy Completion Report (CASCR) Reviews in Fiscal 2005 LICUS

Of the four IEG CASCR Reviews available thus far for LICUS, and that covered at least part of the period since the start of the LICUS Initiative, three were rated moderately unsatisfactory or unsatisfactory and one was rated moderately satisfactory.

Table R.1: Country Assistance Evaluations for Fiscal 2005 LICUS

Country	CAE date	Period	Outcome	Sustainability	Institutional development impact
Cambodia	11/16/2000	1992–99	Moderately satisfactory	Uncertain	Substantial
Haiti	02/12/2002	1986–2001	Unsatisfactory/highly unsatisfactory	Unlikely	Negligible
Papua New Guinea	03/06/2000	1989–99	Unsatisfactory	Modest	Uncertain
Solomon Islands	03/31/2005	1992–2002	Moderately unsatisfactory	Unlikely	Negligible
Zimbabwe	05/21/2004	1990–2000	Unsatisfactory	Unlikely	Negligible

Note: The CAE and the ratings are for the Pacific member countries group, and not for the Solomon Islands in particular.

APPENDIX S: HUMAN RESOURCE PROPOSALS FOR IMPROVING STAFFING IN LICUS

Staff deployment proposals	Progress
Technical promotion criteria to level GH and the managerial selection criteria to include "demonstrated ability to understand the challenges of the poorest countries and to work effectively in such environments." Announced for implementation in 2003, until 2006 this element is to be considered in the promotion criteria. After 2006, demonstration of this competency is proposed as mandatory for promotion.	Generic criteria for GH technical positions under "qualifications, knowledge, experience and competencies" revised in 2004 as follows: Prior work experience should also include (i) work with significant impact in an LIC or (ii) a country office assignment.
Sector Boards to ensure planned rotation and secondment of senior and experienced task team leaders into supporting roles for LICs where needs are not met through the vacancy management system.	Strategic staffing reviews by Sector Boards to assess the health of the internal and external candidate pipeline, plan for cross-vice presidential unit assignments, plan for (re)-entry into the sector of selected staff, identify knowledge and skill gaps among sector staff, and anticipate vacancies plus plan for targeted external recruitment to strengthen skills, experience, and/or diversity of the sector. No specific mention of identifying staffing priorities for LICUS/LICs.
The Bank will examine ways of lessening the difficulties of safety and travel experienced by staff working on LICs.	The Review of Overseas Assignment Benefits points to the need to make some improvements in the benefits package, particularly in mitigating increased living costs and alleviating hardship conditions. A stronger differentiation of cost of living allowances is suggested to provide a better relation to type of posting, staff salary, grade profile, and family size. Meanwhile, changes to the locality premium are proposed to reflect better the hardship conditions and the shift to assigning more senior staff to overseas assignments. A locality premium of 5 percent for duty stations in LICUS with hardship premiums of 20 percent to 25 percent is also introduced, effective April 1, 2005. Rest and recreation travel for difficult locations is re-introduced.
Introduction of special collaboration between research units (DEC and anchors) and staff working on the poorest countries is proposed so that staff get an opportunity to participate in cutting-edge research and analytical work with the special "spotlight" it provides, including publication of their work.	No evidence.
Tangible actions would be supported by "softer" recognition programs, including spotlighting LIC teams in corporate events, meetings with senior management and the Board, and consideration of introducing specific recognition in the President's Award for Excellence Program.	No evidence.

Source: Interviews with the Bank's Human Resource and other staff, 2005.

APPENDIX T: OPERATIONAL POLICIES AND BANK PROCEDURES RELEVANT TO LICUS

OP/BP	Revised/updated	Coverage
OP/BP 2.30 Development Cooperation and Conflict	December 2003	Covers countries vulnerable to conflict, in conflict, or in transition from conflict. Emphasizes the Bank's focus on reconstruction and development, the importance of working with and through other development partners, especially the UN, and providing exceptional financial assistance to help countries emerging from conflict meet their transitional financial needs in a timely manner (OP 2.30 establishes the case for exceptional post-conflict assistance under IDA 13).
OP/BP 8.50 Emergency Recovery Assistance	Revision under way	Currently covers emergencies defined as "extraordinary event of limited duration, such as war, civil disturbance, or natural disasters." The current objectives of emergency recovery assistance are "to restore assets and production levels in the disrupted economy." Revisions to this OP/BP that are under way include expanding coverage of the OP/BP to all events that (i) have caused, (ii) are likely to cause in the absence of immediate preventive action, or (iii) periodically cause a rapid and major adverse economic and social impact, which requires an urgent response from the government. Revisions to the objectives of economic recovery loans include (i) rebuilding and restoring physical assets; (ii) restoring production and economic activities; (iii) preserving human, institutional, and/or social capital; (iv) restoring social activities; (v) preserving or restoring essential services; and/or (vi) supporting preventive measures designed to mitigate or avert the effects of anticipated imminent or future emergencies.
OP/BP 7.30 De facto Governments	July 2001	Covers operations in countries where a de facto government comes into or remains in power by means not provided for in the country's constitution. Ensures continued engagement as long as the Bank is satisfied that the government: is in effective control of the country; recognizes the country's past international obligations; is willing and able to assume all its predecessor's obligations and ensure continued implementation of Bank loans. New operations require an assessment of the financial/legal exposure of the Bank, the number of countries that have recognized the government, and the position of international organizations toward the de facto government.
OP/BP 6.00 Bank Financing	August 2004	Applies to projects in countries for which the Bank has established country financing parameters. Allows for Bank loan proceeds to finance expenditures (including cost sharing, recurrent costs, local costs, and taxes and duties) necessary to meet the development objectives of operations supported by the loan.

Source: World Bank database.

Background work was undertaken on safeguard compliance in Bank projects in LICUS as part of this review. The methodology, overall findings, and conclusions are presented below.

Methodology

The Bank approved 217 projects in LICUS over fiscal 2000–05, of which 184 were assigned an Environmental Assessment (EA) category in accordance with OP 4.01.[1] A random sample of 25 projects was drawn for analysis, stratified by EA category, age,[2] and project size.[3] For each sample project, a desk review was made of at least the following documents: Project Appraisal Document; Integrated Safeguards Data Sheet; Environmental Impact Assessment (EIA)/ Resettlement Action Plan/Indigenous Peoples' Development Plan (if used); Project Status Reports (PSRs)/supervision Aide Memoire; and ICRs (for completed projects). In selected cases, legal documents and/or Project Implementation Manuals were also consulted.

Overall Findings

- *Quality of Safeguard Compliance at Entry.* Overall quality at entry with respect to safeguard policy compliance for the 25 randomly selected projects in LICUS and approved between fiscal 2000 and 2005 was rated at 88 percent moderately satisfactory or better, which shows that safeguards compliance is relatively good (compared with 70 percent for the community-driven development portfolio), though still somewhat short of the "zero tolerance" policy supposedly in effect.
- *Quality of Safeguard Compliance during Implementation.* For implementation, six Category C projects were not rated, as they did not have

issues requiring attention during project execution. For the remaining 19 projects, safeguards compliance during implementation was rated moderately satisfactory and better for only 37 percent of cases (compared with 35 percent for the CDD portfolio), indicating cause for concern.
- *Overall Rating.* The overall rating was a weighted average of the entry and implementation ratings, taking into account the time from Board approval and the seriousness of the safeguard issues being addressed. Overall, 84 percent of projects were rated moderately satisfactory or better.
- *Grants versus Loans.* Some of the LICUS have circumstances that make them ineligible for regular borrowing from the IBRD or IDA, and projects in these countries are funded through grants (from IDA, trust funds, GEF). Grants (or grant/loan combinations) financed 6 of the 25 sample projects. However, the hypothesis that grant-funded projects are reviewed less diligently for compliance with safeguard policies was not supported; in fact, 100 percent of projects with grants were moderately satisfactory or better on the overall rating compared with 78 percent for IDA credits.
- *Large versus Small Projects.* Larger projects appear to have better safeguard compliance (92 percent moderately satisfactory or better on the overall rating) than smaller ones (72 percent), possibly because the larger projects are in the larger countries, which have somewhat better institutional capacity.

Conclusions

While quality at entry needs some improvement, safeguard compliance during implementation warrants much greater attention by the Bank and borrowers. Despite the 2001 changes to the format of the PSR (now called ISR), which should encourage complete reporting on safeguard issues, reporting on safeguards during implementation remains sparse and inadequate. In the great majority of cases, little or nothing is said on the implementation of agreed-on safeguard measures or on any unforeseen problems. Looking beyond the PSRs to mission Aides Memoire or Back-to-Office reports does little to modify this finding.

For LICUS projects under implementation, Bank management should focus on improved safeguard reporting and should assess the level of training needed for effective monitoring of safeguards. The provisions of emergency lending, which push more of the analysis into the implementation phase, do pose some dangers in light of the generally poor monitoring of compliance in this phase. Given the weak implementation capacity in most of the LICUS, particular attention needs to be given to the design, implementation and oversight of institutional strengthening, capacity development, and monitoring and evaluation systems, with respect to safeguards.

Guidelines	Coverage	Status
Fragile States: Good Practices in Country Assistance Strategies	This paper draws together lessons from country strategy development and implementation in fragile states. The principles and approaches presented in the paper are not intended to be prescriptive, but rather to provide a basic framework and menu of tools to facilitate sharing lessons between countries and regions.	Released December 2005
Good Practice Note for Development Policy Lending in Fragile States	This note provides guidance to task teams in applying development policy lending in the context of fragile states. It argues that development policy lending is appropriate in LICUS that exhibit gradual improvement or those transitioning from conflict/political crisis, but not in LICUS that are experiencing deteriorating governance or prolonged conflict/political crisis.	Released June 2005
Guidelines for Preparation, Review and Clearance of LICUS Country Reengagement Notes (CRNs)	CRNs lay out a short-term strategy for countries where the World Bank is actively reengaging beyond the scope of a Watching Brief, but where it has not yet completed the analytical work and dialogue necessary to formulate a full assistance strategy; or where the conditions are not conducive to a normal TSS or CAS approach. The CRN will normally be followed within one year by an update, a TSS, or a CAS.	Released mid-2003
An Operational Note on Transitional Results Matrices (TRM)—Using Results-Based Frameworks in Fragile States	In settings that do not allow for a full PRSP process, the TRM provides a "quick-and-dirty" tool with which to identify key priorities, measure early results, provide a framework in which to embed assistance programs and capacity-building initiatives, and function as a vehicle for donor coordination in challenging situations—ranging from abundant resources and high expectations (Timor-Leste), to little money and a legacy of mistrust (Central African Republic).	Released January 2005
Fragile States: Early Warning Frameworks and Indicators	The note provides a preliminary framework for thinking about early warning indicators of state fragility. It argues that conflict is not a good predictor of state failure and that an alternative approach would be to examine a state's four core functions as the basic framework for understanding state fragility and state failure: (i) resource generation; (ii) management and governance; (iii) accommodation of political dissent and maintenance of security; and (iv) provision of basic social services and infrastructure. A two-stage functional analysis could potentially yield an effective early warning framework: a risk assessment of a state's structural weakness and a monitoring of short-term conjunctural events likely to precipitate failure. It suggests that, going forward, the focus should be on developing reliable short-term conjunctural indicators for each of the four functions because existing long-term structural indicators are already well developed.	Draft, December 2004
Synthesis Note on Leadership Workshops	Prepared in collaboration with the Poverty Reduction and Economic Management Network, the note summarizes the range of leadership activities undertaken in six countries, drawing on these experiences to identify enabling factors and critical choices for consideration when designing leadership interventions in LICUS. Separate leadership notes have been prepared for each of the six countries.	Released December 2004

Source: Guidance Notes, LICUS Unit, World Bank.

APPENDIX W: OVERVIEW OF THE WORLD BANK INSTITUTE'S LICUS ACTIVITIES

The World Bank Institute (WBI) has steadily increased its activities in the three-year period, 2002–05, and has included work in more than 30 LICUS in governance, public finance, education, environment, health, and monitoring and evaluation. WBI's initiatives have focused mainly on rebuilding and strengthening basic economic, social, institutional, and governance policies, with particular attention to building capacity for better governance and improved service delivery. Weak capacity has presented considerable challenges in these fragile states, and World Bank country teams have turned to WBI to engage in capacity development activities to support the implementation of key reforms.

WBI is working with the government of Haiti, for example, to carry out a countrywide governance diagnostic survey as an input into the country's plan to develop a comprehensive anticorruption strategy. A similar survey has been completed in Guinea, where WBI is helping the government develop a long-term governance strategy. As part of the Bank's Africa Action Plan, WBI has committed to working with up to 10 African countries in devising strategies for improved governance. This will include diagnostic surveys in Burundi, the Democratic Republic of Congo, and Niger, among other countries.

WBI is also working with local training institutes to strengthen their capacity to scale up and support the implementation of key development objectives. In Chad, for example, WBI is helping to strengthen local training institutes, which will play a critical role in helping to build the professionalism of the country's revenue management institutions, ranging from the finance ministry to independent oversight and auditing bodies. In Lao PDR, WBI is working with the national civil servants' training institute, which has the objective of building capacity at the central and provincial levels to implement priority reforms under the PRSP. In addition to training trainers and updating their curricula in public financial management, economic development, and project analysis, WBI has also facilitated twinning arrangements between Lao PDR and international institutions such as the Korea Development Institute.

Other WBI work in LICUS has included leadership training, thematic learning programs, and technical assistance. WBI has jointly organized with the country team a series of leadership events in the Central African Republic aimed at engaging multiple stakeholders in short-term action planning to implement the agreed priorities under the PRSP, and engaging national leaders in an experience-sharing and peer-learning event with fellow leaders who have themselves managed similar situations. Similarly, two leadership events for senior government officials in Tajikistan have been organized to expose leaders to international experience and best practices in promoting key reforms. A third workshop will focus on issues of public sector management and administrative/public expenditure reform.

Source: WBI staff, World Bank.

APPENDIX X: OVERVIEW OF THE DEVELOPMENT ECONOMICS VICE PRESIDENCY'S LICUS ACTIVITIES

Development Economics Vice Presidency (DEC) work on sources of conflict and responses to post-conflict situations is ongoing across the research complex and involves significant collaboration with the International Peace Research Institute in Oslo and with Oxford University. A large part of the research has been funded by the Norwegian government. Current work touches on a number of topics. A sample of the papers under way is highlighted here.

Types and Aspects of Conflict

- Transitional Justice and Sustainable Peace
- Manifestations of Violence: Civil Wars, Coups, and Others
- Population Size, Concentration, and Civil War. A Geographically Disaggregated Analysis
- What Is Civil War?

Fragile States and Peace Building

- Interim Institutions and the Development Process: Strategies for Pro-Poor Judicial Reform in Cambodia
- Beyond Fractionalization: Mapping Ethnicity onto Nationalist Insurgencies
- Military Expenditure in Post-Conflict Societies
- Post-Conflict Risks of Conflict Resumption
- Post-Conflict Risks
- The Long-Term Legacy of the Khmer Rouge Period in Cambodia
- Poverty, Social Divisions, and Conflict in Nepal
- DDR and Optimal Aid Allocation in Post-Conflict Countries
- Cheap Guns, More War? The Economics of Small Arms

- Propensity to Civil Disobedience and the Probability of an Armed Struggle in Niger Delta Region of Nigeria
- Neighboring States, Conflict, and Instability
- Systems of Violence in Post-Conflict Societies
- Alternative Measures and Estimates of Peace-Building Success
- Disarming Fears of Diversity: Ethnic Heterogeneity and State Militarization, 1988–2002

Democracy and Conflict

- Moral Hazard, Adverse Selection, and Power Sharing
- Democratic Jihad? Military Intervention and Democracy
- Credible Commitment and Insurgency in Democracies and Autocracies
- Walking the Tightrope: Extending the Franchise in the Presence of Political Competition
- Political Institutions, Horizontal Inequalities, and Civil Conflict

Macro- and Microeconomic Policy Choices in Post-Conflict Countries

- Rwandan Crop Failure and Rural Coping Mechanisms
- Post-Conflict Capital Flight and Return
- Are Non-Poor Households Always Less Vulnerable? The Case of Households Exposed to Protracted Civil War in Southern Sudan
- The Demand for Money around the End of Civil Wars
- Scaling-Up Aid, Real Exchange Rate, and Catch-up Growth in Post-Conflict Countries
- The Aftermath of Civil Wars: An Event-Study Approach to Post-Conflict Transitions

Source: DEC staff, World Bank.

APPENDIX Y: DONOR RELATIONSHIPS

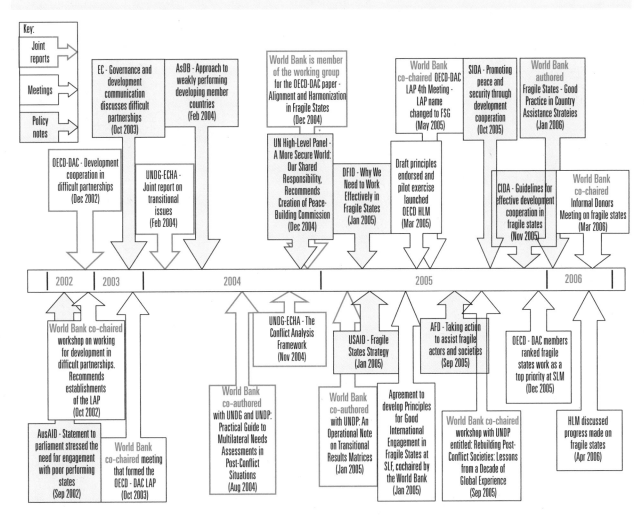

Calendar of major events and key policy papers on fragile states, 2002–06

Key:
- Joint reports
- Meetings
- Policy notes

EC - Governance and development communication discusses difficult partnerships (Oct 2003)

AsDB - Approach to weakly performing developing member countries (Feb 2004)

World Bank is member of the working group for the OECD-DAC paper - Alignment and Harmonization in Fragile States (Dec 2004)

World Bank co-chaired OECD-DAC LAP 4th Meeting - LAP name changed to FSG (May 2005)

SIDA - Promoting peace and security through development cooperation (Oct 2005)

World Bank authored Fragile States - Good Practice in Country Assistance Strateies (Jan 2006)

OECD-DAC - Development cooperation in difficult partnerships (Dec 2002)

UNDG-ECHA - Joint report on transitional issues (Feb 2004)

UN High-Level Panel - A More Secure World: Our Shared Responsibility, Recommends Creation of Peace-Building Commission (Dec 2004)

DFID - Why We Need to Work Effectively in Fragile States (Jan 2005)

Draft principles endorsed and pilot exercise launched OECD HLM (Mar 2005)

CIDA - Guidelines for effective development cooperation in fragile states (Nov 2005)

World Bank co-chaired Informal Donors Meeting on fragile states (Mar 2006)

| 2002 | 2003 | 2004 | 2005 | 2006 |

World Bank co-chaired workshop on working for development in difficult partnerships. Recommends establishments of the LAP (Oct 2002)

UNDG-ECHA - The Conflict Analysis Framework (Nov 2004)

USAID - Fragile States Strategy (Jan 2005)

AFD - Taking action to assist fragile actors and societies (Sep 2005)

OECD - DAC members ranked fragile states work as a top priority at SLM (Dec 2005)

AusAID - Statement to parliament stressed the need for engagement with poor performing states (Sep 2002)

World Bank co-chaired meeting that formed the OECD - DAC LAP (Oct 2003)

World Bank co-authored with UNDG and UNDP: Practical Guide to Multilateral Needs Assessments in Post-Conflict Situations (Aug 2004)

World Bank co-authored with UNDP: An Operational Note on Transitional Results Matrices (Jan 2005)

Agreement to develop Principles for Good International Engagement in Fragile States at SLF, cochaired by the World Bank (Jan 2005)

World Bank co-chaired workshop with UNDP entitled: Rebuilding Post-Conflict Societies: Lessons from a Decade of Global Experience (Sep 2005)

HLM discussed progress made on fragile states (Apr 2006)

Source: LICUS Unit, OPCS, World Bank.

Note: AFD = Agence Francaise de Developpement (French Development Agency), AsDB = Asian Development Bank, AusAID = Australian Agency for International Development, DFID = U.K. Department for International Development, EC = European Commission, FSG = Fragile States Group, HLM = High-level meeting, LAP = Learning and Advisory Process (changed name to Fragile States Group in May 2005), OECD-DAC = Organisation for Economic Co-operation and Development, Development Assistance Committee, SIDA = Swedish International Development Agency, SLF = Senior-level forum, UN-ECHA = United Nations Executive Committee on Humanitarian Assistance, UNDG = United Nations Development Group, UNDP = United Nations Development Programme, USAID = United States Agency for International Development.

As part of this review, three groups of stakeholders were surveyed—Bank staff (including both those in the field and at headquarters), other donors (including international donors and international NGOs), and in-country stakeholders (including government officials, local NGO staff, academics/researchers, and private sector individuals). The aim of the survey was to elicit stakeholder views on the relevance and effectiveness of the Bank's LICUS approach. The Bank staff survey was administered to 1,237 Bank staff working on the 25 LICUS. Bank staff included country staff, sector staff, and network anchor staff as covered in the standard distribution lists of staff working on LICUS. Other donor staff and in-country stakeholders were identified by country directors of each of the 25 LICUS. The survey was sent to all 141 other donor staff and 146 in-country stakeholders identified by the respective country directors. If Bank staff and donor staff worked on more than one LICUS country, they were instructed to answer the survey for the LICUS which they most focused on.

Table Z.1 presents the response rates for each stakeholder group. Thirty-one percent of Bank staff (382), 35 percent (49) of other donor staff,

Table Z.1: Response Rate

	Open surveys[a]	Total sample	Response rate (%)
In-country	24	146	16.4
Donors	49	141	34.8
Bank staff	382	1,237	30.9

a. Number of stakeholders who started the survey but who may not necessarily have completed it, although most did.

and 16 percent (24) of in-country stakeholders responded to the survey. A few adjustments were made to the final data for the analysis: (i) if local NGOs attempted the donor survey, they were moved to the in-country stakeholder group; (ii) stakeholders that attempted only the profile section or less were dropped from the analysis. The two adjustments resulted in 328 Bank staff, 43 donor, and 25 in-country stakeholder surveys. Tables Z.2 and Z.3 present the details by each question for each stakeholder group. *The response rate calculations in this review drop all missing entries, "not applicable" entries, and "do not know" entries from the denominator.*

141

Table Z.2: Responses by Stakeholder Group (total number of respondents)

Question	Response	World Bank	Donors	In-country
I. Respondent Profile (not reported here)				
II. Your Views about the Effectiveness of World Bank Support				
Q1 To what extent do you think World Bank lending and grant support through projects or programs to the LICUS country you most focus on/your country				
Q1.a Has been timely?	To a large extent	109	4	3
	To a moderate extent	118	21	10
	To a slight extent	50	10	6
	Not at all	22	5	2
	Do not know	24	2	2
	Missing	5	1	2
Q1.b Has had an influence on government policies?	To a large extent	66	7	7
	To a moderate extent	126	18	8
	To a slight extent	86	12	6
	Not at all	23	5	1
	Do not know	19	0	1
	Missing	8	1	2
Q1.c Has been coordinated with other donor support?	To a large extent	132	6	4
	To a moderate extent	105	18	9
	To a slight extent	56	14	8
	Not at all	10	4	0
	Do not know	16	0	2
	Missing	9	1	2
Q1.d Has achieved its intended results?	To a large extent	32	2	1
	To a moderate extent	144	12	9
	To a slight extent	82	20	11
	Not at all	13	4	1
	Do not know	49	4	2
	Missing	8	1	1
Q2 To what extent do you think World Bank nonlending support through analytical work to the LICUS country you most focus on/your country				
Q2.a Has been timely?	To a large extent	92	9	6
	To a moderate extent	134	24	9
	To a slight extent	47	4	5
	Not at all	15	1	1
	Do not know	33	4	2
	Missing	7	1	2
Q2.b Has had an influence on government policies?	To a large extent	52	6	6
	To a moderate extent	123	17	8
	To a slight extent	86	13	6

Question		Response	World Bank	Donors	In-country
		Not at all	24	4	2
		Do not know	33	2	0
		Missing	10	1	3
Q2.c	Has been coordinated with other donor support?	To a large extent	93	8	2
		To a moderate extent	105	16	9
		To a slight extent	79	10	7
		Not at all	9	7	1
		Do not know	31	1	4
		Missing	11	1	2
Q2.d	Has achieved its intended results?	To a large extent	32	3	3
		To a moderate extent	121	12	7
		To a slight extent	93	20	11
		Not at all	16	3	0
		Do not know	52	4	3
		Missing	14	1	1
Q2.e	Has had an influence on the Bank's own assistance strategy for the country?	To a large extent	105	10	6
		To a moderate extent	130	15	8
		To a slight extent	32	6	3
		Not at all	15	2	0
		Do not know	33	9	6
		Missing	13	1	2
Q3	To what extent do you think World Bank nonlending support through policy dialogue to the LICUS country you most focus on/your country				
Q3.a	Has been timely?	To a large extent	103	9	3
		To a moderate extent	128	20	10
		To a slight extent	45	8	6
		Not at all	10	2	2
		Do not know	26	3	1
		Missing	16	1	3
Q3.b	Has had an influence on government policies?	To a large extent	52	6	3
		To a moderate extent	136	17	11
		To a slight extent	80	12	5
		Not at all	17	6	2
		Do not know	22	1	2
		Missing	21	1	2
Q3.c	Has been coordinated with other donor support?	To a large extent	98	10	0
		To a moderat extent	122	14	9
		To a slight extent	55	13	9
		Not at all	9	3	1

(*Continues on the following page.*)

Table Z.2: Responses by Stakeholder Group (total number of respondents) (continued)

Question		Response	World Bank	Donors	In-country
		Do not know	25	2	4
		Missing	19	1	2
Q3.d	Has achieved its intended results?	To a large extent	24	1	1
		To a moderate extent	134	18	7
		To a slight extent	89	17	7
		Not at all	16	2	2
		Do not know	45	3	5
		Missing	20	2	3
Q3.e	Has had an influence on the Bank's own assistance strategy for the country?	To a large extent	96	9	3
		To a moderate extent	123	16	7
		To a slight extent	47	5	7
		Not at all	12	4	1
		Do not know	28	8	5
		Missing	22	1	2
Q4	To what extent do you think World Bank non-lending support through technical assistance to the LICUS country you most focus on/your country				
Q4.a	Has been timely?	To a large extent	74	4	6
		To a moderate extent	129	23	7
		To a slight extent	53	5	6
		Not at all	14	4	2
		Do not know	34	6	1
		Missing	24	1	3
Q4.b	Has had an influence on government policies?	To a large extent	36	5	4
		To a moderate extent	117	12	8
		To a slight extent	97	16	8
		Not at all	21	6	0
		Do not know	32	3	3
		Missing	25	1	2
Q4.c	Has been coordinated with other donor support?	To a large extent	72	4	0
		To a moderate extent	103	19	7
		To a slight extent	82	12	12
		Not at all	8	4	0
		Do not know	36	3	4
		Missing	27	1	2
Q4.d	Has achieved its intended results?	To a large extent	30	1	2
		To a moderate extent	113	12	8
		To a slight extent	96	19	9
		Not at all	17	5	0
		Do not know	47	5	4
		Missing	25	1	2

Question		Response	World Bank	Donors	In-country
Q4.e	Has had an influence on the Bank's own assistance strategy for the country?	To a large extent	53	4	3
		To a moderate extent	130	18	9
		To a slight extent	66	5	3
		Not at all	16	3	0
		Do not know	36	11	7
		Missing	27	2	3
Q5	To what extent has the World Bank's work in the LICUS country you most focus on/your country been adequately grounded in an understanding of the country's politics?	To a large extent	113	11	6
		To a moderate extent	135	18	12
		To a slight extent	47	10	4
		Not at all	10	3	1
		Do not know	10	0	0
		Missing	13	1	2
Q6	To what extent has the World Bank supported a focused reform agenda consisting of key actions and reforms in the LICUS country you most focus on/your country?	To a large extent	100	13	8
		To a moderate extent	127	13	9
		To a slight extent	53	10	2
		Not at all	10	3	2
		Do not know	16	3	1
		Missing	22	1	3
Q7	In general, what contribution have the reforms supported by the World Bank made to development in the LICUS country you most focus on/your country?	Large positive contribution	60	6	4
		Small positive contribution	202	27	16
		No contribution	16	3	1
		Small negative contribution	2	1	0
		Large negative contribution	0	1	0
		Do not know	27	4	1
		Missing	21	1	3
Q8	If the World Bank has used nongovernmental or semi-autonomous arrangements to deliver services, what effect have they had on service delivery in the LICUS country you most focus on/your country?	Large positive effect	51	10	7
		Small positive effect	115	11	13
		No effect	15	3	0
		Small negative effect	7	2	1
		Large negative effect	2	0	0
		Do not know	55	9	1
		Not Applicable	54	6	1
		Missing	29	2	2
Q9	What effect have the nongovernmental or semi-autonomous arrangements supported by the World Bank had on the development of long-term government capacity in the LICUS country you most focus on?	Large positive effect	25	5	3
		Small positive effect	97	10	16
		No effect	48	10	1
		Small negative effect	12	1	1
		Large negative effect	7	0	0
		Do not know	56	9	1
		Missing	83	8	3

(Continues on the following page.)

Table Z.2: Responses by Stakeholder Group (total number of respondents) (continued)

Question		Response	World Bank	Donors	In-country
Q10	Overall, what contribution has the World Bank's assistance made in helping to develop long-term government capacity in the LICUS country you most focus on/your country?	Large positive contribution	54	5	6
		Small positive contribution	199	26	14
		No contribution	20	8	2
		Small negative contribution	3	0	0
		Large negative contribution	0	1	0
		Do not know	23	1	1
		Missing	29	2	2
Q11	To what extent has the World Bank adequately pursued collaboration with other donors in the LICUS country you most focus on/your country?	To a large extent	147	11	4
		To a moderate extent	109	15	13
		To a slight extent	30	10	3
		Not at all	0	3	0
		Do not know	15	1	3
		Missing	27	3	2
Q12	To what extent has the World Bank adequately pursued collaboration with international partners in the diplomatic, peace-building, and peace-keeping areas in the LICUS country you most focus on/your country?	To a large extent	116	9	7
		To a moderate extent	85	8	10
		To a slight extent	42	9	1
		Not at all	9	1	0
		Do not know	30	5	4
		Not applicable	17	5	1
		Missing	29	6	2
Q13	To what extent has the World Bank clearly defined what constitutes "success" in the LICUS country you most focus on/your country?	To a large extent	45	2	3
		To a moderate extent	144	16	13
		To a slight extent	57	7	3
		Not at all	29	8	1
		Do not know	25	5	3
		Missing	28	5	2
Q14	To what extent has the World Bank defined clear and monitorable indicators to measure "success" in the LICUS country you most focus on/your country?	To a large extent	48	7	5
		To a moderate extent	128	11	10
		To a slight extent	74	8	5
		Not at all	19	5	0
		Do not know	24	9	2
		Missing	35	3	3
Q15	With what frequency has progress toward "success" been monitored by the World Bank in the LICUS country you most focus on/your country?	Frequently or twice a year	101	11	9
		Once a year	93	12	6
		Once in 2 years	30	2	2
		Never	19	5	1
		Don't know	23	6	2
		NA since no indicator	4	2	1
		New project	3	1	0
		Adhoc	4	1	0

Question		Response	World Bank	Donors	In-country
		Based on project agreement	1	0	0
		Missing	50	3	4
III. Your Views about the Relevance and Evolution of the World Bank's Approach					
Q1	In the last three years, to what extent has the World Bank's approach to development been relevant to the key issues facing the LICUS country you most focus on/your country?	To a large extent	110	13	2
		To a moderate extent	115	14	12
		To a slight extent	50	8	3
		Not at all	5	3	0
		Do not know	14	0	2
		Not applicable	2	2	1
		Missing	32	3	5
Q2	Still thinking about the last three years, what change has there been in the World Bank's approach to development in the LICUS country you most focus on/your country				
Q2.a	Effectiveness of lending and grant support (through projects or programs)	Large positive change	58	5	4
		Small positive change	143	16	14
		No change	42	10	3
		Small negative change	4	2	0
		Large negative change	1	0	0
		Do not know	26	5	0
		Missing	54	5	4
Q2.b	Effectiveness of nonlending support (through analytical work, policy dialogue, and technical assistance)	Large positive change	60	10	4
		Small positive change	139	17	14
		No change	45	6	1
		Small negative change	4	1	0
		Large negative change	0	1	1
		Do not know	27	4	2
		Missing	53	4	3
Q2.c	Grounding of World Bank work in an understanding of the country's politics	Large positive change	70	11	8
		Small positive change	114	16	7
		No change	64	7	3
		Small negative change	6	2	1
		Large negative change	0	1	0
		Do not know	22	2	2
		Missing	52	4	4
Q2.d	Support for a more focused reform agenda consisting of key actions and reforms	Large positive change	67	10	7
		Small positive change	118	14	9
		No change	66	8	4
		Small negative change	3	2	0
		Large negative change	1	1	0

(Continues on the following page.)

Table Z.2: Responses by Stakeholder Group (total number of respondents) (continued)

Question		Response	World Bank	Donors	In-country
		Do not know	21	3	1
		Missing	52	5	4
Q2.e	Attention to building long-term government capacity	Large positive change	60	5	6
		Small positive change	124	19	12
		No change	67	9	3
		Small negative change	6	1	0
		Do not know	18	4	1
		Missing	53	5	3
Q2.f	Effectiveness in pursuing donor collaboration by the World Bank	Large positive change	97	12	5
		Small positive change	120	14	11
		No change	33	6	1
		Small negative change	1	1	0
		Large negative change	1	0	0
		Do not know	23	5	3
		Missing	53	5	5
IV. Your Knowledge of the World Bank's LICUS Approach					
Q1	To what extent are you familiar with the World Bank's LICUS approach?	To a large extent	82	7	3
		To a moderate extent	132	16	10
		To a slight extent	55	11	6
		Not at all	15	4	2
		Missing	44	5	4
V. Your Overall Impressions					
Q1	In your opinion, to what extent are World Bank staff who work on the LICUS country you most focus on/your country competent?	To a large extent	132	22	7
		To a moderate extent	99	8	11
		To a slight extent	27	3	3
		Not at all	3	2	0
		Do not know	19	3	0
		Missing	48	5	4
Q2	What contribution has the World Bank's field office made in supporting the development of the LICUS country you most focus on/your country?	Large positive contribution	150	14	5
		Small positive contribution	101	16	16
		No contribution	11	4	0
		Small negative contribution	4	2	0
		Large negative contribution	0	1	0
		Do not know	14	1	0
		Missing	48	5	4

Question		Response	World Bank	Donors	In-country
Q3	What contribution have the visiting World Bank missions made in supporting the development of the LICUS country you most focus on/your country?	Large positive contribution	123	9	10
		Small positive contribution	118	19	10
		No contribution	6	4	1
		Small negative contribution	5	2	0
		Do not know	25	4	1
		Missing	51	5	3
Q4	What contribution has the World Bank's overall program made in supporting the development of the LICUS country you most focus on/your country?	Large positive contribution	83	11	7
		Small positive contribution	159	20	13
		No contribution	14	1	2
		Small negative contribution	1	1	0
		Large negative contribution	0	1	0
		Do not know	17	4	0
		Missing	54	5	3
Q5	In comparison with other donors, has the contribution of the World Bank's overall program in supporting the development of the LICUS country you most focus on/your country been:	Greater	148	14	5
		Equal	64	12	9
		Smaller	30	10	4
		Do not know	24	2	4
		Missing	62	5	3
Q6	Without World Bank support, do you think the development of the LICUS country you most focus on/your country would have been:	Greater	2	1	0
		Equal	32	8	5
		Smaller	205	27	14
		Do not know	26	2	3
		Missing	63	5	3
Total number of respondents			328	43	25

Table Z.3: Responses of the World Bank Staff on Internal World Bank Support for LICUS Work

Question		Response	World Bank (N = 328)
Q1	To what extent do you think the Bank's operational policies and procedures listed below are adapted to the low capacity or higher risk environment of the LICUS country you most focus on?		
Q1.a	Project preparation	To a large extent	40
		To a moderate extent	86
		To a slight extent	66
		Not at all	51
		Don't know	20
		Missing	65
Q1.b	Project supervision	To a large extent	43
		To a moderate extent	77
		To a slight extent	70
		Not at all	46
		Don't know	24
		Missing	68
Q1.c	Procurement procedures	To a large extent	27
		To a moderate extent	61
		To a slight extent	75
		Not at all	67
		Don't know	30
		Missing	68
Q1.d	Financial management procedures	To a large extent	32
		To a moderate extent	66
		To a slight extent	79
		Not at all	50
		Don't know	34
		Missing	67
Q1.e	Legal framework	To a large extent	28
		To a moderate extent	62
		To a slight extent	72
		Not at all	54
		Don't know	43
		Missing	69
Q2	Is the overall level of Bank Budget (BB) available to the LICUS country you most focus on adequate given the opportunities and challenges facing the country?	More than adequate	11
		Adequate	68
		Less than adequate	159
		Don't know	21
		Missing	69

Question		Response	World Bank (N = 328)
Q3	To what extent has the Bank's lending and grant support (through projects or programs) in the country you most focus on been given adequate Bank budget and senior management attention for the following:		
Q3.a	Been given adequate Bank Budget (BB) relative to other priorities	To a large extent	45
		To a moderate extent	77
		To a slight extent	69
		Not at all	45
		Don't know	25
		Missing	67
Q3.b	Attracted adequate senior management attention or involvement	To a large extent	66
		To a moderate extent	81
		To a slight extent	75
		Not at all	18
		Don't know	19
		Missing	69
Q4	To what extent has the Bank's non-lending support (through analytical work, policy dialogue, and technical assistance) in the country you most focus on been given adequate Bank budget and senior management attention for the following:		
Q4.a	Been given adequate Bank Budget (BB) relative to other priorities	To a large extent	34
		To a moderate extent	83
		To a slight extent	74
		Not at all	34
		Don't know	30
		Missing	73
Q4.b	Attracted adequate senior management attention or involvement	To a large extent	44
		To a moderate extent	84
		To a slight extent	75
		Not at all	20
		Don't know	32
		Missing	73
Q5	When working on a LICUS country, what has been your experience in each of the following human resource matters? Have the following improved, remained the same, or worsened:		
Q5.a	Your overall career prospects in the Bank (promotions, obtaining good jobs in the future, etc.)	Improved	41
		Remained the same	134
		Worsened	38
		Don't know	49
		Missing	66

(Continues on the following page.)

Table Z.3: Responses of the World Bank Staff on Internal World Bank Support for LICUS Work (continued)

Question		Response	World Bank (N = 328)
Q5.b	Your overall financial compensation (salary increases, hardship allowances, etc.)	Improved	23
		Remained the same	186
		Worsened	21
		Don't know	32
		Missing	66
Q5.c	Realism in expectations by Bank Management about what can be accomplished	Improved	41
		Remained the same	149
		Worsened	39
		Don't know	32
		Missing	67
Q5.d	Level of support from Bank Management	Improved	50
		Remained the same	155
		Worsened	33
		Don't know	22
		Missing	68
Q5.e	Efforts made by the Bank to ensure your personal security and safety	Improved	91
		Remained the same	126
		Worsened	20
		Don't know	24
		Missing	67
Q6	To what extent has the Bank's LICUS Unit been effective with regard to:		
Q6.a	Providing access to Trust Funds for LICUS	To a large extent	40
		To a moderate extent	57
		To a slight extent	37
		Not at all	28
		Don't know	93
		Missing	73
Q6.b	Providing substantive support for country strategy development and implementation	To a large extent	35
		To a moderate extent	55
		To a slight extent	48
		Not at all	29
		Don't know	87
		Missing	74
Q6.c	Providing substantive support for projects	To a large extent	19
		To a moderate extent	55
		To a slight extent	46
		Not at all	44
		Don't know	89
		Missing	75

Question		Response	World Bank (N = 328)
Q6.d	Providing substantive support for research or analytical work	To a large extent	20
		To a moderate extent	52
		To a slight extent	53
		Not at all	44
		Don't know	85
		Missing	74
Q6.e	Unlocking procedural or policy difficulties at Headquarters	To a large extent	13
		To a moderate extent	47
		To a slight extent	52
		Not at all	50
		Don't know	91
		Missing	75
Q6.f	Facilitating donor collaboration and harmonization advice	To a large extent	33
		To a moderate extent	42
		To a slight extent	45
		Not at all	43
		Don't know	92
		Missing	73
Q6.g	Getting visibility and support from Senior Management	To a large extent	25
		To a moderate extent	55
		To a slight extent	42
		Not at all	38
		Don't know	91
		Missing	77
Q7	To what extent is the technical input you get from WBI:		
Q7.a	Sufficient	To a large extent	17
		To a moderate extent	37
		To a slight extent	38
		Not at all	77
		Don't know	82
		Missing	77
Q7.b	Of good quality	To a large extent	23
		To a moderate extent	40
		To a slight extent	32
		Not at all	64
		Don't know	90
		Missing	79
Q7.c	Timely	To a large extent	20
		To a moderate extent	34
		To a slight extent	34

(Continues on the following page.)

Table Z.3: Responses of the World Bank Staff on Internal World Bank Support for LICUS Work (continued)

Question		Response	World Bank (N = 328)
		Not at all	70
		Don't know	93
		Missing	77
Q8	To what extent is the technical input you get from DEC:		
Q8.a	Sufficient	To a large extent	10
		To a moderate extent	26
		To a slight extent	34
		Not at all	62
		Don't know	111
		Missing	85
Q8.b	Of good quality	To a large extent	20
		To a moderate extent	38
		To a slight extent	20
		Not at all	47
		Don't know	117
		Missing	86
Q8.c	Timely	To a large extent	10
		To a moderate extent	21
		To a slight extent	31
		Not at all	61
		Don't know	116
		Missing	89
Q9	Does the support of the Bank's LICUS Unit complement, duplicate, or conflict with that of the Conflict Prevention and Reconstruction Unit?	Complementary support	33
		Some duplication	34
		Lot of duplication	14
		Conflicting/contradiction	11
		Don't know	156
		Missing	80

APPENDIX AA: STATEMENT BY THE EXTERNAL ADVISORY PANEL

The Panel welcomes this rich and thought-provoking report and the opportunity to share some of its impressions. The subject—how to manage support by the donor community to LICUS—is of major importance, given the number of fragile states, the hardships endured by their inhabitants, and the spillovers to neighbors, as well as the fact that in certain instances such states may form a breeding ground for terrorism.

The Bank and other members of the international donor community have grappled for several years now with the question of how to help LICUS emerge from their frequently desperate situations. Given the defining characteristics of LICUS, weakness of governance, institutions, and policies, and the outcome of earlier research and experience that financial assistance against such a background tends to be ineffective, it was clear that useful engagement with these countries would require a new framework. The Bank is to be commended for having played and for continuing to play a leading role in developing such a framework.

The Panel was impressed by the methodology of the IEG report. It believes that the right questions have been asked and that the combination of analysis, common sense, and the underpinning of findings by wide-flung surveys has resulted in highly relevant lessons and recommendations. To no small extent this is also thanks to interaction with management that has clearly been fruitful.

While one may argue in general with a rush to evaluate before the necessary data are available, in this case an evaluation with a carefully restricted scope is very useful. The report is right to point out that the question of ultimate effectiveness of Bank interventions cannot yet be addressed.

However, in our language, effectiveness in the more limited sense of whether the Bank has been doing what it says it wishes to do and whether this can be done better is worth examining now, as is the question of the relevance of the formal determinants of LICUS and of their performance. Addressing these questions rigorously is essential to assess later, when adequate data are available, whether the approach chosen delivers acceptable outcomes in the use of scarce development resources.

The Bank has made commendable progress in its engagement with LICUS and in the performance of closed projects (see chapter 2 and appendix Q). However, the donor community has shifted the goal posts for intervention with the relatively recent, intensified, and explicit focus on state building and, where relevant, conflict prevention. This shift is logical in the context of the problems posed by LICUS. The Panel agrees with IEG, however, that the Bank needs to undertake major efforts to fit in with the new focus.

While the narrowing of the focus to state and peace building should induce the Bank to move away from overly broad reform agendas, which "do not augur well for effectiveness," the Bank's effectiveness in the area of governance and capacity building needs to be improved. IEG is right to recommend that the Bank spell out concrete strategies and policies for this purpose. That, at the country level, strategies need to be underpinned by internalized socio/political analysis may appear self-evident, but in practice proves to be difficult. Without such analysis, Bank engagement as well as that of other donors runs the risk of being ineffective and wasteful of resources. Without wishing to attribute responsibility, the recent experience in Timor-Leste appears to illustrate the point.

IEG also rightly stresses that capacity building must be a major part of state-building programs and that the Bank's track record indicates a need to strengthen the design and delivery thereof. The lesson that country ownership and absorptive-capacity constraints apply as much to knowledge products as to financial products does not make the challenge any easier. The Panel is convinced that unless weaknesses in state and capacity building are overcome, future outcomes will be disappointing, distorting judgments on the usefulness of multilateral and bilateral donor support to LICUS.

The joint responsibility of donors in the areas of state building and conflict prevention and across the range of issues involved in supporting LICUS once again leads to an obvious lesson: the need for donors to coordinate to provide more effective support jointly and severally. And once again the simple lesson is difficult to translate into systematic practice at the country level. Yet, as IEG's report brings out, the failure to do so can mean the difference between a whole that is larger or smaller than the sum of the parts, between effective and ineffective support.

The Panel agrees with IEG on the importance of further work on criteria by which to identify LICUS and on the need for a break-down by business models. Similarly, performance indicators require elaboration in order to determine the kinds and amounts of support to be given. Post-conflict LICUS are already treated very differently from the others, and have proven to be fertile recipients of certain kinds of financial aid. Careful specification could also strengthen decision making vis-à-vis resource-rich countries. Moreover, without such criteria and indicators, monitoring and evaluation will not have at its disposal the toeholds needed for learning adequately from experience and for timely adjustment of country strategies.

The Panel agrees with the lessons drawn on how to improve the Bank's internal organization to meet the challenges posed by LICUS more effectively. Criteria for successful performance of staff in LICUS, where the traditional criteria only partly apply, need to be elaborated. Also, IEG's point is well taken that the selection of people for work on LICUS must take account of their willingness and ability to communicate and collaborate effectively inside the Bank and with other donors and the recipients.

The Panel has high regard for how the Bank has immersed itself in the challenging and risky area of support for LICUS. It welcomes the positive interaction between practice and evaluation, as evinced in the present report. In the Panel's view, IEG's comments are balanced and its recommendations sensible. Implementing them will not be easy, but is necessary to improve the effectiveness of Bank support to LICUS, as well as that of other donors. We would be surprised if further progress based on inescapable realities does not materialize. Such progress is all the more necessary because the tipping point between success and failure with equal effort lies much closer to failure in LICUS than in other countries. Adoption of the eminently practical lessons and recommendations of IEG can shift the tipping point onto more favorable terrain. The possibility of emergence from extreme fragility of the state and the associated misery of its inhabitants will be greatly enhanced.

Olayinka Creighton-Randall
Former Coordinator of the Campaign for Good Governance
Freetown, Sierra Leone

John Githongo
Senior Associate Member St. Antony's College
Oxford, United Kingdom

Gunnar Sørbø
Director Chr. Michelsen Institute
Bergen, Norway

Pieter Stek
Former Executive Director of the World Bank Group
Ohain, Belgium

APPENDIX BB: MANAGEMENT RESPONSE

Introduction

Management welcomes IEG's review of the effectiveness of Bank support to Low-Income Countries Under Stress (LICUS) and is grateful for the review team's effort to incorporate many of management's comments in the review. As the review indicates, fragile states represent a critical challenge for the Bank and other development actors and make up an increasingly significant segment of the Bank's portfolio. The review provides useful analysis of a wide range of issues and contributes substance to the Bank's understanding of difficult engagements in fragile states. Management also notes that early conclusions of the IEG evaluation were useful in feeding in to the Good Practice Note on Country Assistance Strategies in fragile states (World Bank 2005e) and would like to thank the IEG team for its close cooperation in this regard.

As the review notes, the Bank has played a leading role in global policy development on fragile states. In pointing to several areas for future improvement, the review reinforces important messages for the Bank's engagement in fragile states that were set out in the LICUS Update (World Bank 2005h), which the Board endorsed on January 17, 2006. Management therefore agrees with IEG on many of the principles and ideas raised in the review, some of which have been the subject of *Fragile States: Good Practices for Country Assistance Strategies* and other guidance and good practice notes issued by OPCS. (By way of illustration, Attachment A provides a matrix showing key issues raised in the review and guidance on that issue that has been provided in one of the notes issued by the Fragile States Group [formerly the LICUS Unit] in OPCS.)

Key Issues of Agreement and Divergence

This Management Response first outlines the areas in which management agrees with the review and then discusses areas in which management believes that IEG has missed critical factors or could have given a fuller account of efforts the Bank is already making.

A. Areas of agreement

Management agrees with many of the review's findings, and the review serves as a powerful, targeted, and well-timed renewal of these arguments. Indeed, many of the areas are already part of an ongoing work program.

Improved institutional response. Management concurs with IEG's diagnosis of the various institutional bottlenecks where the Bank needs to redouble its efforts to restructure for a better performance. Increased field presence in fragile states, better incentives and skills development for staff, and improved surge capacity are all critical challenges that the review correctly highlights; these were areas of attention at the January 2006 Board discussions. Since then, the Fragile States Group has been addressing this set of issues in the review "Strengthening the Organizational Response to Fragile States," to be completed in fiscal 2007. The review examines issues of particular importance, including achieving the right level of field presence through incentives for staff, and the organization and capacity necessary to support the needs of country teams. Likewise, IEG has rightly identified some of the Bank's procedures as barriers to rapid responses. Right-fitting aid allocations to ensure positive, not perverse, incentives to countries is a complex and Bank-wide challenge. And while management concurs with IEG that LICUS face the problem of too little or too much aid, it also would draw attention to the considerable progress made since the LICUS Initiative first raised these concerns (see Management Action Record).

Differentiated approach. Management welcomes IEG's emphasis on the particular challenges that countries in "deterioration" or "prolonged crisis/political impasse" and post-conflict countries transitioning from the immediate post-conflict phase pose for the Bank and other donors. The Bank's Fragile States Group is now working with partners in OECD-DAC's Fragile States Group to take a more detailed look at differentiating approaches by business models, as the LICUS Update explains. Recent experience in such countries has highlighted the need to articulate common messages from the international community and focus both on national unity and accountability within the state-building agenda and on longer-term capacity building.

Learning space. Management also welcomes the review's emphasis on lesson learning as a critical part of the Fragile States Group's role. Regular LICUS learning seminars, often cohosted by SDV or PREM, provide a forum for informal exchange among practitioners and outside experts across a balanced agenda of themes and country cases. The Fragile States Group has also organized more targeted events with country teams to address in real time specific issues of interest—as recent examples, a review of political economy factors in Ethiopia and Sudan and a discussion of development policy operations in deteriorating governance situations. In addition, the Fragile States Group has regularly produced Good Practice Notes, most recently on harmonization and alignment.[1] Management concurs that there is increasing demand for operational guidance for field actors and innovative approaches that have a proven track record for capacity development; however, it notes that substantial operational guidance and learning activities have already been provided, and more are in the work plan articulated in the LICUS Update.

B. Areas of divergence

Overall, the review brings out less clearly the positive trends in performance data and some interesting and innovative approaches that the LICUS Initiative has encouraged and supported. Three areas of particular concern are the review's presentation of performance data and country examples; its discussion of state building, governance, and capacity development; and its assessment of selectivity and prioritization, results measurement, and in-country donor collaboration.

1. Performance data and country examples

Management notes that the review tends to bring out a relatively negative side of the picture; for example, the summary makes use of 18 country examples, 17 of which are negative. While management welcomes identification of weak spots where they exist, it would note that many Bank country teams have also innovated and found successful modes of engagement that others can learn from. *Fragile States: Good Practices in Country Assistance Strategies* (World Bank 2005e) records 25 of these cases, ranging from the use of nontraditional partnerships to secure a robust economic intervention in Liberia to a results-focused strategy in Tajikistan (World Bank 2005e), but they are not reflected in IEG's review.

Project performance data. While the country cases dominate, the summary discussion downplays data on project performance. When unbundled, the data provided in the review for project performance and at-risk projects reveal a positive year-on-year trend, both absolutely and vis-à-vis non-LICUS low-income countries.[2] In 2005 projects in LICUS actually achieved higher levels of performance than projects in non-LICUS low-income countries, a testament to the efforts of country teams working under difficult conditions. Management views this as a positive trend that should be supported and sustained as a real step to more effective engagement. However, the summary makes only cursory mention of it, despite the fact that the LICUS Update (World Bank 2005h) identified project performance as one of the key indicators of the Bank's performance in LICUS (see section below on results measurement).

Data clarity. The review also gives the impression that it is basing judgments on some implementation evaluations that relate to operations begun before the initiative.[3] Management recognizes that three years does not allow for much data to be gathered; however, the use of pre-initiative data and country examples could have been more clearly separated from newer data. Sidebar texts do little to clarify this confusion; for example, one reads that "IEG ratings for LICUS CASs completed thus far have mostly been unsatisfactory" (chapter 2) despite the fact, noted in the text, that of these only one was for a period fully postdating the initiative.

2. State building, governance, and capacity development

Management agrees that the state-building agenda addresses the critical areas of capacity and governance head on. However, the review repeats the formula that the Bank "has made a traditional area of weakness [governance and capacity development] a central part of its focus" and often couples this idea with the concept of overambition, which it further ties to the areas of selectivity and results measurement. In fragile states, governance and capacity are central to longer-term stabilization and development and require early and sustained engagement from the international community. Management agrees that in these countries the state-building agenda is an enormous challenge for governments and other stakeholders, as well as for the international community. The fact that these are hard goals to achieve does not mean the Bank should not make them central to the agenda. The very reason for adopting a state-building agenda that puts these issues front and center is that in the past the international community has been too ready to ignore the task of making state institutions more effective and accountable to their people, focusing instead on delivering quick fixes through parallel and unsustainable structures.

Importance of state building. In adopting this stance the Fragile States Group is in line both with international partners and with other parts of the Bank. The OECD-DAC Principles of Good International Engagement in Fragile States state (principles 3 and 11) that state building should be a focus and that this in turn requires a long-term commitment to capacity development. Among other groups in the Bank, the PREM public sector governance team has undertaken critical analysis of the failings of past capacity development efforts that bolster, not undermine, the rationale for state building:

> *By the early 1990s the realization began to dawn that policies themselves were built on an underpinning of social, political, and state institutions and that weaknesses in this institutional foundation could undercut the economic policy reform agenda in three ways: by short-circuiting efforts at policy change, by failing to provide a robust platform of credibility and conflict resolution for market activity, and by being unable to provide complementary physical and social infrastructures* (Levy and Kpundeh 2004).

Thus many experts see state building as a response to the failure of past development initiatives to see the bigger context in which the technocratic policy reforms advocated by the Bank and others would inevitably fail. The fragile states work has attempted to place these approaches within a broader political context to ensure greater impact, ownership, and sustainability; emphasize Bank staff's knowledge of basic administrative systems; and balance invisible and visible results to maintain political momentum for reform.[4]

Capacity development and governance. The review is relatively dismissive of the Bank's record on capacity development and governance—which have become areas of increasing focus under the LICUS Initiative. It is beyond the scope of this response to address this claim; however, it should be noted at least that the record is more nuanced. The Sector Strategy Implementation Update on Public Sector Governance concludes, among other things, that the overall quality of economic and sector work (89 percent) and country analytic and advisory activities (97 percent) for projects on public sector governance is significantly higher than Bank averages (84 percent and 91 percent, respectively), and that within the public sector governance portfolio, the success rate of public financial management operations was approximately 84 percent, regardless of the larger governance environment (World Bank 2005e, 2005k). While there are no easy solutions in the field of state building, management notes that there *is* a role for the Bank to identify catalytic entry points for reform where the Bank also has a comparative advantage.

3. Selectivity and prioritization, results measurement, and in-country donor collaboration

As the review notes, prioritization and sequencing, donor collaboration, and effective monitoring are all critical components of a successful reform agenda in a fragile state. The review marks the implementation experience in all three areas as low. Management would highlight three responses.

Donor coordination. Regarding donor coordination, the review tends to downplay the achievements of the Bank that management feels has been highly innovative in terms of instruments deployed, such as the transitional results matrix, the LICUS Trust Fund, and country examples of joint strategies. The LICUS Trust Fund mandates multidonor approaches; the Transitional Results Matrices used in the Liberian, Haitian, Timorese, and Central African Republic transitions all supported strong coordination at the country level among actors within a government-owned matrix. Joint country strategies have been completed in Cambodia, Togo, Somalia, and Nigeria and are under way for the Democratic Republic of Congo and the Central African Republic (a proportion that is at least as high as that for joint strategies in non-LICUS low-income countries). In addition, the Comprehensive Development Framework report notes that "improved coordination among external partners around the TRM is providing a basis for strengthening government leadership of development assistance coordination" (World Bank 2005c). (Attachment A highlights where the Bank has provided guidance on selectivity and prioritization issues.)

Selectivity and prioritization. Selectivity and prioritization are logical corollaries of an emphasis on state building that encourages development actors to take a comprehensive perspective on the context while taking action along a "critical path" of feasible reforms. The review highlights one CAS that was not particularly selective—that of São Tomé and Principe, which covers a period straddling the initiative's inception. Management would highlight that several country teams have more recently adopted innovative approaches with tighter prioritization and sequencing, both in the Bank's work with national counterparts on overarching recovery strategies and in the Bank's own CAS processes. The Central African Republic, Tajikistan, Cambodia, Liberia, Nigeria, Togo, and Zimbabwe are examples of interim strategy notes or CASs that have adopted a conscious LICUS approach with strong selectivity and prioritization.

Results measurement. Management concurs that results measurement must be a critical element of the LICUS approach. At a central level the Fragile States Group in OPCS has focused on CPIA and IEG data on project performance, both of which have improved consistently since the initiative began (the LICUS Update [World Bank 2005h] provides comprehensive reporting). At the country level, results measurement is as per Bank norms and depends critically on the availability of budget and staffing to support identification of results in national development plans and Bank assistance strategies. These are issues that the Fragile States Group is addressing both through its strategic advice to country teams on selectivity, reform sequencing, and results focus and through its strategic staffing report—which advocates for more dedicated staff posted in the field, where identification of key results for the national recovery strategy and the Bank's strategy needs to occur. Management concurs with the view that the identification of indicators to monitor progress against peace building is at an early stage in the international community and is committed to working with other actors at the OECD-DAC and the United Nations Peace-Building Commission to further a common sense of progress measurement.

Management Action Record

IEG recommendation	Management response
Clarify the scope and content of the Bank's state-building agenda and strengthen the design and delivery of capacity development and governance support in LICUS. Given its weak record on capacity development and governance, as well as its focus now on the more ambitious and complex state-building objective in LICUS, the Bank needs to clarify its areas of comparative advantage vis-à-vis other donors and adopt innovative approaches that ensure better capacity and governance outcomes. Innovative approaches need to be developed to achieve a better fit between the Bank's interventions and the capacity of a LICUS to perform core state functions; ensuring implementation of focused and well-sequenced interventions in LICUS environments, where virtually every aspect of capacity and governance may need significant improvement; and effectively monitoring capacity and governance outcomes.	***Partly done, partly ongoing*** In January 2006 *Fragile States: Good Practice in Country Assistance Strategies* (World Bank 2005e) was discussed with and endorsed by Board. The paper gives more detailed and differentiated guidance on country strategy and operations than other agencies have given to date, clarifying both the Bank's comparative advantage within the sphere of state building ("core economic and development competences") and setting out innovative practices that can have a positive effect on capacity development. The Fragile States Group (formerly the LICUS Unit) is responsible for disseminating the good practice to support country team application of the lessons in the implementation of their programs in fragile states. This work is ongoing and integrated, as a priority, into the work program for fiscal 2007—see the LICUS Update also endorsed by Board in 2006 (p. 9). In addition, the Fragile States Group will roll out, during fiscal 2007, a program of learning activities based on examples of innovative approaches taken from the Good Practice Note. The Bank has organized two key state-building events. One in September 2005 convened a group of national reformers in New York from post-conflict situations for two days of facilitated discussions on state building. The second, in January 2006, convened a mixture of academics and policymakers to discuss state building with Bank staff in a one-day learning session. Both sessions provided a forum for intensive debate on core state functions, ways to match assistance with capacity, and how international organizations should engage. The September session has resulted in a joint work plan with the UNDP on state building that includes country-level work, policy research, and thematic workshops for lesson learning and discussion. Funding is in place and activities are under way, including research on peace agreements and state building, post-conflict planning processes and state building, as well as country work involving Sudan.

IEG recommendation	Management response
	This work, which supports considerable clarification of the definition, objectives, and division of labor of state building, will also feed into OECD-DAC's planned work around state building as part of the Fragile States Group work stream and will help the Bank play a role in shaping this agenda. The activities of OECD-DAC's work stream are to be defined in the first half of fiscal 2007 and activities to begin in the second half of fiscal 2007. By the end of calendar year 2008 the work is expected to have helped support the development of policy clarification on many of these issues. The forthcoming (first half of fiscal 2007) publication *Aid that Works: Successful Development in Fragile States* contributes some practical insights into project-level approaches for fragile states. It explores in particular the role of local-level governance institutions, the potential for complementarity between short-term results and long-term capacity development, and the importance of "bringing the state back in." Management agrees to support the conclusion of these activities according to their respective schedules. In management's view, these actions will provide a substantive response to the recommendations made.
Develop aid-allocation criteria for LICUS that ensure that these countries are not under- or over-aided.	***Ongoing/Not agreed***
The Bank needs to conduct a technical review of the cumulative effect of the various adjustments to the performance-based allocation system on aid volumes to LICUS. Aid-allocation criteria that reflect the Bank's objectives in LICUS and ensure that these countries are not under- or over-aided need to be developed. Whether and to what extent the criteria should be based on factors other than policy performance (such as levels of other donor assistance, assessment of potential risks and rewards, and regional and global spillovers) needs to be examined, keeping in mind that aid is limited and trade-offs will have to be made.	Management believes that the current IDA allocation system reflects fairly on the one hand the consensus in the larger development community that a performance-based system is needed to steer scarce resources where they are most likely to alleviate poverty most effectively, and on the other hand the IDA donors' specific views on how much allocations should be increased in stronger-performing countries. Accordingly, the weaker performers—broadly constituting the LICUS group—receive smaller allocations per capita. Within this broad framework there is already a recognition of some of the points raised by IEG, as evidenced by special allocations for (a) countries coming out of severe conflict, (b) qualifying regional projects, and (c) in exceptional cases countries reengaging with IDA. IDA donors no doubt will continue to raise points about the performance-based allocation system. One point relates to the role of governance. A technical note on this area is being prepared for discussion during the IDA14 Mid-Term Review in

IEG recommendation	Management response
	November. In the meantime, management continues to see broad support for the current approach described above and does not think that reopening basic allocation questions would be helpful in preserving the broad policy consensus that should underpin a strong IDA15 replenishment.

Strengthen internal Bank support for LICUS work over the next three years.

Ongoing/Agreed in part

Two aspects of internal Bank support need attention. First, staffing numbers, skills, and incentives for working on LICUS need to be prioritized. Ensuring adequate incentives to attract qualified staff—both at headquarters and in field offices—to work on LICUS will require giving clear signals of what is deemed to be success in LICUS, what outcomes staff will be held accountable for, how much risk it is reasonable to take, how failure will be judged, and how overall performance evaluation ratings and staff career development will take these into account. As in Olympic diving, where the scoring system factors in both the technical perfection as well as the difficulty of the dive, staff performance in LICUS should be similarly judged by assigning due weight to the extent of challenges presented by varying LICUS environments. Signaling the importance of LICUS work throughout the management hierarchy will also be required.

This is being addressed through the review *Strengthening the Organizational Response to Fragile States,* now in final draft and to be completed in fiscal 2007. The review examines issues of particular importance, including achieving the right level of field presence through incentives for staff and the organization and capacity necessary to support the needs of country teams. Discussions are under way with all the Regions on how to strengthen the field presence in fragile states. The Fragile States Group will update management and the Board with recommendations and their attendant cost estimates in fiscal 2007. Following discussion of this paper, OPCS will also take steps to strengthen the Bank's surge capacity, staff guidance, and training in fragile states, in line with the IEG recommendations.

Apart from incentives, the Bank needs to ensure that staff working on LICUS have relevant skills, such as in public sector management, are capable of seeking and using political knowledge, and are willing and able to work in interdisciplinary teams. Current plans to address these issues in the forthcoming Strengthening the Organizational Response to Fragile States are welcome, even if late. More systematic thinking is needed on staffing decisions for LICUS within the context of the Bank's overall staffing, recognizing that assigning more and better-qualified staff to work on LICUS would likely mean trade-offs for other Bank country teams. Trade-offs to benefit LICUS may or may not be justified depending on the Bank's objectives for LICUS as well as other Bank clients' need for assistance.

Work is now under way to develop a comprehensive program of critical skills training based on the assessed need for staff in field offices. This training program—which management considers to be the response to this recommendation—is to be rolled out in fiscal 2007 and will include modules for basic public administration reforms, including the budget function, as well as gaming scenarios to test Bank staff response skills in complex or rapid transitions.

Second, the organizational structure for LICUS and conflict work needs to be streamlined. The Bank needs to ensure an efficient organizational arrangement that removes duplication and fragmentation of support between the LICUS Unit and the Conflict Prevention and Reconstruction Unit.

Discussion of the overlap of roles and responsibilities between the Fragile States Group and CPR in SDV hides the useful collaboration that is taking place between the two teams. Notably, these include joint management of the LICUS Trust Fund grants, collaboration on post-conflict needs assessment work, and peer-review functions. Management needs to ensure that all its priorities on fragile states are covered and cannot commit to a change in structure.

IEG recommendation	Management response
Reassess the value added of the LICUS approach after three years. The value of the LICUS category and approach, including the operational usefulness of the business models, needs to be independently evaluated after three years, when sufficient experience on the outcomes of the approach will be available. At that time, it should be possible to address the more fundamental question of whether and to what extent Bank assistance can effectively support sustainable state building. Continued Bank support for the LICUS category and approach should be based on the findings of that reassessment.	*Agreed*

Attachment A. Review Recommendations Already Covered in Bank Guidance

IEG review	Reference to policy notes
Executive Summary The review focuses on selectivity and prioritization of reform efforts in fragile states. For example: p. xxx: The review notes the importance of selectivity and prioritization of reform agendas and within the Bank's CASs, stating: "[E]ven if collective donor selectivity is not immediately achieved, the Bank itself needs to ensure focus and selectivity in its own assistance program…." and p. xxviii: The review emphasizes the need for donors, including the Bank, to understand that "in the absence of a clear and relevant reform agenda, early successes of engagement may be short lived and contribute little to the achievement of country strategy objectives."	Selectivity and practicality of approach is also a pillar of the Bank's core guidance on fragile states. For example, the Good Practice Note on Transitional Results Matrices (TRM GPN) notes five "core principles for developing TRMs"—the first two of which are "Simple" and "Selective," noting both the strong forces against selectivity in fragile states and the risks faced by an overambitious reform strategy. The TRM GPN also states that "the desirable end result [of developing a TRM] is a matrix that focuses on a few key reform goals that will generate visible results and strengthen a platform for further reform and reconstruction." In addition, the Good Practice Note *Fragile States: Good Practice in Country Assistance Strategies* (CAS GPN) clearly sets out criteria for prioritization of reforms: "Building on the zero generation reform approach laid out by the LICUS task force, parameters used to determine priorities in different fragile states have included: (i) actions necessary to lock in promising reforms or lay the basis for future improvements in state delivery; (ii) actions necessary to prevent potential instability; (iii) actions necessary to build popular momentum for reform by generating visible results." In addition, the CAS GPN notes, "Efforts to build state capacity and accountability in all fragile states will tend to put particular emphasis on the *prioritization* needed to continue improvement in state performance or prevent failure of key functions" (p. 3, para 11).
p. xviii: The review states that "In the deterioration and prolonged crisis or impasse business models, given that there is often little consensus between donors and government on development strategy, engagement needs to include policy dialogue aimed at creating an opening for reform, and simultaneously work on a reform agenda should a window of opportunity arise."	The CAS GPN notes "restarting dialogue" as one of the priorities for prolonged crisis countries, stating that "in some situations of prolonged conflict or political impasse, relatively noncontroversial development issues may provide an entry point for constructive dialogue between the parties to a conflict." In deteriorating governance countries, the CAS GPN notes that the Bank can provide "input on specific economic issues which are important for mediation efforts and may serve as a way to restart dialogue."
p. xxx: The review notes that "since capacity to use aid effectively in post-conflict LICUS is low and governance is often poor, the focus from day one also needs to be on the development of capacity and improvement of governance, not just physical infrastructure."	The CAS GPN notes the importance of early capacity-building efforts: "In close collaboration with the International Monetary Fund, the Bank plays a key role in rebuilding capacity on economic policy, public financial management systems, and civil service reform or strengthening. It is therefore critical that the Bank is involved in the immediate post-conflict period (and indeed prior to this), when many critical decisions on the size, scope, and parameters o f public administration will be taken. Assistance in this area may include policy dialogue, analytical work, capacity building and support to recurrent expenditures: since state institutions are often new or extremely weak, much stronger knowledge of basic public financial and administrative systems is needed than

IEG review	Reference to policy notes
	in the Bank's regular IDA clients. The Bank is also engaging more closely with leadership capacity building in the early stages of post-conflict transitions, in recognition that leadership that is new to peace-time government may require exceptional support to make this transition successfully."
	The TRM GPN states: "As important as the early and visible delivery of tangible benefits can be, there are other much less visible actions that must be initiated early on, even though their benefits will not be felt for some time. Strategic and planning efforts must not be delayed; sector visioning, strategy development and policy formulation, definition of institutional capacity needs and planning for the associated capacity development" (p. 7).
Chapter 2 p. 21: The review states: "Critical to the Bank's effectiveness is its ability to reflect sound political analysis in its strategy adequately. This has been an area of weakness in the Bank."	The CAS GPN emphasizes the importance of political understanding: "The Bank should continue to encourage country teams to incorporate analysis of the political economy… in both CAS/ISN processes and upstream project preparation" (p. 8).
p. 26: The review claims: (a) "Building stronger state institutions and governance are not merely technocratic processes involving the state, but…"	The CAS GPN states, "It is therefore important that institution-building initiatives avoid purely technocratic approaches, devoting considerable attention to the process of decision making and implementation, and to well-designed participation and widespread communication of reform initiatives" (p. 5).
(b) "…requires social transformations including those of civil society and the relationship between the state and civil society. Bank approaches need to be adequately informed by such considerations."	The CAS GPN also highlights the importance of demand-side reform: "A vibrant civil society and private sector are critical for effective governance: indeed, without a strong private sector to generate jobs, incomes and tax revenues, or without popular and civil society demand for accountable services, public sector reforms are unlikely to be sustained. Assistance for 'state-building' therefore includes support for private sector and civil society development, in all fragile state contexts" (pp. 5–6).
Chapter 4 p. 61: The review claims: "Other areas where the Bank needs to further develop its operational approach include …address linkages between politics, security, and development…."	The CAS GPN lays out for the first time a coherent framework for addressing the political, security, and development nexus from the Bank's perspective: "Moving forward, there is justification to extend successful country experiences in linking development and peace building to a deeper and more systematic consideration of these linkages in the Bank's operational engagement. Recognizing the need for peace-building to be nationally driven and the constraints posed by the Bank's mandate and expertise, an emphasis on responsiveness to requests from national counterparts for support; maintaining a focus on the Bank's core economic and development competences; and partnerships with other institutions should be the underlying principles of assistance in this area. In particular, experience from country programs indicates that: • Political economy and conflict analysis are important to inform the selection and sequencing of priorities for country assistance strategies, as well as project design issues. The Bank should continue to encourage country teams to incorporate analysis

IEG review	Reference to policy notes
	of the political economy and conflict dynamics in both CAS/ISN processes and up-stream project preparation.

- The Bank plays an important role in supporting various cross-cutting development processes where peace building may emerge as a priority such as post-conflict needs assessments, recovery plans and results frameworks, PRSPs, public expenditure and governance assessments, multidonor budget support operations, multi-sector/multidonor trust funds and donor-coordination processes. These processes are by their nature integrative: precluding peace and security issues and institutions from consideration, or placing them on a separate track, creates the real risk of diminishing their importance, missing opportunities for synergy, or ignoring factors which may undermine longer-term development outcomes. The Bank's role in engaging with political and security sector institutions should focus on its core economic and development competences (such as generic development planning or public finance capacity building), developing as appropriate partnerships with other donors or institutions that have expertise in specialized technical reform or capacity building in the peace and security areas.

- While retaining an emphasis on the Bank's core economic and development activities, there is scope to increase emphasis on peace-building goals. Peace building is a valid goal to use in country assistance strategies, where sustaining a fragile peace, preventing escalation of conflict or addressing crime and violence which constrain the welfare and development opportunities of the poor have emerged as national priorities. Activities which contribute to peace-building goals are not only those which directly touch on the security sector, such as demobilization and reintegration of ex-combatants. All economic and development activities infrastructure, human and social sector development, economic management, private sector and agricultural recovery, etc. can potentially be selected or designed to contribute to peace-building goals.

Bank assistance strategies and programs can also include the development of partnerships with other donors and national counterparts which combine respective technical capacities to support peace-building priorities. For example, the Bank may work with the UN (or other institutions taking the lead on political governance and peace building, including civil society organizations) to provide economic inputs or training to the parties to peace and national reconciliation talks; constitutional reform processes; or economic and development training to political parties and parliamentarians, provided that in all cases this dialogue is nonpartisan and part of a multidonor effort.

This approach allows the Bank to make a more systematic contribution to the evolving international partnership for peace-building. It acknowledges that the Bank is still learning about the linkages between peace-building and development; signals a respect for the mandate and expertise of other international institutions; and recognizes that close partnerships are needed" (pp. 7–9).

APPENDIX CC: CHAIRMAN'S SUMMARY: COMMITTEE ON DEVELOPMENT EFFECTIVENESS (CODE)

On July 26, 2006 the Committee on Development Effectiveness (CODE) considered the report *World Bank Support to Low-Income Countries Under Stress: An IEG Review* and the draft Management Response. The statement by the External Advisory Panel on the IEG review was circulated as background document.

Background. The Bank outlined its approach to Low-Income Countries Under Stress (LICUS) in 2002. In January 2006 the Board considered the LICUS Update, together with the staff guidance note *Fragile States: Good Practices in Country Assistance Strategies*. The LICUS Update called for: (i) increased attention to peace- and state-building goals in fragile state assistance strategies; (ii) stronger partnership with other organizations; and (iii) stronger Bank organizational response. In January 2006, the Board also supported the replenishment of the LICUS Trust Fund created in 2004. The LICUS Trust Fund is the only fund that can provide significant assistance to recovering countries in non-accrual status with the Bank, although there are other trust funds to support LICUS, including the Post-Conflict Fund. In the past year, the Board discussed several LICUS country assistance strategies, including for Afghanistan, Kosovo, Tajikistan, Timor-Leste, and Sudan (update), and a group of Executive Directors visited the Central African Republic.

Main Findings and Recommendations of the IEG Review. IEG found that the LICUS Initiative has increased Bank attention to these countries, but implementation experience to date has been mixed, although it is too early to assess full outcomes. It noted that significant challenges remained, including the need to: (i) increase selectivity and prioritization required in donor and Bank reform agendas; (ii) improve Bank effectiveness in fragile states in deterioration and prolonged crisis or impasse; (iii) improve the Bank's donor coordination at the country level to match its strong coordination at the international policy level; (iv) clarify the Bank's central goals in fragile states, state and peace building; (v) finalize and implement critical human resource reforms (for example, staffing, incentives); and (vi) take stock of the various adjustments made over the years to the Performance-Based Allocation System (PBA), whose cumulative effect on financing for fragile states is not clear. The four IEG recommendations were: (i) clarify the scope and content of the Bank's state-building agenda and strengthen the design and delivery of capacity development and governance support; (ii) develop aid-allocation criteria for LICUS that ensures that countries are not under- or over-aided; (iii) strengthen internal Bank support for LICUS work over the next three years; and (iv) reassess the value added of the LICUS approach after three years.

Draft Management Response. Management welcomed the IEG review, noting that many points reinforced the key messages in the LICUS Update, and echoed the issues considered in *Fragile States: Good Practices for Country Assistance Strategies*. It noted that the preliminary conclusions of the IEG evaluation had been particularly useful in helping staff refine the fragile state business models presented to Board in January. However, management found that the IEG review could have been more balanced in reflecting positive trends in the performance data and country examples; discussing state building, governance, and capacity building; and assessing selectivity and prioritization, results measurement, and in-country donor collaboration. Country team speakers presented a range of examples of application of fragile state approaches and international partnerships in country strategy and operations, as well as underscoring the importance of senior management attention and staffing issues. Management emphasized the newness of the LICUS Initiative whereby the Bank is learning by doing and the need to level the expectation given the difficulties faced in fragile states and the high-risk–high-reward nature of work. It elaborated on Bank efforts to address much of the IEG findings, providing country examples. Management partially agreed to IEG recommendation (iii) and noted its ongoing work on strengthening the organizational response to fragile states. Management disagreed with IEG recommendation (ii), and believed the current IDA allocation system fairly reflects the consensus in the larger development community and the IDA donors on the need for a PBA system to ensure aid effectiveness.

Overall Conclusions. The Committee welcomed the opportunity to discuss the IEG review and the draft Management Response. While it may be too early to draw definitive conclusions about outcomes, given the complexity of issues faced in fragile states, speakers considered it imperative to learn from experience on a frequent ongoing basis. The IEG review was commended for being informative and incisive, raising critical issues, and promoting substantive and constructive dialogue acknowledged by both IEG and management. CODE also appreciated the presentation of country experiences by operational staff.

The Committee strongly supported continued Bank engagement in fragile states, and several speakers expressed appreciation for the dedicated staff working in difficult environments. While encouraged by the preliminary findings and early successes of the Bank's engagement, members agreed with IEG that there is little room for complacency. Emphasizing the importance of "raising the game" in implement-

ing the LICUS Initiative, speakers' comments focused on the following: role and comparative advantage of the Bank especially in peace and state building; possible refinements of the existing business models and use of instruments; need to strengthen the knowledge base; aid-allocation mechanism and possible need for its adjustment; measurement of results; and donor coordination. There was consensus regarding the importance of strengthening internal support for LICUS (for example, staffing, incentives, and organizational structures).

Next Steps. The IEG review (including the Management Response and CODE Chairman's Summary) will be disclosed in September 2006, in absence of a request for a full Board discussion. There was agreement to reassess the value added of the LICUS approach after three years, as recommended by IEG.

The main issues raised during the meeting were the following:

General Comments. Several speakers noted that it was too early to assess the outcome and cautioned against drawing hasty conclusions; they viewed the report as more about learning than an assessment. Others were disappointed about poor funding for and slow and regionally variable implementation of the Board-endorsed LICUS guidelines, although a number of speakers also highlighted the risk and uncertainty of fragile states, the challenge of producing results, and the narrow difference between success and failure in difficult country environments. *Staff commented on the tradeoffs between speed, good governance, and capacity development in providing support to fragile states and on the need to better address them.* A member asked about the prioritization and sequencing of the IEG recommendations, while another speaker requested IEG to review the messages included in the summary of the report, to make sure that they match the analysis. *IEG considered clarifying and monitoring of the state-building agenda as most important, followed by making the resource allocation more systematic, and addressing internal* *organizational issues.* A speaker expressed appreciation for the Norwegian Aid Agency's cooperation and support to the preparation of the IEG review.

The Bank's Role. Speakers strongly endorsed the Bank's continued engagement in LICUS and the focus on state building. They had questions about the comparative advantage of the Bank, the scope and content of the Bank's state- and peace-building agenda, conflict prevention, promotion of macroeconomic stability, and capacity development and governance support. In this connection, one speaker observed that the fundamental issue is the alignment between the security and development agenda. Some other speaker noted that these countries face periodic setbacks, such as Timor-Leste, which was referred to in the IEG review and the Statement by the External Advisory Panel. This speaker viewed that while lessons should be learned from such crises, setbacks should be considered a normal part of engagement in fragile situations, and not necessarily an indication of failure of donor assistance, including of the Bank. Where countries are able to rapidly recover within their constitutional structures and without descending into state failure, this institutional resilience demonstrates a positive result of international investment in institution building. Some members cautioned against overly optimistic expectations, especially the fiduciary aspects and absorptive capacity. Other speakers stressed selectivity and prioritization, addressing gender issues and continuous efforts in monitoring, evaluation, and measuring results.

Management considered state capacity and accountability as core issues faced by fragile states. It referred back to the LICUS Update of January 2006, where it clarified the basis of the Bank's engagement in state and peace building (based on country ownership, the Bank's core economic and development competencies, and partnerships with other donors to address peace, security, and development linkages in an integrated manner). Management also stressed that there have been more Bank

successes in this area, particularly in-country donor partnerships and capacity development in public finance systems, than implied in the IEG review, and provided examples.

Instruments of Support. A number of speakers suggested refining the existing business model, tailoring the approach to varied country situations within the LICUS group, and effective use of various Bank Group instruments, especially the analytical and advisory activities. Some members also emphasized the importance of the knowledge base of LICUS, particularly the analysis of political economy, drawing on existing information, involving local stakeholders to build country ownership, and outsourcing as necessarily. The need to strengthen the quality and relevance of analytic work and of sharing of experiences was emphasized. *Management emphasized that the Bank is adjusting its support and use of instruments to match the changing country context. It also assured the Committee of its efforts to work with countries and donors in delivering economic sector work and technical assistance, building on available information—a point that had also been emphasized in the LICUS Update. Management responded in affirmative to a member's question about whether the new Operational Policy on Emergency Lending will address the procurement and financial management issues faced in fragile states; the OP will be accompanied by appropriate guidelines.*

Classification of Countries. Some members sought more transparency in classifying countries as LICUS or fragile states. A few of them proposed introducing a criterion to define "fragility" of a country, while one sought more involvement of partner government in the classification of countries as fragile states. The Chair requested IEG to review the use of term "LICUS" in its report in view of the recent broad preference to refer to these countries as "fragile states." A speaker proposed monitoring "countries at risk," reporting annually to the Board. *Management acknowledged that the Bank does not* have a strong system of analyzing the risks of fragility, which it was prepared to examine further.

Aid-Allocation System. Diverse views were expressed with respect to IEG's recommendation to develop aid-allocation criteria for LICUS to ensure these countries are not under- or over-aided. While some speakers suggested clarifying whether LICUS are under- or over-aided, taking into consideration the countries' absorptive capacity, others observed that this matter is beyond the Bank's control, given the importance of other donor allocations. *On the issue of absorptive capacity, management mentioned that two changes in IDA 14 had been made to address the needs of fragile state: (i) stretch the resource allocations for post-conflict countries, based on research that indicates improvements in absorptive capacity three to four years after the end of conflict; and (ii) introduce an exceptional provision for countries newly re-engaging with the international community. It also echoed a member's emphasis on need for sustained and predictable financial support for fragile states, noting that some of these countries (for example, Timor-Leste) do face periodic setbacks, and the Bank and donors need to be prepared to stand by these countries throughout.*

Many speakers thought the PBA mechanism could be adjusted or fine tuned. However, a member wanted to maintain the current system while others cautioned against major adjustments and allocation criteria based on factors other than performance. The need for a clearly articulated and defined framework for allocation was also stressed. One member requested management views on IEG findings about the "patched-up" nature of the current aid-allocation system for fragile states. The limitations of the CPIA were discussed, including the need to react quickly to quick turnaround or sharp deterioration of the country situation. *Management agreed with IEG that at each round of IDA replenishment, some adjustments are made to the allocation system. Accordingly, there should be a periodic review of it, including ways to simplify and enhance transparency, while*

maintaining focus on governance. Management assured CODE that the issues of time lag of CPIA and resource allocation for turnaround situations were on its radar screen, but there was no easy solution given the careful due process required for CPIA. Speakers looked forward to the IDA 14 Mid-Term Review, which was expected to address some of these issues.

Partnership. Members commented on strengthening donor coordination, assessing effectiveness of partnerships, and ensuring the Bank's country assistance complements that of the UN and other donors. *Staff provided examples of donor coordination in Sudan, Liberia, and the Central African Republic;* speakers appreciated hearing about the improvements in this area. *In response to the interest expressed in UN-Bank cooperation, management said there have been improvements, and in countries such as Democratic Republic of Congo, Timor-Leste, Liberia, and Haiti, the UN brings their expertise in political governance and security sector reform, while the Bank contributes to economic recovery and public finance and civil service reforms under an integrated strategy or results framework .*

Internal Coordination. Many speakers asked about roles and responsibilities, overlaps, and the pros and cons of merging the LICUS Unit and the Conflict Prevention and Reconstruction (CPR) Unit. A few of them noted the confusion among external partners and the need to strengthen the case for maintaining two separate units. Some also wondered about the implications, if any, of the new Sustainable Development Network (SDN). Other questions related to the link between the LICUS and other Bank initiatives (for example, Africa capacity building) and the effective use of Trust Funds, which could be assessed. *Management responded that the CPR Unit in the Social Development Department is a technical unit that works with Regions, while the LICUS Unit was established to reinforce support for fragile stages through enhanced cross-sectoral coordination. It had a more positive view about the collaboration between the two units than IEG, but also accepted the* *need to further consider the IEG recommendation in the context of the recently constituted SDN. Management expected the new SDN would enhance the synergy between social, environment, and infrastructure to support CPR work, as well as better linkage with Hazard Risk Management Team (also under SDN), in places where conflict and natural disasters converge, such as in Aceh.*

Staffing. Speakers stressed the need for change in organizational culture and improved deployment of internal resources to support fragile states, commenting on issues related to deployment of experienced staff in the field, the setting up of supportive incentive systems (for example, promotion, family support, special benefits), and more transparency regarding allocation of staff resources for LICUS. *Management elaborated on recent efforts to differentiate incentives between service in LICUS and other countries by introducing better locality premium, hazard pay, and R & R; improving reentry guarantees; establishing LICUS service as a criterion for technical promotion at level H; and accommodating family needs. At the same time, management acknowledged that more needed to be done, and Operations Policy and Country Services and Human Resource Departments, together with the Regions, were working to further improve the incentive structure for LICUS assignments.* A member asked management to commit to a timetable for presenting concrete proposals to address internal organizational issues, to which *management responded that draft paper on strengthening the organizational response to fragile states is expected to be ready later in 2006.*

Pietro Veglio
Chairman

ENDNOTES

Chapter 1

1. The events of September 11 prompted the Bank to look anew at its mission and mandate. President James Wolfensohn was quick to articulate that the poverty reduction mission was more important than ever, because "failed states" with territory outside the control of a recognized and reputable government offered fertile soil on which terrorism could thrive (World Bank 2004c).

2. Chauvet and Collier (2004) estimate that the economic cost (cost in terms of growth) for a country that starts out as LICUS and has likely prospects of a turnaround averages 4.6 times its initial GDP, and the economic cost to the typical neighbor is 3.4 times its initial GDP.

3. See, for example, World Bank 2002, 2003a, and UNCTAD 2000. The weak past performance of Bank operations in LICUS is also demonstrated by IEG project, Country Assistance Evaluation, and CAS Completion Report Review ratings (appendixes Q and R).

4. Both DFID and OECD-DAC have identified fragile states as countries in the bottom two quintiles of the Bank's CPIA, as well as those "not rated" on the CPIA. One difference with the Bank, which uses the CPIA (see appendix A for definition) rating for Public Sector Management and Institutions in addition to the overall CPIA rating in defining LICUS, is that DFID and OECD-DAC only use the latter.

5. The fiscal 2005 list of LICUS was created using the fiscal 2004 Gross National Income (GNI) threshold of $865 or less per capita. The overall CPIA rating is used first as a filter, and then the CPIA rating for Public Sector Management and Institutions is considered. Appendix A provides the definition of CPIA.

6. In fiscal 2005, countries without CPIA ratings were Afghanistan, Liberia, Myanmar, Somalia, Timor-Leste, and the territory of Kosovo.

7. Severe LICUS have an overall and governance CPIA of 2.5 or less; core LICUS have an overall and governance CPIA of 2.6–3.0; and marginal LICUS have an overall and governance CPIA of 3.2.

8. While fragile states continue to be a tightly defined group, the Bank has recognized that fragility is not clear cut and has pointed out that higher-income countries facing the aftermath of conflict, genocide, or social instability (such as the Balkans), more strongly performing countries facing rising conflict risks (for example, Nepal), and strongly performing states facing fragility in particular subnational regions (as in India, the Philippines) have found elements of the donor debates on fragile states useful (World Bank 2005h).

9. The 25 countries classified as LICUS by the Bank in fiscal 2005 had a population of 432 million in 2003. The population figures would increase if countries classified as LICUS in other fiscal years are also included. Income data are available for 8 of the 25 LICUS and are for different years. Social indicators are birth-weighted averages for 23 of the 25 LICUS for which these data are available.

10. Although 36 percent of total lending went to 18 non-post-conflict LICUS, the lending within this group was concentrated in a few countries (Nigeria, 60 percent; Cambodia, 11 percent; Lao PDR, 9 percent; and Uzbekistan, 7 percent) (appendix I). Of the 18 non-post-conflict LICUS, 7 were in non-accrual (indicated in table 1.1).

11. The administrative budget is more evenly distributed than lending across the LICUS group. However, the variation within each of the two LICUS groups (post-conflict LICUS and non-post-conflict LICUS) is higher for the administrative budget than for lending (appendix I).

12. Donors agreed to the principles of international engagement in January 2005 at the Senior-Level Forum on Aid Effectiveness in Fragile States, co-sponsored by the Bank, OECD-DAC, the European Community, and the United Nations Development Program (OECD 2005c). http://www.oecd.org/dataoecd/59/55/34700989.pdf.

13.The term *capacity building* is used in this review only when discussing a document that specifically used the term. In all other instances, the term *capacity development* is used as the Bank is increasingly using this term.

14. This includes the Multi-country Demobilization and Reintegration Program, which accounts for $500 million and covers Angola, Burundi, the Central African Republic, and the Democratic Republic of Congo.

Chapter 2

1. Interim Strategy Note (ISN) is the umbrella term for Transitional Support Strategies and Country Reengagement Notes. When a normal Country Assistance Strategy approach is not conducive because of country circumstances, the Bank may prepare an ISN. For details, see "Definitions and Data Sources" in appendix A.

2. If India were included, the per capita lending for non-LICUS LICs would be $3.4 in fiscal 2000–02, and $3.6 in 2003–05.

3. The World Bank's policy places all IBRD loans and IDA credits to a country in non-accrual status if payment on any loan or credit is overdue by more than six months.

4. Kosovo and Timor-Leste were exceptions to the debt-distress grant eligibility criterion, and are thus eligible for grants (see IDA 2005).

5. The ratio of administrative budget to lending declined in LICUS (from 0.042 in fiscal 2000–02 to 0.039 in fiscal 2003–05), indicating a lower administrative budget for each dollar lent in LICUS in fiscal 2003–05. While the ratio for non-LICUS LICs was lower (0.022) than for LICUS (0.039) in fiscal 2003–05, the ratio for non-LICUS LICs increased (from 0.020 in fiscal 2000–02 to 0.022 in fiscal 2003–05) (table 2.1).

6. According to surveys for 79 percent of Haitians, radio is the main source of information; for 13 percent, it is word-of-mouth; for 10 percent, it is TV; and for only 4 percent, it is newspapers.

7. In 2001, the name of the Post-conflict Unit was changed to the Conflict Prevention and Reconstruction (CPR) Unit. The CPR Unit has increased conflict analysis that examines the causes of conflict, but continuing work is needed in this area.

8. World Bank. Project No. P064821, PID (2000); ICR (2005).

9. Including the fiscal 2005 CAS, the CAS Completion Report, and the report to the 2004 Consultative Group Meeting.

10. A SWAp supporting public financial management reform is scheduled for early fiscal 2006.

11. CPIA 12—Property Rights and Rule-based Governance; CPIA 13—Quality of Budgetary and Financial Management; CPIA 15—Quality of Public Administration; CPIA cluster D—Public Sector Management and Institutions; average CPIA cluster A–C—Economic Management, Structural Policies, Policies for Social Inclusion/Equity.

12. Doing Business: http://www.doingbusiness.org/

13. Investment Climate Survey: http://iresearch.worldbank.org/ics/jsp/index.jsp

14. Public Expenditure and Financial Accountability: http://www.pefa.org/

15. Global Integrity Index: www.globalintegrity.org

16. Polity: http://www.cidcm.umd.edu/

17. Transparency International: http://www.transparency.org/

18. Management feels that the evaluation does not take sufficient account of commitment to country-level donor coordination by the World Bank in fragile states and would draw attention to the joint Country Assistance Strategies completed in Nigeria, Cambodia, Somalia, and Togo and under planning in the Democratic Republic of Congo and the Central African Republic; joint Transitional Results Matrixes in Liberia, Sudan, the Central African Republic, and Haiti; and multidonor trust funds and harmonized budget support in Afghanistan, Timor Leste, and Sudan and now under planning in the Central African Republic.

19. Formerly known as the Joint Learning and Advisory Process on Difficult Partnerships.

20. The results of a survey for 2004 among members of the Development Assistance Committee rated the fragile states partnership among the top five networks for quality. On a scale of 0 (unsatisfactory) to 4 (outstanding), the survey found the quality of the partnership's work to be 3.4 and its impact 3.08 (3.5 and 3.2 in 2003).

21. Interviews with respondents in the United States, the Netherlands, and France.

22. Each pilot country will be managed by a single or pair of donors. For example, the pilot program in Sudan will be managed by Norway and the program in Somalia will be managed jointly by the World Bank and the United Kingdom.

23. The UNDG brings together operational agencies in the UN system working on development at the country level.

24. The strategy documents reviewed were: Afghanistan TSS (2003), Angola ISN (2005), Cambodia CAS (2005), Central African Republic CRN (2004), Republic of Congo TSS (2003), Democratic Republic of Congo TSS (2004), Haiti TSS (2004), Kosovo TSS (2004), Liberia RFTF Revision (2005), Nigeria DfID/WB Joint Strategy (2005), Papua New Guinea (2005), Somalia CRN (2004), Sudan JAM Synthesis Framework (2005), Tajikistan CAS (2005), Timor-Leste CAS (2005), and Zimbabwe ISN (2005).

25. Zimbabwe fieldwork undertaken for this review, IEG.

26. QAG defines its realism index as the ratio of problem projects to projects at risk.

27. There is an improving trend in the overall CPIA rating and the CPIA rating for the Public Sector Management and Institutions cluster over the same period. However, the deteriorating trend in the KKZ indicators may be a more robust result, because the KKZ indicators are a statistical compilation based on data from several organizations (including the Bank's CPIA), while the CPIA ratings are based on assessments by Bank staff only. Furthermore, the improvement in the overall CPIA rating and the CPIA rating for the Public Sector Management and Institutions cluster in fiscal 2004 are at least partially explained by the refinement undertaken by the Bank to the bottom of the CPIA spectrum in fiscal 2004. In some countries, 100 percent of the improvement in the CPIA rating for the Public Sector Management and Institutions cluster results from this refinement.

Chapter 3

1. The security and reconciliation cluster of the Post-Conflict Progress Indicator (PCPI; appendix A), which covers public security, reconciliation, and disarmament/demobilization, and reintegration, would be an example of peace-building variables for post-conflict countries.

2. For example, DFID/DAC.

3. Kanbur (2005), for instance, proposes enriching the CPIA formula by including measures of the rate of improvement of desired outcome variables over a given period of time up to the point of assessment.

4. This assumption relies, most notably, on the findings of influential papers by Burnside and Dollar (1998)

and Dollar and Pritchett (1998), which claim to have established empirically a positive relationship between measures of policy and institutional quality and the effectiveness of aid in bringing about poverty reduction.

5. During fiscal 1993–95, for every $1 per capita lent to IDA borrowers overall, about $1.20 was allocated to the top CPIA-quintile performers and about $0.85 per capita to the lowest quintile. But by fiscal 1998–2000, the spread had widened to $2.10 versus $0.60 per capita. By the time the LICUS Initiative was formulated in 2002, the relationship between aid and governance had strengthened to the point that a standard deviation increment on the CPIA translated into nearly 100 percent more assistance (Dollar and Levin 2004). The link between IDA commitments and the IDA Country Performance Ratings continued improving throughout fiscal 2002–05 (IDA's commitments, disbursements, and funding for fiscal 2003–05).

6. For instance, Beynon (2003), Lensink and White (2001), Dalgaard and Hansen (2001), Hansen and Tarp (2001), Guillamont and Chauvet (2001), Easterly, Levine, and Roodman (2003), Roodman (2004), and Rajan and Subramanian (2005).

7. Their governance indicators are only marginally worse (and in some cases following an improving trend) than in other countries receiving more aid.

8. A technical review paper on governance in the PBA system is under way at the request of IDA deputies for discussion during the IDA 14 Mid-Term Review in November 2006.

Chapter 4

1. Refers to Grade E and above staff working on education and training, energy, environment, forest/tree crops, health/nutrition/population, highway, irrigation, industry, power, private sector development, public sector development, rural development, senior management, social development, social protection, transportation, urban, and water/sanitation.

2. A few donors suggested that Bank staff would benefit from the UNDP training course for Resident Representatives.

3. For complete text of OP/BP 8.50, see http://web.worldbank.org/WBSITE/EXTERNAL/TOPICS/EXTSOCIALDEVELOPMENT/EXTCPR/0,,contentMDK:20486236~menuPK:1260741~pagePK:148956~piPK:216618~theSitePK:407740,00.html.

4. For complete text of OP/BP 6.0, see http://wbln0018.worldbank.org/Institutional/Manuals/

OpManual.nsf/1337075cf0d5ba638525705c0024aa3a/2c
b575f62255c53a85256e8a0078068c?OpenDocument.

5. In semistructured interviews, Bank staff were, however, more positive than indicated by the Stakeholder Survey about the LICUS Unit's contribution to harmonization/alignment (for example, through Transitional Results Matrices).

6. Only two staff above the GF level, one GE level staff, one A–D level staff, three secondees, two junior professional associates, and one extended-term temporary; staff data provided by LICUS Unit, July 2005.

7. Bank staff may have factored operational usefulness into their assessment of quality.

Appendix H

1. The objectives of the Enhanced HIPC Initiative are, first, "to deal comprehensively with the overall debt burden of eligible countries by removing their debt overhang within a reasonable period of time and providing a base from which to achieve debt sustainability and exit the rescheduling cycle," and, second, to free up resources for poverty reduction (World Bank and IMF 2006b).

2. HIPC decision point is the date at which a heavily indebted poor country with an established track record of good performance under adjustment programs supported by the International Monetary Fund (IMF) and the World Bank commits to undertake additional reforms and to develop and implement a poverty-reduction strategy. A country may start to receive interim relief at this point. HIPC completion point is the date at which the country successfully completes the key structural reforms agreed at the decision point, including the development and implementation of its poverty-reduction strategy. The country then receives the bulk of debt relief under the HIPC Initiative without any further policy conditions (*Steps of the HIPC Initiative: A Guide,* available at h t t p : / / w e b . w o r l d b a n k . o r g / W B S I T E / E X TERNAL/TOPICS/EXTDEBTDEPT/0„contentMDK:20655535~menuPK:64166739~pagePK:64166689~pi PK:64166646~theSitePK:46904 3,00.html).

3. In September 2004, the Boards of IDA and the IMF decided to extend the "sunset clause" of the Enhanced HIPC Initiative to end-2006, as well as to identify countries that at the end of 2004 had estimated debt burden indicators above the enhanced HIPC Initiative thresholds. As of April 2006, staff identified 11 countries as potentially eligible for the HIPC Initiative.

(Three others, including Lao PDR, a fiscal 2005 LICUS country, were found to meet the indebtedness criteria, but have stated that they do not wish to avail themselves of the HIPC Initiative.) In addition to these 11 countries, others could be added on a case-by-case basis if their data are verified to meet the relevant criteria. For instance, Afghanistan, also a fiscal 2005 LICUS country, would then be included in the list if, upon reconciliation of its debt, its debt indicators are found to be above the relevant thresholds (World Bank 2004a; World Bank and IMF 2006b).

4. In the sense that the oil windfall produces sovereign resource rents that can generate dysfunctional rent-seeking behavior.

5. Lower policy quality (CPIA) implies lower sustainable debt thresholds and, implicitly, a higher grant component.

6. For instance, the HIPC Initiative has reduced debt ratios by half, on average, in 18 countries. But debt sustainability, the primary objective of the initiative, remains elusive. In 11 of 13 countries with available data, the key indicator of external debt sustainability has deteriorated since completion point, and in 8 of these countries the ratios once again exceed HIPC targets (IEG 2006b).

Appendix L

1. In Angola, for instance, related analytical work includes the Public Expenditure Management and Financial Accountability Review, Oil Diagnostic Study, Corporate Social Responsibility Report (with a focus on the oil sector), and the Oil Revenue Management Study.

2. In the Democratic Republic of Congo, mining sector management issues are addressed through public financial management studies, including the Public Expenditure Review, Country Procurement Assessment Report, Public Enterprises Reform Study, Financial Sector Assessment Program, Country Financial Accountability Assessment, Institutional and Governance Review, and Country Economic Memorandum.

Appendix M

1. The sample is not restricted to LICUS and includes a total of 83 operations.

2. There is a potential upward bias in the ratings of adjustment operations because of the nature of policy actions against which performance is monitored. For instance, the ratings could incorporate the suc-

cessful passage of necessary legislation. Whether this legislation is being applied in practice is more difficult to observe unambiguously, which could result in the overestimation of the result.

3. The sample included projects approved in fiscal 2000 or thereafter, for which IEG ratings already exist: 31 operations in total, of which 9 are adjustment and 22 are investment.

4. Including marginally unsatisfactory, unsatisfactory, and highly unsatisfactory.

5. It is important to note here that SWAps should not be viewed as a direct alternative to DPL in the sense that DPL is a lending instrument whereas SWAps are an approach to development program planning and implementation that can rely on various lending instruments (including budget support).

Appendix O

1. The Institutional and Governance Review has also been included in the list of LICUS core diagnostic reports because the 2002 LICUS Task Force Report identified the IGR as an essential piece of ESW for LICUS.

Appendix P

1. QAG has carried out six assessments of quality at entry and five of quality of supervision. Three assessments for both were conducted prior to fiscal 2000. Because QAG conducts these reviews for a very small sample of projects, results for pre-fiscal 2000 are compared with results of fiscal 2000 onward.

Appendix U

1. Category A: The project is likely to have significant adverse environmental impacts that are sensitive, diverse, or unprecedented. Category B: The project's potential adverse environmental impacts on human populations or environmentally important areas are less adverse than those of Category A. Category C: The project is likely to have minimal or no adverse environmental impacts. Category FI: The project involves investment of Bank funds through a financial intermediary in subprojects that may result in adverse environmental impacts.

2. The sample was stratified by two periods: projects approved over fiscal 2000–02, and projects approved over fiscal 2003–05.

3. An IBRD/IDA commitment level of $13 million was used to divide "large" from "small" projects.

Appendix BB

1. Other Good Practice Notes, as noted in IEG's review, include World Bank 2005f and 2005k; and World Bank and UNDP 2005.

2. IEG notes that these results are not necessarily fully attributable to the LICUS Initiative, as only one project covered by these ratings was approved in the period following its inception.

3. IEG notes that the report is referring to the CASCR Review ratings for those CASCRs that covered at least part of the period since the inception of the LICUS Initiative—of the four such CASCRs reviewed by IEG, three were rated moderately unsatisfactory or unsatisfactory, and one was rated moderately satisfactory.

4. See, for example, World Bank, 2005e, pp. 3–6, and World Bank, 2005h, pp. 10–13. See also the LICUS Web site for knowledge work on political economy and state building, including the joint PREM-OPCS workshop on state building.

BIBLIOGRAPHY

Beynon, Jonathan. 2003. "Poverty-Efficient Aid Allocations: Collier/Dollar Revisited." Economic and Statistics Analysis Unit Working Paper No. 2, Overseas Development Institute, London.

Birdsall, Nancy, and Devesh Kapur. 2005. *The Hardest Job in the World: Five Crucial Tasks for the New President of the World Bank.* Washington, DC: Center for Global Development.

Boesen, Nils, and Ole Therkildsen. 2003. *Between Naivety and Cynicism. A Pragmatic Approach to Donor Support for Public Sector Capacity Development.* Copenhagen: Danida.

Burnside, Craig, and David Dollar. 1998. "Aid, Policies and Growth." Policy Research Working Paper No. 1777, World Bank, Washington, DC.

Carnegie Endowment for International Peace. 2004. *States at Risk—Stabilization and State-Building by External Intervention.* Washington, DC.

Chauvet, Lisa, and Paul Collier. 2005. *Policy Turnarounds in Failing States.* Oxford, U.K.: Oxford University Press.

———. 2004. *Development Effectiveness in Fragile States: Spillovers and Turnarounds.* Oxford, U.K.: Oxford University Press.

Cliffe, Sarah, Scott Guggenheim, and Markus Kostner. 2003. "Community-Driven Reconstruction as an Instrument in War-to-Peace Transitions." CPR Working Paper No. 7, World Bank, Washington, DC.

Collier, Paul. 2005. *Is Aid Oil? An Analysis of Whether Africa Can Absorb More Aid.* Oxford, U.K.: Centre for the Study of African Economics, Oxford University.

———. 2003. *Breaking the Conflict Trap: Civil War and Development Policy.* Washington, DC: World Bank.

Collier, Paul, and David Dollar. 2002. "Aid Allocation and Poverty Reduction." *European Economic Review* 45: 1–26.

———. 2001. "Can the World Cut Poverty in Half? How Policy Reform and Effective Aid Can Meet International Development Goals." *World Development* 29 (11).

Collier, Paul, and Anke Hoeffler. 2002. "Aid, Policy and Growth in Post-Conflict Countries." Policy Research Working Paper No. 2902, World Bank, Washington, DC.

Dalgaard, Carl-Johan, and Henrik Hansen. 2001. "On Aid, Growth, and Good Policies." CREDIT Research Paper No. 00/17, Centre for Research in Economic Development and International Trade, University of Nottingham, U.K.

DFID (Department for International Development). 2005. "Why We Need to Work More Effectively in Fragile States." DFID Policy Paper. London.

Dollar, David, and Victoria Levin. 2004. "The Increasing Selectivity of Foreign Aid, 1984–2002." Policy Research Working Paper No. 3299, World Bank, Washington, DC.

Dollar, David, and Lant Pritchett. 1998. *Assessing Aid—What Works, What Doesn't, and Why.* Washington, DC: World Bank.

Easterly, William, Ross Levine, and David Roodman. 2003. "New Data, New Doubts: A Comment on Burnside and Dollar's Aid, Policies, and Growth` (2000)." NBER Working Paper No. 9846, National Bureau of Economic Research, Cambridge, MA.

Foreign Policy and the Fund for Peace. 2005. "The Failed States Index." *Foreign Policy* (July/August).

François, Monika, and Inder Sud. 2006. "Promoting Stability and Development in Fragile and Failed States." *Development Policy Review* 24 (2): 141–60.

Grindle, Merilee S. 2004. "Good Enough Governance: Poverty Reduction and Reform in Developing Countries." *Governance: An International Journal of Policy, Administration, and Institutions* 17 (4): 525–48.

Guillamont, Patrick, and Lisa Chauvet. 2001. "Aid and Performance: A Reassessment." *Journal of Development Studies* 37 (6): 66–87.

Hansen, Henrik, and Finn Tarp. 2001. "Aid and Growth Regressions." *Journal of Development Economics* 64: 547–70.

Hassan, Fareed. 2004. "Lessons Learned from World Bank Experience in Post-Conflict Reconstruction." IEG Conference Note, World Bank, Washington, DC.

IDA (International Development Association). 2005. *Additions to IDA Resources* (14th Replenishment). *Working Together to Achieve the Millennium Development Goals.* Report No. 31693. Washington, DC: World Bank.

———. 2004. *IDA's Performance-Based Allocation System: Update on Outstanding Issues.* Report No. 27837. Washington, DC: World Bank.

———. 2002. *Additions to IDA Resources* (13th Replenishment). *Supporting Poverty Reduction Strategies.* Report No. 34298. Washington, DC: World Bank.

IEG (Independent Evaluation Group–World Bank). 2006a. *Assessing the Effectiveness of the Bank's Fiduciary Work: An Evaluation of Country Financial Accountability Assessments and Country Procurement Assessment Reports, July 1999-December 2004.* Washington, DC: World Bank.

———. 2006b. *Debt Relief for the Poorest: An Evaluation Update of the HIPC Initiative.* IEG Study Series. Washington, DC: World Bank.

———. 2006c. "Timor-Leste: Community and Local Governance Project" (P069762), "Second Community Empowerment Project" (P072356), "Third Community Empowerment and Local Governance Project" (P075342), "Agricultural Rehabilitation Project" (P070533), and "Second Agriculture Rehabilitation Project" (P073911). World Bank, Washington, DC.

———. 2005a. *Capacity Building in Africa: An OED Evaluation of World Bank Support.* Report No. 34351. IEG Study Series. Washington, DC: World Bank.

———. 2005b. *The Effectiveness of World Bank Support for Community-Based and -Driven Development.* IEG Study Series. Washington, DC: World Bank.

———. 2003a. *Debt Relief for the Poorest: An OED Review of the HIPC Initiative.* IEG Study Series. Washington, DC: World Bank.

———. 2003b. *Extractive Industries and Sustainable Development: An Evaluation of World Bank Group Experience.* A Joint IEG-World Bank, IEG-IFC, and IEG-MIGA evaluation. IEG Study Series. Washington, DC: World Bank.

———. 2002. *Social Funds: Assessing Effectiveness.* IEG Study Series. Washington, DC: World Bank.

———. 2000. "Utilization of Project Implementation Units (PIUs). Lessons and Practices." Washington, DC.

———. 1998. *The World Bank's Experience with Post-Conflict Reconstruction.* IEG Study Series. Washington, DC: World Bank.

Kanbur, Ravi. 2005. "Reforming the Formula: A Modest Proposal for Introducing Development Outcomes in IDA Allocation Procedures." Discussion Paper No. 4971, Center for Economic Policy Research, Washington, DC.

Koeberle, Stefan, and Zoran Stavreski. 2005. "Budget Support: Concept and Issues." Paper presented at the Practitioners' Forum on Budget Support, Cape Town, South Africa, May 5–6.

Lensink, Robert, and Howard White. 2001. "Are There Negative Returns to Aid?" *The Journal of Development Studies* 37 (6): 42–65.

Levin, Victoria, and David Dollar. 2005. "The Forgotten States: Aid Volumes and Volatility in Difficult Partnership Countries (1992–2002)." Summary Paper for DAC Learning and Advisory Process on Difficult Partnerships, OECD-DAC, Geneva.

Levy, Brian, and Sahr Kpundeh, eds. 2004. *Building State Capacity in Africa: New Approaches, Emerging Lessons.* Washington, DC: World Bank Institute.

Mitra, Saumya. 2004. "Aid and Development." Comments at the conference on the Future of Intervention: Intervention, Legitimacy and the Reconstruction of Statehood. Berlin, July 13.

OED (Operations Evaluation Department, The World Bank). See IEG.

OECD (Organisation for Economic Co-operation and Development. 2005a. "Chair's Summary: Senior Level Forum on Development Effectiveness in Fragile States." Development Cooperation Directorate and Development Assistance Committee. Paris: OECD.

———. 2005b. "Piloting the Principles for Good International Engagement in Fragile States." Draft Concept Note, Development Cooperation Directorate and Development Assistance Committee. DCD (2005)11/REV1, Paris.

———. 2005c. "Principles for Good International Engagement in Fragile States." OECD-DAC Draft Paper, Development Cooperation Directorate and Development Assistance Committee, DCD (2005)8/Rev2, Paris.

———. 2005d. *The DAC Fragile States Agenda: Progress and Issues Development.* Paris.

———. 2005e. "Work Plan for the Fragile States Group (FSG) 2005–2006." Development Cooperation Directorate, DCD(2005)12/REV2, Paris.

———. 2003. "Draft Mandate and Terms of Reference for the Joint Learning and Advisory Process on Difficult Partnerships." Paris.

Ottaway, Marina. 2003. *Democracy Challenged. The Rise of Semi-Authoritarianism.* Washington DC: Carnegie Endowment for International Peace.

———. 2002. "Rebuilding State Institutions in Collapsed States." *Development and Change* 33 (5): 1001–24.

Perlez, Jane. 2006. "From Bad to Worse in East Timor." *International Herald Tribune*, May 31.

Rajan, Raghuram, and Arvind Subramanian. 2005. "Aid and Growth: What Does the Cross-Country Evidence Really Show?" NBER Working Paper No. 11513, National Bureau of Economic Research, Cambridge, MA.

Reuters. 2005. "Lots of Fanfare, Billions of Dollars and Not Much to Show." April 3.

Rogier, Emeric. 2005. *Designing an Integrated Strategy for Peace, Security and Development in Post-Agreement Sudan.* The Hague: Netherlands Institute of International Relations.

Rohland, Klaus, and Sarah Cliffe. 2002. "The East Timor Reconstruction Program: Successes, Problems and Tradeoffs." Conflict Prevention and Reconstruction Working Paper No. 2, Report No. 26361. World Bank, Washington, DC.

Roodman, David. 2004. "The Anarchy of Numbers: Aid, Development, and Cross-country Empirics." Working Paper No. 32, Center for Global Development, Washington, DC.

Schiavo-Campo, Salvatore. 2003. "Financing and Aid Management Arrangements in Post-Conflict Situations." CPR Working Paper No. 6, World Bank, Washington, DC.

UNCTAD (United Nations Conference on Trade and Development). 2000. *The Least Developed Countries Report, 2000: Aid, Private Capital Flows, and External Debt.* New York.

UNDG (UN Development Group) and The World Bank. 2005. "Operational Note on Transitional Results Matrices, Using Results-Based Frameworks in Fragile States." Washington, DC.

UNDG (United Nations Development Group), UNDP (United Nations Development Program), and The World Bank. 2004. *Practical Guide to Multilateral Needs Assessments in Post-Conflict Situations.* Report No. 29822. Washington, DC: UNDG, UNDP, World Bank.

UNDP (United Nations Development Program). 2005. *Human Development Report: International Cooperation at a Crossroads.* New York.

Unsworth, S. 2003. "Better Government for Poverty Reduction: More Effective Partnerships for Change." Consultation document, Department for International Development, London.

Van de Walle, Nicolas. 2005. *Overcoming Stagnation in Aid-dependent Countries.* Washington, DC: Center for Global Development.

World Bank. Forthcoming a. *Aid That Works: Successful Development in Fragile States.* Washington, DC.

———. Forthcoming b. *Strengthening the Organizational Response to Fragile States.* Washington, DC.

———. 2006a. "Are We Really Getting Rid of PIUs?" World Bank, Washington, DC. http://web.worldbank.org/WBSITE/EXTERNAL/TOPICS/EXTCDRC/0,,contentMDK:20845819~pagePK:64169192~piPK:64169180~theSitePK:489952,00.html

———. 2006b. *Annual Report on Portfolio Performance: Fiscal Year 2005.* Quality Assurance Group. Washington, DC.

———. 2006c. "Cambodia: World Bank Releases Latest Statement and Update." News Release No. 2006/493/EAP. June 26.

———. 2006d. *Global Monitoring Report 2006: Strengthening Mutual Accountability, Aid, Trade, and Governance.* Washington, DC.

———. 2006e. *IDA's Implementation of the Multilateral Debt Relief Initiative.* Vol. 1. Washington, DC.

———. 2005a. *Building Effective States—Forging Engaged Societies.* Report of the World Bank Task Force on Capacity Development in Africa. Washington, DC.

———. 2005b. *Country Assistance Strategy for the Kingdom of Cambodia.* Report No. 32118-KH. Washington, DC.

———. 2005c. *Enabling Country Capacity to Achieve Results—2005 CDF Progress Report.* OPCS Report No. 34102. Washington, DC.

———. 2005d. *Engaging Civil Society Organizations in Conflict-Affected and Fragile States: Three African Case Studies.* Washington, DC.

———. 2005e. *Fragile States: Good Practices in Country Assistance Strategies.* Report No. 34790. Washington, DC.

———. 2005f. *Good Practice Note for Development Policy Lending: Development Policy Operations in Fragile States.* Report No. 32636. Washington, DC.

———. 2005g. *Low-Income Countries Under Stress (LICUS) Implementation Trust Fund: Request for Replenishment and Special Support for Sudan.* Report No. 34831. Washington, DC.

———. 2005h. *Low-Income Countries Under Stress: Update.* Report No. 34789. Washington, DC.

———. 2005i. *Meeting the Challenge of Africa's Development: A World Bank Group Action Plan.* Washington, DC.

———. 2005j. *World Development Indicators.* Washington, DC.

———. 2005k. *Good Practice Note for Development Policy Lending: Development Policy Operations and Program Conditionality in Fragile States.* Washington, DC.

———. 2005l. *Papua New Guinea Interim Strategy Note.* Washington, DC.

———. 2005m. "World Bank Operational Manual." Washington, DC.

———. 2004a. *Enhanced HIPC Initiative: Possible Options Regarding the Sunset Clause.* Washington, DC.

———. 2004b. "The LICUS Challenge." Corporate Day Presentation. Washington, DC.

———. 2004c. "The Role of the World Bank in Conflict and Development: An Evolving Agenda." CPR Seminar Series. Washington, DC.

———. 2004d. "Workshops for Leaders, and Leadership Workshops: Support for Meeting the Challenges of Transition." Synthesis Note on Leadership Workshops 2001–2004. Washington, DC.

———. 2003a. *Low-Income Countries Under Stress: Implementation Overview.* OPCS Report No. 27536. Washington, DC.

———. 2003b. *Low-Income Countries Under Stress: Implementation Trust Fund.* OPCS Report No. 27535. Washington, DC.

———. 2002. *World Bank Group Work in Low-Income Countries Under Stress: A Task Force Report.* Report No. 26903. Washington, DC.

———. 1998. *Post-Conflict Reconstruction: The Role of the World Bank.* Report No. 17752. Washington, DC.

———. 1997. *World Development Report 1997: The State in a Changing World.* Washington, DC.

World Bank and International Monetary Fund. 2006a. *Heavily Indebted Poor Countries (HIPC) Initiative — Listing of Ring-Fenced Countries That Meet the Income and Indebtedness Criteria at End 2004.* Washington, DC: World Bank and IMF.

———. 2006b. *HIPC—Status of Implementation.* Washington, DC: World Bank and IMF.

World Bank and United Nations Development Programme (UNDP). 2005. *An Operational Note on Transitional Results Matrices: Using Results-Based Frameworks in Fragile States.* Washington, DC, and New York: World Bank and UNDP.